The World of Science
and the
Rule of Law

It is essential, if man is not to be compelled to have recourse, as a last resort, to rebellion against tyranny and oppression, that human rights should be protected by the rule of law . . .

Preamble, Universal Declaration of Human Rights, 1948.

The lack of conformism and the deep intellectual honesty characteristic of Plyushch the scientist were characteristic of his usual behaviour in life.

Anonymous, from Russian samizdat

The World of Science
and the
Rule of Law

A study of the observance and violations
of the human rights of scientists
in the participating states
of the Helsinki Accords

BY

JOHN ZIMAN, FRS

PAUL SIEGHART

JOHN HUMPHREY, CBE, FRS

OXFORD UNIVERSITY PRESS
1986

Oxford University Press, Walton Street, Oxford OX2 6DP

Oxford New York Toronto
Delhi Bombay Calcutta Madras Karachi
Kuala Lumpur Singapore Hong Kong Tokyo
Nairobi Dar Es Salaam Cape Town
Melbourne Auckland

and associated companies in
Beirut Berlin Ibadan Nicosia

OXFORD is a trade mark of Oxford University Press

British Library Cataloguing in Publication Data
Ziman, John
The world of science and the rule of law: a study
of the observance and violations of the human
rights of scientists in the participating states
of the Helsinki Accords.
1. Scientists—Legal status, laws, etc.
I. Title II. Sieghart, Paul
III. Humphrey, John, 1915–
341.4'81'08805 JC571
ISBN 0-19-825516-0

Library of Congress Cataloging in Publication Data
Ziman, J. M. (John M.), 1925–
The world of science and the rule of law.
Includes index.
1. Civil rights (International law) 2. Scientists—
Legal status, laws, etc. I. Sieghart, Paul.
II. Humphrey, J. H. (John Herbert), 1915–
III. Title.
K3240.4.Z56 1986 341.4'81 85–24662
ISBN 0-19-825516-0

Printed in Great Britain by
Biddles Ltd, Guildford and King's Lynn

PREFACE

The origins of this work go back to a discussion on freedom in science, in the Council for Science and Society, as long ago as 1975. John Ziman, from his professional experience as an academic physicist and his personal interests in the social relations of science, saw this as a normative issue affecting the integrity of the whole scientific community. Paul Sieghart, the Council's founder, from his professional experience as a lawyer and his involvement in the theory and practice of international human rights law, pointed out that these issues were already governed by binding legal rules. We were so impressed by the insights to be gained by combining these two perspectives that we persuaded the Council to let us set up a small working party to report on the subject. That report—*Scholarly Freedom and Human Rights*—was published in 1977, and showed that the scientific and legal perspectives were indeed complementary aspects of a single consistent and coherent set of principles.

But how well could these principles be applied in practice? We became involved in various activities related to the 'Helsinki process', in which both science and human rights figure prominently. From our Council colleague John Humphrey, a medical scientist, we learnt of the problems of verifying 'reliable information' about particular cases, and organizing international action to support the victims of persecution and oppression. We then began to talk of making a survey of the actual situation in this particular 'Helsinki' group of countries, to estimate the extent of the problems, and to focus concern and action on them in our various communities. But that would obviously have to be a major piece of research, for which none of us could then have spared the time.

This project would have remained a dream had it not obtained one of the first Awards for work on 'Freedom under the Law' from the Airey Neave Memorial Trust, established in memory of a great and courageous parliamentarian whose devoted work in the cause of freedom was tragically cut short when he was assassinated within the precincts of the very Palace of Westminster in which he had served his constituents and his country for so long. With this generous support, we were able to commission Dr. Peter Tahourdin, CBE, in the summer of 1981 to research the subject in detail and to prepare it for publication. His scientific training, and his long and distinguished career in the British Council, not only enabled him to bring to this task an unrivalled experience of the scientific and cultural life of many countries: he also brought immense enthusiasm and integrity in unearthing the facts, and a lucid and lively pen in setting them down on paper. His tragic death on 8 April 1983, after nearly a year of grave ill health in which he had not spared himself to press on with the work to which he had become deeply committed, robbed us of a delightful friend and an invaluable colleague.

To a large extent, this is the book that Peter Tahourdin was striving to complete. He left us with a mass of detailed information, and first drafts of many of the present chapters. Several further chapters were then drafted by Dr. Nihal Jayawickrama, who brought his legal skills to work on them. We also obtained invaluable critical comments and advice from Eric Stover, a staff member of the Committee for Freedom and Responsibility in Science of the American Association for the Advancement of Science. For all this work, the Rector and authorities at Imperial College of Science and Technology in London generously gave us free office space, access to their excellent facilities, and general support. We owe a great debt to them all, as well as to the many individuals and organizations, too numerous to list, who willingly supplied us with information, materials, and references.

Nevertheless, we are very conscious that working this material up into a publishable text took far longer than we had anticipated when we took that task over ourselves in January 1984. We should particularly like here to record our appreciation of the helpful and sympathetic support that we have received throughout from the Committee of the Airey Neave Memorial Trust, who have followed the project with consistent interest, and with real concern for its ultimate success. We take personal responsibility for all that we say in this book; but without their help much of it could not have been said at all. Whether the following pages justify the confidence they have shown in us will be for the reader alone to decide.

JOHN ZIMAN
PAUL SIEGHART
JOHN HUMPHREY

London, March 1985

CONTENTS

I

INTRODUCTION

The Helsinki Accords

On 1 August 1975, in the capital of Finland—chosen for its non-aligned symbolic position between East and West—thirty-five men ceremonially signed six very long documents. The men were the 'High Representatives' of the USA, the USSR, Canada, and all but one (Albania) of the thirty-three sovereign states of Europe—ranging from the UK, France, Italy, and the two Germanies, to Monaco, the Holy See, and San Marino. The roll-call included Gerald Ford, Leonid Brezhnev, Helmut Schmidt, Pierre Trudeau, His Beatitude Archbishop Makarios III, Valéry Giscard d'Estaing, Harold Wilson, Janos Kadar, Aldo Moro, Edward Gierek, Nicolae Ceausescu, Gustav Husak, and Josip Broz Tito. The documents were the English, French, German, Italian, Russian and Spanish versions of a single text. Its full title is the Final Act of the Conference on Security and Co-operation in Europe, but it has become much better known as 'the Helsinki Accords'.

These Accords took over two years to negotiate. No single peace treaty had ever formally brought the second world war to an end; Europe remained riven between the two major power blocks, as well as accommodating, at little comfort to themselves, a few 'neutral and non-aligned' states; and the main object of the Helsinki exercise was to give formal recognition to Europe's post-war frontiers, and to enshrine in a single text the elements of the then still fashionable policy of *détente*.

Tucked away at the very end of the text are two brief sentences. The first says that 'the text of this Final Act will be published in each participating state, which will disseminate it and make it known as widely as possible'. By and large, the participating states carried out that promise, and as a result more people in both East and West have now heard of the Helsinki Accords than of almost any other modern international document, except perhaps the Universal Declaration of Human Rights.

However, the very next sentence says that the text 'is not eligible for registration under Article 102 of the Charter of the United

Nations', which is an oblique way of saying that it is not a binding international treaty, and therefore imposes no *legal* obligations on any of the states whose High Representatives adopted it with such solemnity. In international law, therefore, it constitutes no more than a 'gentlemen's agreement'—of the kind once defined by an English judge as an agreement between parties none of whom is a gentleman, and each of whom expects the others to be bound by it without wishing to be bound himself. None the less, as we shall come to see, this particular set of Accords is in fact underpinned by some quite rigorous legal obligations.

Divided into three 'baskets' and some odds and ends, the text covers a wide range of topics: military security and disarmament; industry, trade, and commerce; transport and tourism; the environment; and the special problems of the Mediterranean. But its most detailed sections are devoted to two subjects which are seldom considered together: on the one hand science and technology, on the other human rights. These are the particular concerns of this book.

The text of the Helsinki Accords is uncompromising in its support for the human rights of all the inhabitants of the participating states. Thus, for example, Basket I contains a set of ten principles to guide the relationships between these states. Principle VII includes clauses such as this:

'The participating states recognize the universal significance of human rights and fundamental freedoms, respect for which is an essential factor for the peace, justice and well-being necessary to ensure the development of friendly relations and co-operation among themselves as among all states.'

Principle X goes on to say that:

'The participating states will fulfil in good faith their obligations under international law, both those obligations arising from the generally recognized principles and rules of international law and those obligations arising from treaties or other agreements, in conformity with international law, to which they are parties.'

Since almost all the thirty-five Helsinki states are in fact now parties to one or more treaties which spell out these human rights in great detail, this apparently vague 'gentlemen's agreement' is in fact supported by a number of very specific legal obligations by which the parties to it are bound. Any accusation that human rights are not being respected in one or other of these states is therefore today no longer a matter of politics, but of law.

The numerous references to science and technology in the Helsinki Accords are equally fundamental to its purpose. Section 4 of Basket II, for example, starts by affirming that the participating states are:

'*Convinced* that scientific and technological co-operation constitutes an important contribution to the strengthening of security and co-operation among them, in that it assists the effective solution of problems of common interest and the improvement of the conditions of human life . . .'

It goes on to specify more than a dozen fields—agriculture, energy, medicine, public health, etc.—in which this co-operation is to be achieved. Similarly, in Basket III it sets out in detail the means to be employed in order to improve the exchange of information between research workers, and to facilitate travel by scientists between the participating states. This is a strong reminder of the transnational network of science and technology that now binds all nations together.

Unfortunately, none of these initiatives in support of 'security and co-operation' has developed as well as was hoped when the Helsinki Accords were signed. The accusations and recriminations between many of the 'Helsinki' countries for failing to respect certain human rights have become a major issue of international affairs. Transnational technological co-operation and scientific exchanges have also languished, with reciprocal suspicions about threats to national security. Although these disappointments are perhaps only symptoms of the failure of the whole process of *détente* in Europe, they are not unconnected with one another. International co-operation in science is easily damaged by attacks on the human rights of individual scientists—and yet, for reasons that we shall later explore in detail, scientists are particularly vulnerable to just such attacks. The intellectual freedom that is essential for the growth of knowledge cannot be separated from all the other freedoms—civil and political, social, economic, and cultural—that the Helsinki Accords affirm.

For this reason, it seemed natural to make a detailed study of the extent to which the 'Helsinki' states have *in fact* carrried out their solemn promises in the vital area where these two great themes intersect. Such a survey of the principles and practices governing the human rights of scientists in a relatively small group of countries might not at first sight seem of great significance to the hopes and fears of the rest of the world today; but we propose to show that this is one of those apparently narrow topics through which one can see into much larger fields of aspiration and concern.

Generalized rhetoric flows all too glibly on such matters, and it is therefore essential to grasp realities by reference to particular cases. This book reports what has happened to particular individuals, in particular countries, in relation to particular human rights. We have drawn these cases from the best information available, but we know that it is not complete, and cannot guarantee that it is accurate in every detail. Although there are many more problems than we can describe here, we believe that those we have chosen to illustrate are a fair sample of the relevant facts, and fairly represent the trends of recent years—that is, from the mid 1970s to the early 1980s. The reasons for limiting this survey to a limited professional group and a limited group of countries will be explained later in this chapter.

A straightforward survey of these uncomfortable facts might well be considered enough in itself to evoke protests and calls for remedial action. But it is essential that it should be seen in a larger setting. Each case—and this is the main thrust of our argument—needs to be interpreted in a framework of *law*. Before beginning our investigation, we therefore need to look more closely at both science and the law of human rights, and at their connections and intersections.

Science and human rights

At first sight, science and human rights would seem to have as little in common as chalk and cheese. One thinks of science as objective, sceptical, hard-headed, above politics and beyond ethics; one thinks of human rights as subjective, idealistic, soft-hearted, embedded in political and social realities, and forming part of the discourse of morality. In fact, as we shall see, there is no justification for either of these stereotypes. For all its claims to objectivity, science is not a disembodied activity: it is a human enterprise, conducted by human beings interacting in a complex social network with each other, and with the societies in which they work. And whatever may have been the case about human rights in the past, today they have acquired a sharply defined and objective framework in which can be set the performance of many human enterprises, including the pursuit of science.

The dependence of science on the *personal* liberties of its practitioners—that is, on the extent to which they are able to exercise certain rights of free speech, and openly criticize accepted opinions—is a commonplace of history. The most thoughtful scientists have always recognized this truth, and have given generous support to the rights of their fellow scientists, at home and abroad. The life and circumstances of Andrei Sakharov, for example, would undoubtedly have been crueller still had it not been for the appeals of innumerable scientists and scientific organizations from all over the world. The brutalities practised in recent years against scientists (among others) in Chile, Argentina, and Uruguay have aroused similar widespread protests—sadly, with similarly limited results—though those who have been able to flee abroad have been helped to re-establish themselves. But this is nothing new. Refugee scientists from tyrannical regimes have long been welcomed as colleagues and offered scientific employment in countries far from home. There is plenty of good will for such supportive action— although, as we shall show, much more is needed, and much more could be done than is usually realized even in well-informed scientific circles.

Many of the endeavours, by scientists and others, to safeguard science as a world-wide enterprise requiring freedom of thought, communication, and travel have been hampered by conflicting opinions on the scope and validity of what are the basic freedoms which are theirs by right. Oppressive governments have been able to exploit these uncertainties, and thus to stifle or frustrate concerted action in support of the victims. What has been missing is the realization that when the concept of freedom is defined in terms of human rights, it has two important features in common with science.

One is that both seek for consistency, and for ways of expressing general regularities of behaviour in concise terms. In the case of human rights, the diverse precepts collected under this heading have been refined into a consistent set of rules designed to constrain the behaviour of a part of the social world—that is, into a set of agreed prescriptive 'laws' limiting the exercise of political or economic power over individuals. Science likewise aims to formulate as concisely and accurately as possible generalizations about the behaviour of the natural world which will stand the test of observation and experiment—though scientists nowadays usually do not choose to dignify these by the term 'laws', since they have learnt from their collective experience that even the most apparently valid generalizations may not prove to be strictly true when particular phenomena are examined very closely, or on very different scales.

A second common feature is that both science and human rights have a universal and transnational quality. Whatever some philosophers may say, a scientific 'truth', once sufficiently established to become part of the 'reliable knowledge' accepted by the scientific community,[1] is effectively independent of any particular place, culture, tradition, or economic or political system. Having passed as many tests as can be devised for it by the scientific community, it is accepted as a valid statement of what is probably true wherever scientific concepts are applied anywhere. This is now also true in principle of human rights; as we shall see, there is today in force a complete international code of human rights law, composed of closely defined rights, freedoms, and duties, agreed upon by the international community of nations, which is independent of any particular place, culture, tradition, or economic or political system, and which has been accepted as an international standard of reference for the exercise of civil, political, economic, social, and cultural activities throughout the world.

These structural parallels between scientific knowledge and the code of human rights law can be very illuminating. By their aid, it is possible, at least in principle, to assess objectively the performance of any modern government in the field of human rights, indicating unambiguously where this performance is deficient. Just as any deviation from a scientific law is not to be explained away by mere local prejudice, so any deviation from the international code of human rights law is not to be justified by mere political or moral preference. In both cases, human judgment may be called for in establishing the precise facts of the matter, but this judgment is not undermined, from the start, by unstated and indeterminate assumptions. The laws to which the facts are to be referred clearly imply what facts are to be sought, and how they should be interpreted in practice.

These are large claims, which we shall try to make good through-

[1] Ziman J. M., *Public knowledge* (Cambridge University Press, 1967).

out the rest of this book. But if they are correct, then they indicate a major step forward towards the full protection of human rights, for scientists and for all other people. These rights are now defined, in a form designed for legal application, in instruments negotiated between, and formally adopted by, the governments of very many of the world's countries. Rather than having to discuss human rights in the language of sympathy, morality, and political aspiration, where all values and opinions are subjective and controversial, we can now base our analysis on this single standard code, which is written in language that is as precise and objective as it can be. The code may be regarded as weak, or over-zealous, on any particular point: but like the great body of scientific knowledge it is the outcome of long and arduous work, and presently represents the nearest one is likely to get to a collective, consensual, prescription. It has rendered obsolete most of the ill-defined and highly debateable catalogues of human rights that people tend to construct when they approach this subject individually from a sentimental, moralistic, or politically motivated point of view.

The 'Helsinki' group of nations

The international code of human rights law is now so well defined that one could in principle apply it to any country in the world. But such an exercise would meet with certain practical difficulties if it were attempted world-wide. There are today something over 160 sovereign states in the world, in which somewhere around four and a half billion individuals are treated with more or less (and far too often still decidedly less) than the respect due to their human rights under the rules laid down in the international code. For many of those states, and even more of their inhabitants, 'reliable knowledge' about that treatment is hard to come by. Much of the information which does become available about the Far East or Latin America, for example, is at best patchy and selective, and at worst hopelessly partisan and coloured by the ideological preconceptions of the reporter. For the time being, therefore, a survey that can claim to be objective is best confined to a manageable set of countries, and a defined section of their inhabitants, both chosen for the reliability of the knowledge which becomes available about them.

Fortunately, scientists in the 'Helsinki' states present just such a set. The states range in size from the two great superpowers to three tiny sovereign cities. They include a number of countries with 'capitalist' and a number with 'communist' economic and political systems (some, but not all, of which also belong to NATO or the Warsaw Pact respectively), as well as some which are 'neutral' and 'non-aligned'. They include the more 'developed' of the world's nations, especially in the fields of science and technology, and have strong and sophisticated scientific institutions. Their scientists are competent to contribute to transnational science at the most advanced level, and are often known personally or by repute to one another as fellow members of 'the one world of science'. Because of this, information about them travels across national frontiers more quickly and freely than it does about most other people. Because they form an educated élite which is generally fairly close to, yet formally separate from, government, they are more exposed than most people to infringements of their human rights, and (as we shall see) more vulnerable than most to some of these infringements. And because science plays such an important role in today's world, and the well-being of mankind depends ever more on its proper pursuit, the consequences of infringements of the human rights of scientists may affect far more people than just the individuals directly concerned.

A significant factor in our choice was the existence of much well-attested information about individual scientists and the conditions of scientific life in all these countries. We are thus able to cite *public* sources for practically all the detailed information in our survey. This information is not necessarily complete, but at least readers may judge for themselves, on the basis of the reputation of such sources, how far any particular item is worthy of credence.

Nevertheless, the initial decision to restrict this study to the thirty-five 'Helsinki' countries was taken with regret. What is presented here should be considered as a partial account of a larger subject. It ignores the situation in a number of countries of major standing in the scientific world, such as Japan, India, and China—not to mention other countries such as Israel, South Africa, South Korea, and Brazil where advanced science and technology are significant factors in a politically tense national life. A world-wide study would also focus on the situation in certain Latin American countries—especially Argentina, Chile and Uruguay—where recent years have seen some appalling violations of the human rights of many people, including scientists and scholars. Although the basic information for a study of these countries is available in several public sources[2], our reason for excluding this in the present book is our limited supply of time, and of research facilities.

What is so special about scientists?

We must remove one possible source of misunderstanding at this point. The reader might well ask: what is so special about *scientists* in relation to their rights? Is science such a uniquely valuable profession that it ought to have its own charter, spelling out the particular rights and liberties that its members should enjoy in order to perform their duties? Plenty has been written about the *responsibilities* of scientists, as the guardians of natural knowledge, as technological innovators, and as policy advisors; should these notable responsibilities perhaps be codified, and matched against a corresponding code of rights?

We advocate no such élitist attitude. It goes without saying that when scientists, as a consequence of their professional work, find themselves in positions of high responsibility, they must be expected to act according to high moral principles. But these circumstances are so diverse, and the proper action in each case depends on so many considerations, that a formal code of behaviour—a 'Hippocratic Oath' for scientists—could never cover them adequately, nor be enforceable. In the end, there is probably no effective guidance other than the personal ethics by which they live, whether founded on humanistic values or on a transcendental religion. In other words, they must behave as well as any other men or women should in the same circumstances and with similar special knowledge, but with no special regard to their professional status as 'scientists'.

By the same token, scientists must be scrupulous not to claim *for themselves* rights that would not be available to other people in the world around them. Though they are often singled out for critical intelligence, diligence, imaginative creativity, and other personal attributes, and are usually given a very lengthy and arduous training that would distinguish them from, say, machine operators, shop assistants, or customs officials, their individual human rights are neither greater nor less than those of any other member of society. But just as infringements of the human rights

---

[2] For example, in various reports published by the American Association for the Advancement of Science.

of a doctor or a lawyer may damage many patients or clients, so infringements of the rights of a scientist which stifle creativity or invention may damage much more than the scientist himself. In a sense, therefore, scientists also hold their individual rights on trust for others. So our approach is to ask what rights do *all* people have, by simple virtue of their humanity, and how far would these rights—if conscientiously observed—safeguard the pursuit of science?

As will become apparent later, our analysis comes to what may at first appear a surprising conclusion. With only one exception—the lack of a right to enter a country of which one is not a citizen, for professional scientific purposes—*all the rights necessary for the free and effective pursuit of science are already covered by the existing international code of human rights law.* There is no need for a special 'charter' for science, balancing special privileges against special responsibilities. The rights already guaranteed in principle to *all* men and women, in all countries, cover all the professional needs of scientists. If the international code of human rights law could be properly enforced, then the pursuit of science would also be quite adequately protected.

One conclusion of this book is the remarkable consistency between the social structure of science and the legal framework of international human rights law. This consistency is seldom appreciated, but it emerges clearly from a detailed investigation and comparison of the two systems.[3] Once established in general, this consistency can be applied to the study of the realities of scientific freedom in any particular place, from the perspectives of the individual, the advancement of knowledge, and the rule of law, knowing that there is no inherent contradiction between these three different perspectives.

Problems of objectivity

Quite apart from the obvious differences between the constitutional, institutional, legal, and administrative systems of thirty-five different countries, a survey that attempts to cross the political divide which splits Europe also runs into a number of other problems. At the most superficial level, there is a problem about certain labels. In the Western 'Helsinki' countries, those of

[3] See *Scholarly Freedom and Human Rights* (Council for Science and Society; London, 1977).

the East are frequently called 'communist', a term generally used as one of opprobrium. In return, and with similar opprobrium, the Eastern countries are apt to call the Western countries 'capitalist'. In fact, neither of these labels provides an accurate description of the economic systems concerned. The Eastern countries do not themselves claim that they have yet achieved communism; they prefer to call themselves 'socialist', though it is at least arguable that 'state capitalism' would be a better description. Likewise, the Western countries do not see themselves so much as capitalist, but rather as 'mixed economies' in which free markets and free enterprise coexist with various degrees of public ownership, public intervention, and public regulation, and they prefer to call themselves 'liberal'—a term to which the other side is apt to add the word 'bourgeois', with pejorative intent. Similar disputes arise over the label 'democratic' which each side attaches to itself, and in which it claims to outperform the other.

In order to keep the emotive content of our survey to a minimum, we have tried wherever we can to avoid the use of labels which one side or the other regards as a term of abuse. Instead, we have generally used the term 'East' (or 'East European') where we have wanted to group together the seven Warsaw Pact states (the Soviet Union, Poland, Czechoslovakia, the German Democratic Republic, Hungary, Romania, and Bulgaria) as well as Yugoslavia; and 'West' for all the rest—even though we know that Sweden and Finland lie north, and Greece south, of the 'Eastern' bloc, and that Turkey and Cyprus lie east of all of it except the USSR. Where we have nevertheless used words like 'communist', 'capitalist', 'socialist', and 'liberal', we have tried to remember to put them into quotation marks.

Obviously, we cannot be oblivious to the political and military rivalries between the two major blocs, which tend to bias any commentator towards a partisan attitude on one side or the other. Science and international human rights law may both be transnational in scope and application, and provide objective languages and sets of basic principles which transcend the differences between economic systems. But we are not so naïve as to suppose, or so disingenuous as to pretend, that we can look on the European scene from an entirely detached point of view. Political oppression, the flouting of law, and the distortion of truth are matters which are apt to arouse moral concern, passionate feeling, and action, rather than detached contemplation. We believe, indeed, that the facts will speak well enough for themselves. But by studying the defects on both sides, we may better understand our own position, and also uncover certain disquieting trends even in countries that are fully committed to transnational science and freedom under the law.

2

SCIENCE AND SCIENTISTS; RIGHTS AND HUMAN RIGHTS

One world of science

Science is not just a matter of doing experiments with elaborate apparatus, and inventing subtle theories to explain the results. Of course it demands extremely careful observations with sensitive instruments, and a combination of imaginative insight and scrupulous logic to understand precisely what is going on. Scientists all over the world have to learn their subject thoroughly, and be trained in laboratory techniques, before they can even begin to do research. But if science has any 'method' it is in the way that it brings to bear on any question the attention of a whole *community* of well-informed critics.[1]

Everyone knows that scientists are always hoping to make original discoveries. But this would get out of hand if it were not continually curbed by communal criticism. Suppose, for example, that a scientist in Chicago reports the observation of an unusual effect. Scientists working on the same problem in Geneva, say, or Moscow, will try to repeat the experiment and see whether they get the same result: unless they succeed, the original observation will not be accepted as a genuine discovery. Or suppose that a scientist in Cambridge wants to publish a novel idea about, say, the origin of life: he knows that he must make a very strong case for it, because scientists in Paris and Stockholm who have spent their lives studying the same question will take a lot of convincing that he is right. Philosophers argue endlessly about whether entities described by scientists such as electrons are 'real', or even whether science-based knowledge is more 'true' in principle than any other set of beliefs about the world: they would all agree, however, that the hallmark of science is *organized scepticism* applied to all new and to many old ideas.

This creative tension between originality and scepticism can only be maintained if new and old facts, new and old arguments,

[1] See, e.g., Ziman, J. M., *Public Knowledge* (Cambridge University Press, 1967); *An Introduction To Science Studies* (Cambridge University Press, 1984).

are freely exchanged between scientists in public. One of the firmest traditions of science, dating back to the seventeenth century, is that it is a *communal* activity, devoted to the creation of a reliable and convincing body of *public* knowledge about the natural world. Individual scientists may do much of their research in private, but what they come to know in that way adds nothing to the body of 'scientific' knowledge until it has been disclosed to other scientists, and accepted by those able to judge best.

For this reason, the *communication* system of science is vital to its health. In principle, this system should be absolutely open: anybody, anywhere, might contribute a crucial observation or an incisive comment. In practice, modern science is so sophisticated that such contributions almost always come from people who already know a lot about the subject. But the question whether a particular observation or comment merits attention depends on whether it really makes a significant contribution to knowledge, not on whether it is made by a professional scientist or an amateur, by a professor or a student, by an American or a Russian. By its very nature, the communication system of science is bound to be *transnational*, in order to focus the widest possible body of expert opinion of each subject of scientific interest.

The process by which new scientific ideas are thus generated and tested may take many years. Even when a piece of scientific knowledge is regarded as well established, it may be impossible to prove that it is absolutely 'true'. All one can say is that every effort has been made to test its validity at every point, and that it is now accepted by almost all the scientists in the world who are acquainted with it. In other words, it displays the *consensuality* and *universality* which are characteristic of mature scientific knowledge.

This account of science as a social institution is obviously highly schematic: for example, the consensus of the scientific community on any particular point is seldom complete, even when a controversial matter seems to have been finally settled. It is also highly idealized: now that science has become a major factor in industry and war, other considerations—such as commercial secrecy and national security—affect its progress. This is very evident as one moves from relatively academic subjects, such as astronomy, to those closely linked with technology, such as solid state physics. Nevertheless, it cannot be denied that the reliability and credibility of scientific knowledge derives ultimately from the way it is gained and tested, through the combined efforts of the members of a world-wide community, who are both (usually friendly) rivals and yet perforce co-operate in a vast common enterprise.

The scientific community

Not only is the *scientific enterprise* universal and transnational: the more experienced of those who take part in it are also conscious of their membership of a universal and transnational *scientific community*. This was well illustrated by the positive response of scientists in many countries to the plight of their German Jewish colleagues before the Second World War. For most active scientists (apart from those corrupted by National Socialism), there could only be one world of science, whose members read each other's papers, corresponded regularly on scientific questions, met at conferences, attended lectures and seminars, collaborated formally as equals, were employed as research assistants, or studied for higher degrees, almost regardless of the accidents of geography and nationality. These professional contacts often developed into deep and lasting personal friendships. When such friends were in mortal peril, it was natural to do anything possible to save them. This sympathy was extended to other scientists whom one did not happen to know personally, but who were in similar need of help. In short, the communal spirit of science was a potent factor in the humanitarian help given during the 1930s to many of its members, from the most famous professors such as Albert Einstein to many more humble lecturers and students.

Communal spirit remains a powerful factor in the humanitarian activities of scientists. The community of interest that transcended the national frontiers of Europe in the 1930s now extends over all the continents, from Japan to Brazil, from Iraq to New Zealand. It is, of course, a much larger and more sophisticated community today than it was fifty years ago, but it is even more transnational in its network of communications, its travel itineraries, its job opportunities, and its personal friendships—and it remains transnational in its humanitarian impulses. Scientists everywhere recognize their moral duty to aid their companions in an enterprise whose scope is world-wide.

The facts presented in later chapters of this book demonstrate the continuing need for such solidarity among the members of the scientific community. Many are content to remain oblivious to this need, but for those who are aware of it, peace of mind requires that they do something, however little, in support of friends or respected professional acquaintances in other countries—a public protest, say, at the imprisonment of a Polish scientist whom one knew from personal acquaintance to be an honest if outspoken sort of man, or at the disappearance of a very able Argentinian scientist who had been a particularly gracious host on a visit to that country. It is therefore scarcely surprising that scientists, with their strong transnational links from person to person, have been in the forefront of such humanitarian action in the past few decades. But the point to be emphasized, especially to non-scientists, is that the spirit of communalism and universalism exhibited by this sort of action is not a mere humanitarian sentiment: it is an aspect of the spirit of science itself.

Scientists and their governments

All over the world, scientists are nowadays exceptionally dependent on their governments; in fact a large proportion of them are, directly or indirectly, state employees. In 'socialist' countries such as the Soviet Union, this applies to all scientists, whether engaged in higher education, academic research, or industrial research and development. In 'capitalist' countries the proportion might seem much smaller, but it can seldom be much less than 25 to 30 per cent, since it includes the large numbers of industrial scientists who are engaged in contract work for the government—especially in the field of defence.[2]

This dependence can expose scientists to some rather special pressures. Science is fostered, supported, or employed by modern governments primarily for practical purposes. Scientists are generally engaged to work towards explicit goals, such as making useful inventions, improving agriculture, curing diseases, and so on, rather than for the production of knowledge for its own sake. Since many of the policies of a national government are directly competitive with the policies of the governments of other nations, these goals are often mainly patriotic or commercial. There is therefore ample scope for conflicts of loyalties between 'the one world of science' and the many separate worlds of the nations—

[2] Rotblat, J. (ed.), *Scientists, the Arms Race and Disarmament* (UNESCO, Paris; Taylor & Francis, London; 1982).

not to mention the worlds of commercial corporations—where scientists actually work and live.

It is tempting for the government of a country to think of its scientists as a national resource, to be used mainly for the benefit of that country, and to rank that consideration above their roles as individuals and as participants in world science. For example, it is often important for scientists to be able to move from country to country, temporarily or even permanently, for instance to join a unique research group, but this may be blocked by a government, on the ground that the scientist in question is indispensable to the nation, or might even betray secrets to a potential enemy or commercial competitor. In a world composed of nation states prepared to defend their interests by war, there is no denying the legitimacy of national interests, especially where military security is at stake. But their profession puts many scientists into a situation where there may be a sharp conflict between these interests and their role as citizens of the one world of science—and, in some cases, even their responsibilities as decent human beings.

The vulnerability of scientists

The objectivity of science, and its disengagement from direct political issues, does not protect scientists as individuals from political attack. Unlike lawyers, journalists, and religious leaders, they may not always be in the front line of ideological battle; but as the proponents of objectivity and scepticism they are often prime targets of attack. One must not be misled by the relative rarity of such attacks. As the case of Galileo demonstrated to the world of learning, by muzzling a single prominent individual a whole community can be coerced into subservience to authority; by this one prosecution, the Inquisition effectively cowed Italian scientists for a century or more. Scientific hypotheses are often tentative in their formative stages, and are easily suppressed by defenders of vested interests, whether academic or ideological.

Scientists are not only vulnerable to coercion for expressing deviant *technical* views; they may also become objects of suspicion simply because they constitute a well-educated and relatively independent group in society, and sometimes turn their inquiring minds to the political and social problems around them. This has been the situation, for example, in several Latin American countries, where academic scientists have often been severely maltreated on the suspicion that they are sympathetic to radical or rev-olutionary forces; paradoxically, it is also the situation in the Soviet Union, where a substantial proportion of the leading political dissidents are scientists.

These are some of the reasons why scientists are especially exposed to attacks on their personal and professional freedom. As we shall see in Chapter 3, they are also particularly sensitive to some restrictions which might do others less harm. This is why we cannot disregard the cases of political or religious dissidents who just 'happen' to be scientists. For example, as a consequence of his outspokenness about much wider issues than freedom of scientific communication, Andrei Sakharov in the Soviet Union has been largely prevented from playing his proper part as a research scien-tist of international renown. Some people argue that he has now become more of a 'politician' than a 'scientist', and that this would debar him from support by any strictly 'non-political' scientific body unless he were a member of it. Any learned society must decide for itself whom it judges worthy of its support, but no such distinction is to be found in the code of international human rights law. As we shall see in Chapter 7, the sentence of internal exile, which was imposed on Sakharov without regard for his national or international legal rights, has effectively destroyed his professional career: the particular reason why he has suffered this manifestly unjust treatment cannot be a reason for not considering his case.

Nevertheless, we do not intend the theme of this book to extend over the whole human rights domain, which encompasses almost every vexed issue in every corner of the globe, from terrorism in Northern Ireland to freedom of the press in China. We shall keep to cases that are somehow related to science, whether through the cause which the victim defends, or through the means by which his or her rights are violated. The case of Sakharov is doubly relevant here, not only because he 'happens' to be an extra-ordinarily gifted scientist whose career has been unjustly destroyed, but because he has stood up with great courage for the transnational conception of science—and has, as a consequence, been personally deprived of just those rights, such as freedom of communication, which are essential to that conception.

Beyond that, scientists and their professional scientific organ-isations may have adequate and legitimate reason to protest at, say, the imprisonment and torture of some innocent Uruguayan professor, even if neither the supposed motive nor the actual means of the injustice has anything to do with his scientific work. Violations of the international code of human rights law ultimately affect everyone, and so provide ample justification for scientists generally to show their humanitarian solidarity with a fellow scientist in desperate trouble. As we shall see in the final chapter, the important question in such matters is how best to mobilize support and sympathy, and how to know what action is likely to be most effective, rather than to engage in theoretical analysis of who owes what sympathy to whom.

What do we mean by 'science'?

So far, we have referred to 'science' and 'scientists' without defining what we mean by these terms. We intend to keep mainly within the 'natural' sciences—mathematics, physics, chemistry, biology, geology, and so on—and their associated technologies, such as engineering, clinical medicine, and agricultural development. The limits are hard to define, because the world of science and scholarship extends into social studies and the humanities. Indeed, in languages other than English the word for 'science' embraces them both.

We are aware that by limiting our survey to scientists we shall exclude most of the worst instances of violations of the human rights of scholars and intellectuals. Those governments that deprive people of their individual human rights bear most heavily on the traditional humanities such as history and philosophy, and on certain branches of the social sciences, where these rights are analysed and celebrated. The study of history, for example, inevitably brings to light the crimes and follies of past governments, and hence, if the historian is at all honest, casts doubts upon the claims of present-day rulers. The historian or literary critic has to speak openly about human values—and invites comparison with the values of the people around him. *Index on Censorship*, the authoritative review with world-wide coverage, shows clearly enough that governments react far more oppressively against those who try to evaluate their performance against stated or historical ideals than against most 'natural' scientists. A selection of cases from *Index*, or from the reports of Amnesty International, recounting the imprisonment and torture of poets, playwrights, novelists, and journalists, would be more striking than the cases presented in this book if our sole purpose were to arouse sympathy for the general cause of human rights around the world.

But our purpose is somewhat different. It is to show that even 'natural' science is founded upon some very important human values such as trust, sincerity, openness, independence of mind, originality, honest scepticism, and respect for the dignity, worth, and integrity of others, and that these values can only be expressed meaningfully by people who are secure in their fundamental rights and liberties. And it is to show that even these elementary rights cannot be taken for granted: they have to be upheld wherever they are threatened. We therefore deliberately restrict our discussion to the 'hard' sciences, in order to be able to make these points without complications arising from political, religious, or other ideological controversies.

Rights and human rights

Having now charted the field of science and scientists which is one part of our concern, we must turn to the other: human rights. In this book, there is neither space nor need to deal with its genesis, history, and content in more than the most summary fashion.[3]

The concept of 'rights' has been a fertile field of discourse for theologians, philosophers, and political scientists over many centuries. What exactly do we mean when we say that someone has a right? How are rights acquired, and how are they lost? Are there some rights which are 'inherent' in, and 'inalienable' by, everyone, so that they need not be acquired, and cannot be lost, by any particular transaction? If so, from what antecedents are these derived? Do they follow from the natural condition of human beings in society, or must their roots be traced to some religious, ethical, or cultural system? Are they coherent and all of a kind, or do they fall into discernible categories? Besides, what is the relationship between rights and laws? Within any given society, who is competent to make laws, and what are the necessary properties of any particular law which require us to obey it?

On all these questions, many different theories have been—and are still being—put forward. Fortunately, in this book we need not concern ourselves with any of them, for although there is still (and probably always will be) wide disagreement on some of them,

[3] The reader who wishes to delve further into this is referred to Sieghart, P., *The Lawful Rights of Mankind* (Oxford University Press, 1985).

there is a very large measure of agreement on at least one proposition: if, within any given community, there is overwhelming (even if not absolutely universal) agreement about the content of a particular law, then the rights and duties which that law confers and imposes are 'positive' values in that community, and the law constitutes a rule of conduct which the members of the community must obey so long as they wish to remain within it. As we shall see shortly, just such an agreement has been reached quite recently among the members of the international community of sovereign states about certain rights and freedoms of their individual inhabitants. For lack of a better label and in order both to mark their universality and to distinguish them from other kinds of rights and freedoms, these are called 'human' rights and 'fundamental' freedoms.

National human rights

Until fairly recently, most laws were made by rulers—traditionally known to international lawyers as 'sovereign Princes'—for their 'subjects'. Today, they are made by the legislative assemblies of nation states, at least ostensibly on behalf of their sovereign peoples. Over many centuries, this process has involved struggles for power, and it still does. One of the leading features of those struggles has been a series of attempts to impose constraints on the absolute power of the law-maker to make what laws he pleased—even if the law-maker was an elected assembly, in order to avoid what Alexis de Tocqueville once called 'the tyranny of the majority'. The great landmarks in that series include famous documents like the English Magna Carta of 1215, the Act of Abjuration of the Netherlands States-General of 1581, the English Bill of Rights of 1688, the French Declaration of the Rights of Man and the Citizen of 1789, the American Bill of Rights of 1791, and the post-revolutionary or post-independence constitutions of many modern states. Underlying those struggles was a variety of theories of 'divine' law or 'natural' law which conferred on individuals certain 'inherent' and 'inalienable' rights which no law-maker could *legitimately* infringe: a principle first encapsulated in the maxim *lex iniusta non est lex* coined by medieval canon lawyers—'an unjust law is not a law'.

By the turn of the present century, most sovereign nations had incorporated into their constitutions a catalogue of rights which, within the limits defined for them, were to be treated as vested in every human individual by virtue of his or her humanity alone. Because the national constitution stands supreme in the hierarchy of national laws, all other laws, whether embodied in civil and penal codes or otherwise, must be consistent with and subordinate to its authority: neither the legislative nor the executive power of the state could infringe it. These rights included such rights as the right to life, to liberty and security, freedom from arbitrary arrest, equality before the law, fair trial, freedom of movement, freedom of religion, and so forth.

It must be emphasized that these rights have one special characteristic: they are defined primarily in relation to the power and authority of the state and its institutions. In general, for every right recognized by law there is a correlative duty imposed on someone other than its holder: if I have a right, someone else (or, it may be, everyone else) has a duty to respect that right. If I have a right to cross the street safely, every motorist has a duty to drive with care. If I have a right to occupy my house or apartment, others have a duty not to enter it without my consent. If my landlord has a right to receive rent for it, I have a duty to pay it on the appointed days. But for the 'universal' or 'fundamental' rights inhering in every human individual, the correlative duty to respect them falls in the first instance on the state, which must not itself infringe them, and must enact the necessary laws, and use its monopoly of power to enforce these, in order to ensure that no one else will infringe them either.

These then were the classical 'civil rights', 'civil liberties', or 'Rights of Man', on the national plane. But there were soon added to them some other rights where the duty of the state was more positive, namely to intervene actively in order to redress economic or social injustices of the kinds which had become manifest during the industrial revolution, and which led to the recognition of rights such as those to public education, health care, municipal housing, unemployment benefit, and social security. These were variously called 'programme rights' or 'welfare rights', and although they owed their development at least in part to early socialist writers such as Proudhon, they were introduced by many countries which have never been 'socialist' in the modern sense.

By the turn of the present century, therefore, what we now call 'human' rights were already quite well protected by the national legal systems of a number of the world's major nations—best of all, perhaps, in the UK, the USA, and France.

International human rights

While all this was going on at many national levels, *international* law took very little notice of it. This was not for lack of any humanitarian concerns, but simply because international law was concerned only with the macroscopic sphere of the legal relations between sovereign Princes or nation states. It dealt with war and peace, diplomatic emissaries, international trade, customs duties, and such-like matters—not with the manner in which a sovereign Prince treated his own subjects within his own realm. Indeed, the doctrine of 'national sovereignty' expressly precluded international law from being concerned with almost anything that went on within a sovereign Prince's territory, or within the relationships between him and his subjects. Not until the late nineteenth century, for instance, did international law have anything to say even about the outlawing of the slave trade, and then only because this formed a contentious part of the trading relationships *between* sovereign states. However, following the First World War, the League of Nations began to concern itself with certain 'humanitarian affairs'—including the promotion of an international Slavery Convention, designed to encourage the world's nations not only to stop trading in slaves, but actually to eliminate the institution of slavery within their own territories. And at about the same time, the International Labour Organization began to promote international treaties designed to reduce the worst excesses of the exploitation of labour.

Then, within a very few years, there occurred not only a series of civil and international wars and occupations—such as those in Spain, Abyssinia, China, and Manchuria—but also two quite horrifying domestic cataclysms: the Nazi holocaust, in which six million Jews perished, together with Gypsies, and later innumerable numbers of Byelorussians, Poles, Balts, Ukrainians, and others; and the wholesale liquidation of 'kulaks' and other groups in Stalin's Russia, where the victims may well have been even more numerous.

These events placed into sharp focus a yawning gap in the world's legal system: there was at that time nothing to make any of these horrors *illegal*, however much anyone's conscience might have been shocked by them. Hitler's Nuremberg laws, which legalized the persecution of the German Jews, had been enacted with all due formality by a constitutionally established legislature of the sovereign German Reich, and the liquidation of the kulaks in the USSR was likewise supported by appropriate legal formulae. And, since both these were sovereign states, what happened within them could not be the legitimate concern of international law.

In order to fill that gap, the international community of nations did something unprecedented in international law: they set up a legally binding code which would impose upon sovereign states legal obligations as to what they could, and could not, legitimately do to their inhabitants—so conferring on those inhabitants individual rights *under international law* against their own states and their public authorities. As one of the great international lawyers of our century, Professor Sir Hersch Lauterpacht, put it in 1950, 'the individual has acquired a status and a stature which has transformed him from an object of international compassion into a subject of international right'.[4]

Components of the code

The international community of nations has no supreme lawmaking assembly. Rather like preliterate villages or tribal communities in many parts of the world, it can only make its laws by consent, which nowadays takes the form of multilateral treaties, variously called Conventions, Covenants, or Pacts. The first such treaty to deal with human rights generally, made just before the end of the Second World War, was the Charter of the United Nations, by Articles 55 and 56 of which the then 56 members of the United Nations (whose number has since swelled to nearly 160) 'pledge themselves to take joint and separate action . . . for the achievement of . . . universal respect for, and observance of, human rights and fundamental freedoms for all without distinction as to race, sex, language, or religion.' Precisely what these 'human rights and fundamental freedoms' were to be was not defined until three years later when, on 10 December 1948, the United Nations adopted the famous Universal Declaration of Human Rights (which we shall call 'the UDHR'), whose 30 Articles contain a comprehensive catalogue of civil, political, economic, social, and cultural rights, without any ranking or distinction between them.

[4] Lauterpacht, H., *International Law and Human Rights* (Stevens; London, 1950) p. 4.

Widely known, eminently quotable, and frequently quoted though it is, one must remember that the UDHR is *not* itself a treaty; in so far as it has any binding force, it can only be because the world's governments regularly cite it with approval (especially when it suits them to use it in criticizing the human rights record of another state with which they have no current strategic alliance or mutual common interest), and because its Preamble refers back to Articles 55 and 56 of the UN Charter, and it can therefore be read as supplying the missing definition of the 'human rights and fundamental freedoms' there referred to. Since virtually all the world's nations are members of the UN (among the 'Helsinki' states, only Switzerland, Liechtenstein, Monaco, San Marino, and the Holy See are not), it is therefore strongly arguable that their 'pledge' in the UN Charter to 'take joint and separate action for the achievement of universal respect for, and observance of, human rights and fundamental freedoms for all' binds them in international law to respect and observe precisely those rights and freedoms which are enumerated in the UDHR.

However, the United Nations did not stop at that point: they went on to draft two more treaties to put the matter beyond any legal doubt. Because of the worsening relations between East and West, this process took a good deal longer: the texts were not agreed until 1966, and they did not come into force until ten years after that. But they have been in force ever since, in the form of two International Covenants, one on Civil and Political Rights, and the other on Economic, Social, and Cultural Rights (which we shall henceforth call 'the ICCPR' and 'the ICESCR' for short). These treaties are drafted with even greater precision than the UDHR, and between them they cover almost exactly the same ground. (The division into two of the UDHR's single catalogue was done at the insistence of the Soviet Union and its allies, but the Preambles to the Covenants themselves make it clear that neither of them has any priority over the other.)

Meanwhile, much quicker progress was being made at a regional level: as early as 1950, the members of the Council of Europe had adopted the text of a European Convention for the Protection of Human Rights and Fundamental Freedoms ('the ECHR') which covers much the same civil and political rights as the ICCPR. This came into force in 1953, and now has all the 21 member states of the Council of Europe as parties. (Some additional Protocols have since been added to it, protecting further rights.) In 1961, the Council of Europe also adopted a European Social Charter ('the ESC') covering certain economic, social, and cultural rights, which came into force in 1965 and now has 15 state parties. In other regions of the world, an American Convention on Human Rights was adopted by the members of the Organization of American States in 1969 and came into force in 1978, and the text of an African Charter of Human and Peoples' Rights was adopted by the members of the Organization of African Unity in 1981, but has not yet come into force.

In Appendix 1 we reprint the full text of the UDHR, and the substantive Articles of the ICCPR, ICESCR, ECHR and ESC. For convenience of reference, we also list in Appendix 2 the rights with which these instruments deal, and the numbers of their relevant Articles.

As well as the global and regional treaties which deal with many rights and freedoms at a time, there are also around twenty specialized treaties dealing in greater detail with just one, or a few allied aspects—such as, for example, the Slavery Convention of 1926 already referred to, or the UNESCO Convention against Discrimination in Education of 1962, to which we shall have occasion to refer in Chapter 4. Apart from these, there is a whole variety of other international instruments called 'Declarations', 'Recommendations', or 'Resolutions', which are not treaties and whose effect is therefore persuasive rather than legally binding. As we have already explained, this is the formal status of the Helsinki Accords, which are not legally binding on the signatory states, but which cite the international instruments relating to the human rights of their inhabitants by which they *are* bound. These Accords are also of great importance because they contain provisions for a regular 'Follow-up to the Conference', in the form of further conferences to be held at regular intervals. The first of these opened in Belgrade in 1977, the second in Madrid in 1980, the third in Ottawa in 1985. Because of this procedure, the performance by these particular 35 states of the promises made in this particular text is being particularly closely monitored, and an unusually full amount of information is available about it.

Contents and effects of the code
Any sovereign state is perfectly free to become, or not to become, a party to an international treaty. It becomes a party not, as one

might expect, by signature, but by a procedure called (depending on circumstances) either 'ratification' or 'accession'. In either case, the state concerned is said to have 'adhered' to the treaty. From the effective date of that adherence, the state becomes legally bound to perform its obligations under the treaty 'in good faith'.

Appendix 3 shows the dates of adherence to the principal human rights treaties for the 35 'Helsinki' countries. As will be seen, 23 of them (including all the Eastern ones) have adhered to both the Covenants, 21 to the ECHR, and 15 to the ESC. Only the Holy See, Monaco, San Marino, and the USA have not yet adhered to any of them.

The three city states are not members either of the UN or of the Council of Europe, so they could not adhere even if they wished to. As for the USA, several reasons are usually put forward why, despite its public championship of human rights, it has not so far adhered to any of these treaties. The first is that the US Constitution, and the US Supreme Court which interprets and applies it, already give ample protection for human rights at the domestic level, and that there is therefore no need to superimpose yet another tier over a system which has been found increasingly effective, over the best part of two centuries, in protecting those civil rights and civil liberties that are enshrined in the constitutional Bill of Rights of 1791. (Indeed, it has been argued that such a step might indirectly amend the Constitution, and so itself be unconstitutional.) Another reason is that the 50 individual States of the Union display a jealous concern not to allow a Federal Government, by adherence to an international treaty, to impose limitations (beyond those already contained in the Federal Constitution) on the laws that their state legislatures might wish to enact. Finally, there is the difficulty of obtaining the necessary two-thirds majority for ratification from the US Senate which jealously preserves, and regularly exercises, its constitutional right to prevent the Federal Government from entering into foreign treaties of which it does not approve.

All these, of course, are arguments founded on the traditional concept of national sovereignty, and have in their time been put forward by many other nations which have eventually adhered to one or more of the treaties concerned. But, as we have already seen, the object of installing the new superior tier of international human rights law is precisely to remove this whole field from the

exclusive jurisdiction of sovereign states, and the price for achieving that objective is therefore necessarily an abridgment, by common consent, of national sovereignty. It is true that states with a
federal structure, and therefore more than one tier of sovereignty
within their territories, have special problems in adhering to such
treaties. But this has not prevented a number of them—such as
Australia, Canada, and India—from adhering to the UN Covenants. Indeed even Switzerland, which has not joined the UN and
is a fiercely federal state whose cantons and communes never miss
an opportunity of defending their old-established sovereign rights
against the federal government, has freely chosen to adhere to the
ECHR.

In the human rights treaties, the state obligations are very clearly
defined. They fall into two distinct categories. For the treaties that
deal with civil and political rights, the state obligation is absolute
and immediate: Article 2(1) of the ICCPR, for example, says that:

'Each State Party to the present Covenant undertakes to respect and to
ensure to all individuals within its territory and subject to its jurisdiction
the rights recognised in the present Covenant, without distinction of any
kind, such as race, colour, sex, language, religion, political or other
opinion, national or social origin, property, birth or other status'.

For the treaties dealing with economic, social, and cultural
rights, the words of obligation are relative and progressive: for
example, Article 2 of the ICESCR provides that:

'(1) Each State Party to the present Covenant undertakes to take steps,
individually and through international assistance and co-operation, especially economic and technical, to the maximum of its available resources,
with a view to achieving progressively the full realization of the rights
recognized in the present Covenant by all appropriate means, including
particularly the adoption of legislative measures.

(2) The State Parties to the present Covenant undertake to guarantee
that the rights enunciated in the present Covenant will be exercised
without discrimination of any kind as to race, colour, sex, language,
religion, political or other opinion, national or social origin, property,
birth or other status.'

The reason for the distinction is simply that, in the case of the
'programme' or 'welfare' rights dealt with by the second of these
Covenants, the ability of a state party to provide them will depend
far more on the state's available economic and other resources than

in the case of civil and political rights, most (though by no means all) of which are rights of 'non-interference'. But this does not mean that either of these sets of rights is any less, or any more, 'universal', 'inherent', or 'inalienable' than the other, nor that there is any ranking of priority between them: it is simply that the correlative obligations imposed on the states differ in these particular respects.

It will be observed that each of these Articles of obligation contains an express prohibition against any form of discrimination. This is of course crucially important in the case of rights and freedoms which are said to be universal, are not acquired by the grant of the state or any other transaction, and cannot be taken away, forfeited, sold, or otherwise 'alienated'. In a sense, non-discrimination is the key to all 'human' rights, and we shall come to appreciate the central role of this provision as our enquiry proceeds.

Having imposed the state obligation, the treaties then proceed to define the precise rights which their state parties are bound to 'respect', 'ensure', 'secure', or 'realize'. In order to do this, they must define the boundaries of the rights and freedoms concerned, since it is a commonplace that, in a human society, few rights or freedoms can be absolute. (The only exceptions in the treaties are the absolute prohibitions of slavery, and of torture or cruel or inhuman or degrading treatment or punishment.) For this purpose, the treaties use the technique of defining, with careful precision, what restrictions and limitations are allowed for the right concerned. It is important to appreciate from the start that this is *not* (as one might be forgiven for thinking at a first reading) a way of taking away with one hand what has been given with the other, but simply a method for delineating boundaries in order that there should not be collisions between different rights, or between the rights of one individual and the legitimate interests of the other members of his or her community. The restrictions and limitations cannot erode the central right: they can only serve to define its limits. The same principle also applies to the opportunity which most of the treaties allow to their state parties to 'derogate' from *some* of the protected rights 'in time of war or public emergency threatening the life of the nation'—but even then only 'to the extent strictly required by the exigencies of the situation.'

These treaties, and the interpretation which they have been

given by a variety of competent international and national organs, now constitute a substantial corpus of international law regulating the rights of individuals against states, and the obligations of states to individuals. Indeed, the measure of this corpus is indicated by the fact that, when one of the present authors attempted merely to state its detailed content without even discussing it, the result occupies nearly 600 pages of close print, with around 1,600 references.[5] There is no point in even attempting to summarize it here: we shall quote the relevant Articles and interpretations as required when we come to consider their importance to scientists in later chapters.

For our present purposes, we need only make one more point about the effect and content of the code. Until it came into force, what were 'human rights'—and indeed whether there were any— was a matter of legitimate dispute, on which different people could come to quite different conclusions depending on their religious, political, ideological, or ethical convictions. Indeed, human rights could scarcely be discussed apart from politics or morality. Today, that is no longer so. What human rights now *are* is conclusively determined by the content of the international code. One may not like what one finds there; one may think it goes too far, or not far enough; one might wish to amend or augment it: on all such questions political, ideological, religious, and ethical debate will doubtless continue. But as to the present contents of the code, the only remaining area of legitimate dispute is that of the precise meaning and effect of its provisions, an area properly reserved to lawyers, who conduct such disputes before the appropriate tribunals, and in their learned journals, in accordance with the specialized rules and techniques which they have developed for this purpose—not unlike scientists among themselves. Like science, the code is, in principle, universal and transnational, unaffected by the ethnic, cultural, political, religious, or economic differences among the nations to which it applies.

In short, for a sovereign state which is bound by the international code, it is today no longer legitimate to dismiss a foreign critic of its national laws and administrative practices with the classic defence of an 'illegitimate interference in its domestic affairs', nor is such a state entitled to defend itself on the ground

[5] See Sieghart, P., *The International Law of Human Rights* (Clarendon Press; Oxford, 1983).

that it starts from political or ideological premises which differ from the critic's; how a state treats its individual inhabitants has today become the legitimate business of the whole of the international community and everyone in it, to be evaluated and assessed by the objective criteria of international human rights law. To that extent, the ancient doctrine of national sovereignty has been abridged by the common consent of the nations themselves.

Enforcement of the code

As we have seen, the primary obligation of the state parties to the human rights treaties is *themselves* to 'respect', 'ensure', 'secure', or 'realize' the rights and freedoms concerned within their own territories. Enforcement of the code is therefore in the first instance something to be done at the national level—and indeed the UDHR, the ICCPR, and the ECHR all require their state parties to provide their inhabitants with 'an effective remedy' for any violations of their protected rights, even if these have been committed by 'persons acting in an official capacity'.

In effect, this provision requires each of the state parties to install, at the domestic level, an effective system for the protection of human rights, and to operate that system under what has long been called 'the rule of law'—that is, to enact only laws which will conform with its international obligations, to operate only within those laws, and to install impartial and independent courts and tribunals from which individuals can obtain redress, *even against the state itself*, for any violations of their protected rights. (The treaties also contain detailed provisions about various other aspects of the rule of law, such as recognition and equality before the law, equal protection by the law, the right to a fair trial, and various aspects of 'due process'.)

In assessing any particular state's performance of its obligations under the code, one must therefore first examine whether its domestic laws and practices adequately protect the rights and freedoms concerned, whether the state adequately enforces these laws and itself abides by them, and whether there are independent and impartial tribunals, accessible to everyone, for the redress of any infringement of these rights, even by the state's own agents.

Provided the state does all that, it will conform with its international obligations, and its inhabitants' human rights will be adequately protected. But what if it does not—if its laws are not good enough, or its own officials do not abide by them, or there is no redress for the resulting human rights violations in its own courts? Here we arrive at what is still the major weakness of the new code, for what is required at this point is some 'effective remedy' at the *international* level. However, just as the international community still lacks a single legislative assembly, so also does it lack an international enforcement agency and even a single international court with compulsory jurisdiction over its members. *International* enforcement of the code—as indeed of all international law—is therefore still rudimentary, and depends more than anything on pressures and sanctions applied by the members of the international community, themselves often under pressure from their electorates and from the increasingly important expression of international public opinion.

But even here there have been important developments. The ICCPR, for example, is subject to the supervision of an international Human Rights Committee, composed of independent experts who do not sit as representatives of their governments. Each of the state parties to that treaty is bound to—and does—render regular reports on the performance of its treaty obligations to this Committee, and its members can—and do—submit the representatives of the states concerned to searching public examinations on these reports. Under an Optional Protocol to that Covenant, more than 30 of the state parties have now recognized the Committee's competence to receive, investigate, and report on 'communications' from *individuals* complaining of infringements of their human rights against the state concerned. It is a measure of the utility of this procedure, established only since 1976, that three countries—Canada, Finland, and Mauritius—have already changed their laws and administrative practices, following adverse findings by the Committee in such cases.

There is no comparable committee to supervise the ICESCR: this task is meant to be performed by the UN Economic and Social Council. However, being a body composed of governmental representatives, it has so far done nothing of any note in this field. By contrast, the ESC is supervised by a European Committee of Experts, whose published Conclusions on the regular reports submitted to it by the state parties have had a substantial and beneficial effect, and have led to many changes in national practices, principally in the field of employment.

But by far the most formidable procedures for supervision—and indeed enforcement—are those which have now been operating for thirty years in the context of the ECHR. Here, two different bodies—the European Commission of Human Rights and the European Court of Human Rights, both located in Strasbourg and composed of independent lawyers—have developed a wealth of international case law on the provisions of that treaty. More than 10,000 individual complaints—in this case termed 'petitions'—have been presented to the Commission, and more than fifty important cases have gone on to the Court. This has jurisdiction to hand down binding judgments against the state concerned, which that state is then bound to carry out. As a result, many states have changed their laws or administrative practices, and hundreds of people have had adverse decisions against them reversed, or been compensated by their governments. In this system, even the most extreme legal positivist would be compelled to admit that individuals can have *enforceable* human rights against their states at the international level.

Nevertheless, the sad fact remains that human rights continue to be violated in many other parts of the world, sometimes in states which are parties to one or other of the relevant treaties. Critics of the modern human rights system often cite this fact in support of the proposition that human rights are only an illusion—that the very concept remains, in Jeremy Bentham's famous words, 'nonsense upon stilts'. Such criticism is founded on an elementary category mistake: the fact that a law is broken, even frequently, puts in question only the adequacy of the means for its enforcement, not the law itself. Chicago has a notoriously high murder rate, but it does not follow either that there is not, or that there ought not to be, a law against murder in the state of Illinois. The international law of human rights undoubtedly exists, but it is a very recent—and indeed revolutionary—development on the legal landscape. As more time passes and as more people get to know it better and begin to use it, it will doubtless become better enforced—though, like all human laws, it will doubtless also continue to be broken in different places at different times.

Other pressures supporting the code
Public opinion plays a very important part in ensuring that laws are obeyed or enforced, and this effect is becoming increasingly

felt at the international level. An important consequence of the coming into force of the international code of human rights law is that it provides a means of focussing criticism on a public authority which violates it. Before 1945, no such forum existed: criticism of the Nazi regime in Germany, for example, could be raised only in the parliamentary assemblies and the press of other countries, or debated ineffectively at the League of Nations. Quite apart from the institutions with legal responsibility to determine such questions, there are now several international fora in which the governments of states which offend against the international code of human rights law can be called to account. Some of these fora, like the General Assembly of the United Nations, are given over mainly to political debates, but their influence can still be considerable. There are also the United Nations Commission on Human Rights and its Sub-Commission, which are not only able to study particular problems affecting human rights and to suggest solutions, but also have procedures for considering communications to the UN Secretary-General of allegations of a consistent pattern of gross violations of human rights. Other UN agencies, such as UNESCO, the World Health Organisation, the International Atomic Energy Agency, etc. have special terms of reference in particular areas of activity, and are able to exert influence in those areas not only through debate but through the allocation and distribution of funds to a wide variety of programmes. Since the members of such agencies are national governments, their actions are inevitably influenced by international politics. Nevertheless, as organs of the United Nations they are bound by the international human rights code which has its origins in the UDHR; indeed, some of them, such as the International Labour Organization, have contributed to the refinement of that code in their special fields.

In particular, UNESCO, as the agency of the UN concerned with science as a social institution, has gone into these issues in some depth. In 1974, the General Conference of UNESCO adopted a statement of Recommendations on the Status of Scientific Researchers ('RSSR') which touches on many aspects of scientific freedom. This document (which we reproduce in Appendix 4) was adopted after considerable debate, involving representatives of governments and learned societies, and its provisions are recommended to member states of UNESCO for legislative action, dissemination to responsible institutions, and subsequent report.

Next, there are non-governmental organizations—international bodies whose members are not national governments or appointed by national governments, but which are recognized as having 'consultative status' with the UN and its agencies. Among those relevant for our purposes are the International Council of Scientific Unions ('ICSU') and the International Commission of Jurists ('ICJ'). ICSU is a federal body of various international unions of different branches of science (themselves composed of national learned societies in each branch) and of national academies of science. In recent years it has established specialized committees concerned with freedom in science (see Chapter 13). The ICJ's principal concern is the Rule of Law, and the observance of human rights throughout the world in accordance with the international instruments.

Another relevant non-governmental organization is the World Federation of Scientific Workers, a federation of national organizations of scientists, including trade unions, professional associations, etc. concerned with the applications of science and the rights, duties and training of scientific workers (see Chapter 13). The Declaration of the Rights of Scientific Workers ('DRSW') adopted by the General Assembly of the WFSW in 1969 contains many references to the needs of scientific freedom. (See Appendix 5.)

What all these bodies have in common is that they are international and so concerned with affairs throughout the world, regardless of national boundaries or the policies of national governments. Although their decisions may have no formal legal or diplomatic authority, they are of considerable relevance to the preservation of scientific freedom. Their special expertise also enables them to propose interpretations, elaborations and refinements of the formal instruments which have grown out of the needs and aspirations of scientists themselves, and thus carry considerable weight within the scientific community. They provide a model for the practices appropriate to 'the one world of science' which must be our ideal.

Having now described how and why the new code was made, and how it works, we must see how its particular provisions apply to scientists and their work.

3

THE RIGHTS AND FREEDOMS
IMPORTANT FOR SCIENCE

All human rights are important

The international code of human rights law covers a great many eventualities, any one of which might happen to anyone, whether a scientist or not, during the course of his or her life. On a particular occasion, it may be very important indeed to have the right to marry whom one will, or the right to fair access to medical treatment, or the right to apply promptly to an impartial judge for release from arrest. But the importance of different rights to different individuals at different times does not determine the relative importance of the rights themselves. The code treats them all as having equal value; it does not rank them in any order of priority; as the UN General Assembly has repeatedly pointed out, they are all 'interdependent and indivisible'.[1]

However, our particular concern in this book is with those rights and freedoms which are specially important for *science*. Scientists as a group do not ask to be thought of as special, in the sense of claiming that they should be given any special privileges. But they are a group of people with a particular type of training, with characteristic types of work to do, and with particular professional needs. Some of these needs can only be met by setting up large organizations to provide the resources and facilities for research, or for advanced education, or for publishing scientific papers. But there are also needs that are essentially individual. Within the international code can be found certain personal rights and freedoms that are of special importance to scientists *in the exercise of their profession*. In this chapter we shall briefly survey these rights, showing how they relate to the pursuit of science, before we report in detail in later chapters on the extent to which scientists are actually able to enjoy them in the 'Helsinki' countries.

Any attempt to single out the human rights and fundamental

[1] For the most recent and comprehensive of these statements, see Resolution 32/130 of 16 December 1977.

freedoms of particular importance to scientists must be to some extent arbitrary. The list which we develop here is a minimum one, and the detailed examination of its separate components in the later chapters will bring in others. Each right stands by itself, but they are all closely linked, forming parts of an indivisible whole. Scientists are of course entitled to all these rights in the same measure as any other citizens, for they are individuals first and scientists second. But in that second capacity, they are peculiarly vulnerable in two respects: even apparently minor restrictions or denials of some of their rights may seriously prejudice their professional development, achievement, and output; at the same time, the relative responsibility, and consequent influence, which they are likely to enjoy in their countries may, if they question established authority or dissent from its policies, more readily attract the kinds of repressive action which gravely violate their human rights not only in a personal but in a professional context. In short, there are some rather special ways in which scientists may become thorns in the flesh of their state's authorities, and some rather special ways in which those authorities can destroy them professionally, even without seeming to destroy them personally.

The 'special' rights and freedoms

The rights and freedoms which are specially important for the pursuit of science could be ordered or classified in various ways. The order in which we take up various topics in this chapter, and in the more detailed chapters that follow, is derived primarily from a practical conception of the scientific life as 'work', undertaken in the course of a 'career'. We hope that this may be more immediately comprehensible to working scientists and others than a classification according to some theoretical notion of the intrinsic importance of the various rights, or the various forms of oppression that arise in practice, or the relative extent to which different rights are enforceable by the legal machinery or by political pressures. It also allows us to emphasize certain characteristic features of scientific research, such as the informal exchange of information and opinion, whose value is not always appreciated by those who have no direct personal experience of this specialized way of life.

A typical scientific career would begin with formal education and training in research. This would be followed by employment in scientific work, where it would be necessary to have access to scientific information, and to communicate the results of research to other scientists. This leads naturally to the expression of opinions about the work of other scientists. To take part in critical discussions of new scientific ideas, scientists need to move around, and to meet together in various groupings. If their work has been well done, they may win a personal reputation and be eventually honoured publicly for their intellectual achievements. Schematically, these are the successive stages in a typical scientific career.

Given that sequence, we shall therefore study the following areas of rights and freedoms in the following order:

1. Education and training;
2. Work and choice of work;
3. Communication;
4. Opinion and expression;
5. Movement;
6. Assembly and association;
7. Honour, reputation, and intellectual achievement.

Before examining these areas more thoroughly in later chapters, let us first look at them briefly here in order to show the importance of each of them in the overall pattern of scientific work.

Education and training

Science is a highly skilled profession, which can be entered only after long years of formal education, followed by a substantial period of training in research. Access to an appropriate education is therefore an essential prerequisite for a scientific career. As Article 26(1) of the UDHR puts it:

'Everyone has the right to education . . . Technical and professional education shall be made generally available . . . '

But higher education calls upon economic resources, and this right is therefore necessarily limited in any given country by its economic and social circumstances. All education is expensive, and that of scientists is particularly long and costly. One could not therefore claim that a government had violated the international code of human rights law simply because one believed that it had not given a sufficiently high priority to scientific education in general.

But what the code does require is that the allocation of such a scarce resource must be carried out without any illegitimate discrimination. The cardinal precept, which the code fully recognizes, is that access to those higher levels of education which are essential for a scientific career must depend on merit and capacity alone. That merit must be scientific, not skill at football or dialectical materialism. And this rule must continue to govern any further training for scientists, after they have already embarked on their careers. Negative discrimination on any other grounds and positive discrimination on nepotic, political, or ideological grounds could be equally effective in preventing a would-be scientist from embarking on this career, and are equally unacceptable. We shall look at this in more detail in Chapter 4.

Work and choice of work

Modern scientific research demands time and material resources for observation and experiment, far beyond those normally available to the part-time amateur. Scientists by and large are paid professional workers, and depend vitally on the availability of suitable employment. This right, again, is proclaimed unequivocally in Article 23(1) of the UDHR:

'Everyone has the right to work, to free choice of employment, to just and favourable conditions of work, and to protection against unemployment'.

As we shall see in Chapter 5, the precise meaning of the 'right' to work is highly debateable. But *freedom* to work is obviously as basic a right for a scientist as it is for anyone else. There is great personal satisfaction in carrying out the highly skilled professional work for which one has undergone a long and arduous training. But the opportunity to enjoy this is bound to depend upon economic realities. In particular, the possibility of choosing in detail the precise area of one's scientific employment cannot be claimed as an absolute right. Plainly it makes good sense for scientists to be employed in scientific work for which their extensive and expensive training and upbringing have prepared them. Within that area, it makes equally good sense to leave them as far as possible to elect for work which matches their inclinations as well as their training and experience. Like most creative people, scientists will be most productive when they feel committed to their work and believe in its value and rightness.

But even if scientists cannot be entirely free to work in any area they choose, they must be entirely free, without suffering any penalties, to follow their conscience and refuse to work in fields to which they are morally or scientifically averse. 'Conscientious objection' in science must be considered a very important right, for the number of areas where there can be valid grounds of objection is already alarmingly large. Scientists, by reason of their special knowledge and experience, may perceive the evils and dangers of certain policies sooner or more sharply than laymen. They may not have the power to change those policies, but it is right and necessary that they should be free to provide the knowledge which should inform such changes, however unpalatable that knowledge may be to the decision-makers. And they have a compelling moral duty to resist the perversion by others of the fruits of their knowledge—such as, for example, the use of certain psychotropic drugs, normally employed in the legitimate treatment of mental illness, for the personality control of people whose opinions are thought to be 'awkward' by the authorities.

A very important item for the defence of scientific freedom is protection of the scientific worker from arbitrary dismissal. A scientist who is dismissed at short notice from a responsible research post in an area where he or she has become expert may not find it at all easy to obtain comparable employment in the same specialized field, and their expertise may thus be wasted. It is true that some very able persons have made significant contributions in widely disparate fields, but this is exceptional. The threat of dismissal is therefore one of the most effective means of personal coercion in the hands of governments or corporate bodies. The code of human rights law is infringed when the true reason for the dismissal is an attempt by a scientist to exercise another important right, such as freedom of expression, or freedom to leave his or her country. This aspect of our enquiry will be more fully covered in Chapter 5.

Communication

Scientific advance requires the free flow of information between scientists. Scientific discovery is an elaborate activity involving many different steps of observation, experiment, analysis of results, formulation of hypotheses, their critical examination and decisive validation. A single scientist may go through all the initial steps in isolation, but validation depends upon others. Any discovery, even if apparently the work of one person or one group, inevitably builds upon a foundation of knowledge accumulated by the collective activity conducted by the scientific community in the public world of science. If scientific knowledge is to be well-founded and reliable, scientists must be in a position to communicate with other scientists who can confirm their observations, check their theoretical analysis, and retest their conclusions independently.

This means in practice that reports of all significant steps in a piece of scientific work must sooner or later be made freely available to all those who can undertake the processes of criticism and verification. The consideration of contrary views and findings, the interpretation of anomalies and paradoxes, the disclosure of supplementary information independently obtained elsewhere, and other elements of dialogue, can then be united in a synergy of experience and intellect. At the least such publication helps to prevent needless duplication of work already done elsewhere, and the pursuit of hypotheses already discredited. At the best it brings to bear a battery of knowledge and experience which greatly exceeds that of the individual participants.

If science is to live up to its norms of 'universalism' and 'transnationalism' (see Chapter 2), the communication of scientific discoveries and hypotheses must be as wide and free as possible. Where basic knowledge is concerned there must be no bar to *publication*, either in print or by word of mouth, and no artificial restriction on *access* to such publication. Even without explicit restraints on the transfer of scientific information, there are barriers enough in the shape of linguistic diversity, shortage of funds for the purchase of books and journals, and so on. Scientists should not only be free, but be positively encouraged, to publish any work of value in such a way that it will reach the greatest number of those able to appreciate and evaluate it, without regard to national boundaries. Similarly, scientists need to have access to the other published work in their areas of interest, and thus be able to take into account all the relevant world literature in their field. A scientist who is unable to give or receive information in his or her field of work might as well not exist so far as the world of science is concerned.

In fact, the right to 'seek, receive and impart information and ideas through any media and regardless of frontiers' is a general human right, set out boldly in the UDHR (Article 19) without particular reference to its importance for science. But information is a valuable commodity in the worlds of commerce and public affairs, and there are many powerful forces seeking to impede its flow. Some constraints are perfectly legitimate, for example when they relate to the security of the state. It is therefore not surprising that the human rights treaties subject this right to a number of limitations. These tend at first sight to look rather formidable, but on careful inspection and reflection most of them turn out to be quite reasonable in the context of a complex, highly ordered social system—which is, after all, the context in which science has to function, and scientists must live and work. In practice, most of these limitations are normally irrelevant to the pursuit of science, and could therefore be ignored in this book. But some of them, when they are interpreted illiberally, can bear very heavily indeed upon scientists, both in their professional work and as responsible citizens. For this reason, the principles and practices associated with the exercise of this right are of particular significance for science, and will be dealt with at length in Chapter 6.

Opinion and expression

In the international code of human rights law, freedom of communication does not stand alone, but is coupled with the right to 'hold opinions without interference'. This coupling implies that whatever opinions one may hold may also be communicated to others, within the due limitations of the code. Indeed, the distinction between 'information' and 'opinion', scientific or otherwise, is often so questionable that they are properly brought under the same heading.

Nevertheless, it is convenient in practice to make this distinction in relation to scientific work. For the working scientist, a general right to express an individual opinion on the scientific results and ideas of others is an indispensible professional requirement which goes somewhat beyond the right to publish one's own results and to have access to the published literature of one's subject. Freedom of opinion and expression is the essential basis for the *critical* activity that keeps science healthy.

That process of comment and criticism will fail in its purpose if it is restricted by irrelevant considerations. The advance of knowledge will not be served, for example, if some work or some individuals are held to be above informed criticism, either by reason of official support for a particular theory, or by reason of the political status of an individual or group. In other words, science will suffer if there is deliberate or arbitrary interference with the freedom of scientists to speak their minds in scientific matters and to pursue directions they believe to be right and productive, subject to the academic conventions of courtesy and constructiveness, simply because their views may not entirely harmonize with those of the central authorities.

Nor can this freedom of opinion and expression be confined to purely technical topics. The traditional scientific norms of originality and scepticism cannot be set aside when a scientist leaves the laboratory or conference hall for the committee room or television studio. Scientific research and technological development are not carried out in a social vacuum, isolated from the commercial, military, political, or other societal interests they are designed to serve. By the nature of their profession, scientists are bound to be caught up in the controversies that naturally erupt around such issues as the development of nuclear power, the conservation of the environment, policies for war and peace, or the appropriateness of technological innovations. It is of the essence of their responsibility to society that they should speak the best they know on such matters—often much more than people without special scientific training could possibly know—and it is of the essence of the international human rights code that they should be free to express their opinions on them, even when these go beyond the technical facts or theories.

The difficulty is, of course, that there is no clear line of demarcation between a quasi-technical issue where the opinion of a scientist with the relevant expertise can scarcely be regarded as 'irresponsible', and an issue of general public concern where scientists are no more competent than other citizens to make a significant comment. Indeed, governments and other authorities are often heard to say that scientists should be 'kept in their place' and should not 'meddle in politics'. If strictly adhered to, this view would deny to scientists their normal rights as citizens to hold and express personal opinions on the public issues of their day. This is one of the points where we would particularly emphasize the general principle that scientists need the same rights as other people, no more and no less. We deal with this part of our concerns in Chapter 7.

Movement

This right too is central to the activity of science, and to the pursuit of a scientist's calling. The publication of papers in journals and books is only one part of the communication system of science.

Free access to the world literature is seldom enough for a meeting of minds on a scientific question. This is partly because the volume of world scientific literature is now so great (for example, the British National Library of Science and Technology alone holds over three million volumes of books and periodicals) that it is extraordinarily difficult to discover all the information that is relevant to a particular piece of research without talking to other scientists in the same field. More generally, however, as J. D. Bernal wrote nearly 50 years ago, 'in spite of the best system of publications that can be devised, physical and mental techniques can generally best be transmitted by direct experience':[2] written communication needs to be supplemented by the more sharply focused activity of personal contact, observation and discussion.

The 'official' communication system of science is indispensible; the 'unofficial' communications that pass by letter or telephone from laboratory to laboratory are just as essential; but most important of all, as a mechanism for the rapid and persuasive transfer of knowledge or opinion, is the physical movement of people. A significant proportion of the time, effort and financial resources of a professional research scientist has to be devoted to meeting and talking with colleagues in other institutions, at home or abroad. These meetings and visits take place on many different scales of time and number of participants, ranging from international congresses involving thousands of people but lasting only a few days, to individual study visits that may extend over years.

It has been borne out by experience that there is no substitute for personal travel as a means for diffusing scientific knowledge throughout the world, and no substitute for personal dialogue and confrontation of opinion in advancing scientific knowledge. Consequently, restrictions on the possibility of international travel are a most serious interference with the activity of science, and a major threat to scientific freedom. Scientists are therefore particularly concerned with the right proclaimed in Article 13(2) of the UDHR:

'Everyone has the right to leave any country, including his own, and to return to his country.'

In principle, this part of the code of human rights is quite strong enough to cover much of the comings and goings of scientists to

---

[2] Bernal, J. D. *The Social Function of Science* (Routledge; London, 1939).

attend international conferences, or to make more extended visits to scientific centres in other countries. Subject to the usual provisos for national security, etc., freedom of movement *within* and *out of* any country is amply guaranteed by the code—though it does not, of course, give a right to the money needed for such travel, which is often a severe practical obstacle to the movement of scientists, especially those in the less developed countries.

What the code does not provide for is the right of *entry* to a country where a scientific meeting is taking place, or where a foreign scientist may have legitimate research interests. There is no doubt that restrictions on the entry of foreign participants at an international scientific conference can be just as damaging to free scientific communication as those that restrict the movement of scientists out of their own countries. This is the one exceptional matter on which scientists might seek some special, internationally agreed right associated with their special professional activities, and going beyond the general rights covered by the code. If we are to continue to believe in 'the one world of science', then we should insist on some formula for 'freedom of entry' for this purpose under international law. And indeed, the Helsinki Accords have a good deal to say about this—but unfortunately not in legally binding form.

However, the general right to leave one's home country—for example, to emigrate permanently in order to better one's circumstances or to escape oppression—is also one that scientists need, in common with all other free people. Indeed, its denial may be particularly painful for a scientist who may already have many friends and professional colleagues in other countries, and can be reasonably confident of finding work consistent with his or her existing skills and experience. Chauvinists sometimes accuse scientists of being 'cosmopolitans', as if they lacked loyalty to their native country; indeed enthusiasm for their research may come uppermost in some scientists' minds, but by the nature of their calling, they at least have the means to make themselves reasonably at home in another country, even if its general culture might be alien to them. We deal with the many different aspects of all this in Chapter 8.

Association and assembly

Freedom of association and assembly is obviously linked with the freedoms of communication, opinion, and movement. It is part of the process of the sharing of knowledge and experience throughout the whole scientific community. Technically, however, these are separate rights, generally protected by different Articles in the international instruments. The right of assembly is essentially physical, and implies the presence in the same place and at the same time of a number of people engaged in a common, lawful, and peaceable pursuit. The right of association is symbolic rather than physical, and implies membership of some body of people sharing a common interest. To belong to a trade union or learned society involves the exercise of the right of association; to attend its meetings involves the exercise of the right of assembly.

Since science is a *collective* human activity, involving personal communication and co-operation, these rights too are of special importance to scientists. Without membership of a learned society, a scientist is deprived of many important professional and intellectual benefits. Without membership of a trade union, he or she may be deprived of material ones. And every scientific conference or seminar, however informal, constitutes an 'assembly'. The protection given to these freedoms by the international code is vital to the health of science and the advancement of knowledge, and we examine this in greater detail in Chapter 9.

Here again, the role of the scientist as, say, a technical expert shades into that of the responsible, free citizen. Although a scientific association such as a learned society may choose to limit itself to specifically scientific questions, this limitation does not put it into a special category from the point of view of the human rights code. Thus, for example, a scientific society may claim as much protection for a meeting to discuss the career prospects of scientists, or even the prospects for nuclear disarmament, as for a meeting on quantum mechanics or the genetic code. As we shall see in Chapter 13, learned societies, national academies and other professional associations of scientists can play a vital role in protecting the rights and freedoms that are essential for science.

Honour, reputation, and intellectual achievement

In considering the processes by which scientific knowledge is advanced, one cannot leave out of account the importance of the personal motivation of the working scientist. Many scientists— perhaps most nowadays—are employed directly by large organizations to undertake research and technological development with quite specific ends, and their rewards normally come in the form of higher salaries or higher status in the organization. But progress in science has always been greatly stimulated by recognition of the achievements of individual research workers—or of identifiable teams of research workers—competing with one another to make important and reliable advances in their field. Without the incentive of personal recognition, the motivation to excel or to remain in the front rank would be diminished.

In 'the one world of science', this competition for recognition by one's scientific peers is maintained by a highly developed system of public procedures. The personal repute that means so much for most scientists is made evident by informal acts, such as the citation of their published work in other scientific papers, or by an invitation to address an international scientific conference. More formal acts of recognition might include the award of a public prize, or election to an honorific academy. Because the actual products of research are often so abstract and intangible—a measured experimental result, a theoretical formula, a mere conjecture with fruitful consequences—these symbols of honour and reputation are peculiarly prized by scientists, and play a very important part in the satisfactory functioning of the scientific community.

The international human rights code covers all these things. Article 12 of the UDHR declares that:

'No one shall be subjected . . . to attacks upon his honour and reputation'

and Article 27(2) says that:

'Everyone has the right to the protection of the moral and material interests resulting from any scientific, literary or artistic production of which he is the author.'

This is one of the few places in the code where the rights of scientists are specifically noted. But this right, again, is not a special privilege, since it applies to the honour, reputation, and achievement of any creative individual in society. If knowledge of his or her work is suppressed, denigrated, or stolen it will deprive them of the respect and honour that should be theirs; and at the more mundane level it will damage their prospects of career advancement and the just material reward they should be entitled to receive. We shall look at this further in Chapter 10.

Having now sought to apply some of the principal provisions of the code to the special circumstances of scientists, it is heartening to find that there is no divergence in principle between the legal and scientific notions of the rights of scientists, which reinforce one another on almost all issues concerning freedom in science. This mutual reinforcement strongly supports the contention, fundamental to the present work, that there exists today for human rights in the field of science an objective code by which all scientists and governments are bound. Now that it is there, we must learn to use it, and indeed that is one of the main purposes of this book. We must next seek to apply it to the limited target of our study—that is, the scientists in the 35 'Helsinki' countries.

4

THE RIGHT TO EDUCATION AND TRAINING

Equal access on the basis of merit

Scientists need to be prepared for their profession by a long period of education and training in research. Access to such an education is therefore the first requisite for a scientific career. And indeed, that access is one of the rights included in the UDHR, Article 26(1):

'Everyone has the right to education . . . Technical and professional education shall be made generally available, and higher education shall be equally accessible to all on the basis of merit.'

The principal global treaty which covers this right is the ICESCR, whose Article 13 recognizes the general right to education enunciated by the UDHR, but then goes on to add the following more specific provisions:

'(2) The States Parties to the present Covenant recognize that, with a view to achieving the full realization of this right:
(a) Primary education shall be compulsory and available free to all;
(b) Secondary education in its different forms, including technical and vocational secondary education, shall be made generally available and accessible to all by every appropriate means, and in particular by the progressive introduction of free education;
(c) Higher education shall be made equally accessible to all, on the basis of capacity, by every appropriate means, and in particular by the progressive introduction of free education;
(d) Fundamental education shall be encouraged or intensified as far as possible for those persons who have not received or completed the whole period of their primary education;
(e) The development of a system of schools at all levels shall be actively pursued, an adequate fellowship system shall be established, and the material conditions of teaching staff shall be continuously improved.'

The status of this Article is a useful reminder of the problems inherent in any attempt to create a 'social' right of this kind for individuals against their states. Since education—particularly higher education—calls heavily on national economic resources, the right to it must necessarily be limited, in any given country, by its economic and social circumstances. The state obligation to provide it is therefore not absolute and immediate, but relative and progressive: 'to take steps . . . to the maximum of its available resources . . . with a view to achieving progressively the full realization' of this right 'by all appropriate means . . . '. That being so, a state could probably only be held to have violated the *general* obligation to provide education if it deliberately starved its educational system of resources that it manifestly had available, unless it could show that it was allocating them to some even more pressing programme. Perhaps the People's Republic of China might have fallen into this category during the cultural revolution, had it been a state party to this Covenant. But such cases must be rare, and there are certainly none among the 'Helsinki' countries.

However, that does not exhaust the force of the Covenant's provisions, for it has a great deal more to say about the manner in which the resources which *are* allocated to education in a particular state are then to be distributed among those who need them. For scientists, the significant point in these Articles is the emphasis they lay on 'merit' or 'capacity' as the single factor in the allocation of scarce resources in higher education. This sole criterion for individual access to advanced scientific education and training must be read together with Article 2(2) of the Covenant, itself based on Article 2 of the UDHR:

'The States Parties to the present Covenant undertake to guarantee that the rights enunciated in the present Covenant will be exercised without discrimination of any kind as to race, colour, sex, language, religion, political or other opinion, national or social origin, property, birth or other status.'

This outright prohibition of illegitimate discrimination is fundamental to the whole operation of the code of human rights law, and is repeated in almost all the treaties. Indeed, some of the specialized ones concern themselves only with this subject. A particularly important example for the present chapter is the Convention against Discrimination in Education, originally negotiated in the forum of UNESCO, and in force since 1962. This defines discrimination in education very precisely as:

'any distinction, exclusion, limitation or preference which, being based

on race, colour, sex, language, religion, political or other opinion, national
or social origin, economic condition or birth, has the purpose or effect
of nullifying or impairing equality of treatment in education, and in
particular:
(a) of depriving any person or group of persons of access to education of
any type or at any level;
(b) of limiting any person or group of persons to education of an inferior
standard . . .'

International law therefore fully supports the policy advocated
in Article 11(a) of the UNESCO Recommendations on the Status
of Scientific Researchers (see Appendix 4):

'Among the measures which Member States should take to assist the
emergence of scientific researchers of . . . high calibre are:
(a) Ensuring that, without discrimination on the basis of race, colour, sex,
language, religion, political or other opinion, national or social origin,
economic condition or birth, all citizens enjoy equal opportunities for the
initial education and training needed to qualify for scientific work . . . '

Discriminatory practices
There is no doubt that all the 35 states covered by our survey
spend very large sums on the primary and secondary education of
their citizens, and they all have adequate and competent institutions for the higher education and advanced training of their
future scientific workers. These institutions are of such diversity,
even in a single country, that it is almost impossible to compare
them between one country and another, or even between one sector
or level of scientific education and another. But measured by any
of the standard indicators—such as educational expenditure per
head of population, or in proportion to the national income—they
are all well above the world average, and there is no indication
that any of these 35 states might be in default of their general
obligation under Article 13 of the ICESCR by failing to take steps
'to the maximum of their available resources' to realize the right to
education of their inhabitants.

But where some of these countries do have shortcomings is in
failing to ensure that access to their institutions of higher education
is based on genuine merit or capacity, measured by accepted academic standards of performance in competitive examinations or
similarly objective criteria of ability. The actual discriminatory
practices that violate the human rights code seem to fall into five
main groups: (1) financial obstacles; (2) nepotism; (3) ideological

requirements; (4) ethnic or religious discrimination; (5) gender or colour prejudice. These categories are not, of course, mutually exclusive. For example, financial conditions overlap with the effects of ethnic or colour prejudice in some countries, and nepotism is often closely associated with ideology.

Financial obstacles

It can be argued—and many people do argue—that higher education should be provided free to everyone who merits it, especially if this is in preparation for a useful career such as scientific research or technological development. This is the official policy in the 'socialist' countries of Eastern Europe, where it is systematically put into practice: no young person who is admitted to an institution of higher education need pay any fees for his or her instruction, and they will receive a modest stipend to cover their living expenses. But in the other 'Helsinki' countries this right is often constrained by financial difficulties: there are fees to be paid for instruction, and there are living expenses to be met by full-time students who are not in a position to earn a working wage. In those countries, it is quite possible that some young people with the appropriate capacities are excluded from higher education in science simply because they cannot afford it.

This situation varies from country to country. In the USA, instruction fees are often quite high, and scholarships are rare in proportion to student numbers: most undergraduate students must be financed by their parents, or work their way through college, or assume a heavy load of personal debt. In some Scandinavian countries there is an official system of student loans, which requires the would-be graduate to mortgage a proportion of the earnings of his or her early postgraduate years. In the UK, all admitted students are entitled to grants covering their fees and (very austere) living expenses, but a large part of this grant may only be notional, consisting of a voluntary 'parental contribution' assessed on the whole family's means. In the other countries of Western Europe, university fees are usually very low, and the general costs of student life may be kept down by government subsidies to hostels and refectories, but there are stipends and scholarships for only a few of the most outstanding students.

In 'expensive' scientific disciplines such as medicine, where the fees may be particularly high, students from poor families may be particularly disadvantaged. And there are other, less direct, financial constraints on entry to higher education in many countries. The poverty of a community in which a child grows up may be reflected in the poor quality of its primary and secondary education, so that the capacity for higher education is not developed, and the merit that ought to be apparent in the competition for entry to a university is hidden. This serious source of educational inequality is still to be found in most of the 'Helsinki' countries (including the Soviet Union), despite persistent efforts by governments to reduce its effect. It is particularly serious in the United States, where education is financed locally rather than federally; this is thought to be the main factor still discriminating there against black people in science.

The formal education of research scientists seldom stops at a first 'bachelor' degree. Postgraduate instruction and supervised training in research may go on for many years, before the award of a Ph.D. or equivalent qualification. At this advanced level, however, poverty is generally no longer a significant barrier to education: anyone who can gain admission to an appropriate course at an appropriate institution can usually rely on a fellowship, or a teaching assistantship, or some other paid employment closely linked to the training organization. In the USSR, science graduates are employed in research posts where they are able to undertake the research needed to submit a dissertation for the higher degrees of 'Candidate' and (eventually, after many years) 'Doctor'. A similar system prevails in Eastern Europe, and indeed in most of the countries of Western Europe. In the UK, students admitted to full-time courses leading to M.Sc. or Ph.D. degrees are awarded meagre studentships which cover their costs for the minimum time needed to complete the course. In the United States, graduate students of proven ability can almost always earn enough to cover their fees and expenses in return for a certain amount of drudgery as teaching or research assistants.

There can be little doubt that financial obstacles still prevent many people from exercising their right to higher education in science, even though they have the inclination and the capacity for a scientific career. In the nature of things, it is impossible to present the evidence for this form of discrimination through individual case studies, since those who have been excluded have had no opportunity to qualify for consideration as scientists in the first place. However, it seems fair to say that, despite many imperfections, no state of the Helsinki group is in really grave breach of its human rights obligations under this heading. Nevertheless, the countries with 'socialist' or 'mixed' economies have a much better record in this respect than those with entirely free-market economies.

The *quality* of scientific education in any country—or in a region of a large country—is necessarily limited by the availability of material facilities, and especially of suitably qualified teachers. As we have seen, the relative and progressive obligation of the ICESCR allows for this. But restrictions on the *content* of such education—by, for example, prohibiting the teaching of a particular branch of science, or of certain widely accepted scientific theses—would violate the various Articles governing freedom of expression and opinion. Cases of this kind will be reported in Chapter 7, which deals with this group of rights.

Nepotism

In many countries of the group, universities admit everyone who has achieved a certain standard of school education, as of right. A typical example is Italy, where there is no constraint on the number of students who may be enrolled for a particular course in a particular university, provided they have passed the general '18 +' school-leaving examinations. But where there is a *numerus clausus*—that is, where only a limited number of students are admitted to a course—the right of admission may be influenced by family connections. Such influence is most needed by those who would not win admission on their academic merits, and if it succeeds it will offend against the rights of those who are displaced by it.

In areas where higher educational facilities are very limited—as in many African countries, for example—nepotism can be a serious obstacle to entry to scientific education according to merit. But the institutions open to would-be students of moderate competence in most of the Helsinki countries are so diverse in standard and prestige that few young people can actually be prevented from entering science by a small amount of nepotism in the admission practices of a small number of élite institutions. Thus, for example, the traditional tendency of some of the older British institutions, such as the Oxford and Cambridge colleges and the London medical schools, to favour the sons and daughters of former members has been cause for concern in the past, but more for its implications for the scholarly integrity of such institutions than for any significant harm that this can do to the rights of tens of thousands of other students who are able to enter equally good institutions elsewhere in the country. In fact, the competition for places at the older élite institutions is now so fierce that the 'old boy' influence is practically negligible by comparison with meritocratic considerations: indeed, there are now complaints that they are starting to practise 'positive discrimination' in favour of those who have *not* been educated privately. One should not however overlook the well-publicized incident at Wadham College, Oxford in 1982, when an overseas student of very doubtful competence was admitted after his father had offered the College a substantial contribution to its endowments. This incident was made public by the protest of a member of the college teaching staff (who was later penalized for 'blowing the whistle' in this way): there is no knowing how many similar cases occur elsewhere, but do not achieve public notoriety.

But the 'old boy' influence is not a peculiarly British vice. Similar nepotistic habits have their effect on admissions to universities in the United States, and in other countries of the group. Under this heading we might for instance include the traditional practice of awarding places—sometimes even scholarships—to outstanding athletes who would certainly not be admitted on their intellectual merits alone. This practice too is probably less common now than it used to be, and in the USA it is often justified by its favourable effect on race relations, and by the charitable donations which it attracts to colleges with outstandingly successful sports teams.

Nor are the 'socialist' countries of Eastern Europe free from such vices. For example, the Czechoslovak University Law of 1980 empowers the Minister of Education to override a negative decision on university entrance, even though this was made on the grounds of the student's lack of the necessary intellectual competence. This power has apparently been exercised to admit the children and other relatives of persons in high political positions. An extension of it was used to give teaching appointments in the law faculty of the Charles University in Prague to, amongst others, the daughters of the President, the Deputy Minister of the Interior, and the former director of the Party newspaper, despite the fact that they had no legal experience.[1] Similar cases have been reported from Bulgaria (see Chapter 8) and from Romania, where membership of the extended family of the ruling Ceausescu clan can be a key factor in gaining access to advanced scientific education, and to the influence that may spring from this.

Ideological requirements

An even more serious infringement of the right to education is ideological discrimination. In many countries it is thought proper to include in the school and university curriculum a certain amount of instruction on politics, religion, and other essentially ideological subjects. In itself, that is no offence against the rights of the students who have to undergo this instruction. Indeed, there is much to be said for broadening the education of scientists to make them more conscious of the place of science in society at large.[2] But such instruction becomes a denial of their right to education when their further educational progress is barred for failing to conform to orthodox opinions in such matters. As we have seen, the UDHR, the ICESCR, and the UNESCO Convention all expressly forbid educational discrimination on grounds of 'political opinion'.

A striking example of the imposition of ideological requirements on higher education is to be observed in Czechoslovakia. Official policy there is summed up in the preamble to the University Law, which states that 'under the direction of the Czechoslovak Communist Party, the institutions of higher education will bring together their total activity in science, upbringing and education into a single whole on the basis of Marxism-Leninism'. To ensure that this happens, the entrance test to the university includes an examination in Marxism-Leninism, which is followed by more compulsory tuition—and more tests that must be passed—throughout the course. It should be noted that these conditions are imposed by universities which have lost their traditional rights as self-governing corporations: their rectors are appointed by the President of the Republic, their deans of faculty by the Minister of Education, and their professors by the rector. All these appointments are made for five years only, and professors and lecturers can be appointed by decree without reference to their academic credentials. Indeed, a diploma from the Military-Political

[1] *Listy*, X, 5, 34 (Rome, 1980).
[2] Ziman, J. M., *Teaching and Learning about Science and Society* (Cambridge, 1980).

Academy or the Police College is ranked with a doctorate for such purposes.[3]

In these circumstances, entry to and succesful graduation from any scientific degree course in Czechoslovakia depends on conformity with the doctrines of the ruling Party. The right of the university to award higher degrees has been usurped by the state, which insists on membership of the Party as an essential condition for a doctorate. This is not, of course, laid down by law or public executive order; it is imposed extra-legally by a simple Party instruction to the officials involved. Educational discrimination in Czechoslovakia was summed up as follows in a paper issued by Charter-77 on 23 January 1977:[4]

'The present system of selection for study at universities is not concerned with an objective evaluation of the abilities, talents and prospects of the candidates, nor with the proper utilization, development and dispersal of talent. Its two basic functions are: firstly, to give reward for political "involvement" and conformity; and, secondly, to punish parents for their political views if they are not in complete agreement with today's political practice.'

The effect is that the political sins of the parents are visited on their sons and daughters: the children of those who have failed to conform are deprived of university education on that ground alone. Thus, for example, Jan Bednar was prevented from taking a university course which he had fully merited academically, simply because he was the son of Olga Bednarova, a notable dissident and member of Charter-77, who was arrested and sentenced in 1979.[5]

Perhaps the most pitiful tale of this kind, for the authorities and the victim alike, happens not to concern a 'natural' scientist. Jiri Hajek, born in 1913, had impeccable socialist credentials. Between the wars, he campaigned against Francoist Spain, fascism, and appeasement. In 1940, the German occupiers sentenced him to twelve years' imprisonment, part of which he served in Nazi camps. For ten years after 1955, he served in the Czechoslovak diplomatic corps, rising to become Deputy Minister of Foreign Affairs, and eventually Minister of Education. In the 'Prague spring' of 1968, he became Foreign Minister. But the Soviet invasion in August of

[3] *Listy*, X, 5, 34–5 (Rome, 1980).
[4] 'Document 4' in *Human Rights in Czechoslovakia: the Documents of Charter-77, 1977–1982* (Commission on Security and Co-operation in Europe of the Congress of the United States; Washington, DC, 1982).
[5] *Prague Winter* (US Helsinki Watch Committee; New York, 1980).

that year led to his expulsion from the Communist Party, the university where he had previously lectured, and eventually even the Academy to which he had been elected as a distinguished scholar of international affairs. Perhaps not surprisingly, he then became one of the founder members of Charter-77.

But the story is really about his son Jan, born in 1964. Having been an outstanding pupil at his primary school, he was refused entry to high school at fourteen 'because of his father's opinions and activities'; that refusal was only reversed when Chancellor Kreisky of Austria personally invited him to continue his education in that country. In 1983, Jan Hajek graduated from his high school as the best of his class, and was formally admitted to the Poly-technical Institute in Prague to study architecture. However, within a fortnight his admission was cancelled by an arbitrary decision of the Deputy Minister of Education, without any reason being given. For a year he worked as a clerk, and then applied to enrol once more at the Polytechnic. This time, he was told that he had failed his examination in mathematics, but no explanation was ever given for that startling finding. He was then offered places for study in Vienna, Oslo, and Rennes. But the Czechoslovak authorities have consistently refused his applications to go there, on the ground that he is liable for military service—for which he has in fact been found medically unfit.[6]

It is worth noting that these actions are often taken under the cover of regulations whose ostensible purpose is to compensate for the potential disadvantages of children from working-class back-grounds in competition for university entry—a worthy purpose which is corrupted by confounding the class status of the family with its political orthodoxy. The directives and operational pro-cedures by which this policy is put into effect are kept secret, but they work rather to exclude students from families who do not fulfil the 'class political criteria' than to include those who are educationally disadvantaged, irrespective of their political or class backgrounds.[7] It is also worth noting that Czechoslovakia is a party to the UNESCO Convention against Discrimination in Education, which forbids discrimination on *any* irrelevant grounds—includ-ing, amongst others, 'political or other opinion', 'social origin', or 'economic condition or birth'.

[6] *Der Spiegel*, No. 7, 1985.
[7] *Prague Winter*, loc. cit.

The ideological conformity required of all students and academics in Czechoslovakia is paralleled in Bulgaria, where the regulations for university enrolment, laid down in 1973, insist upon a written examination in 'General Culture and Political Training'. In Romania, entry to university depends on a recommendation from the Party, thus effectively excluding members of unrecognized religious creeds such as Adventists and certain Baptists.[8] Compulsory instruction and successful examination in Marxism-Leninism is also a necessary qualification for a degree in most of the other East European states, including now Poland, where previously the distinction between political conformity and academic merit had been reasonably respected.[9]

These policies are practised just as systematically in the Soviet Union, where they largely originated, and where they have been thoroughly institutionalized over more than half a century. In recent years, however, the requirement of general ideological conformity has apparently been further extended in the natural sciences. It is a long-established principle that the holder of a teaching post in higher education, or of a relatively senior research post, should be either a Candidate or a Doctor of science. But these degrees are not awarded by a university or other academic body, simply on the recommendation of expert examiners in the subject of the degree. The expert examining body can only *recommend* the award to the Higher Attestation Committee—known by its Russian initials as the 'VAK'—which makes the final decision. Even to get to this level, the candidate and his or her thesis must have passed various political hurdles. The employing institution will have had to provide a satisfactory personal profile of the candidate, signed by representatives of the Party committee and trade union as well as the appropriate scientific superior. A security clearance will be needed from, amongst others, a branch of the KGB known as the First Division. These procedures are obviously open to abuse for motives of personal animosity or professional sectarianism, not to mention excessive zeal by politically minded academics. And at the final level of VAK approval, criteria of political and social reliability can override all other considerations. Directly responsible as it is to the Central Committee of the Party, the VAK does not

[8] *Menschenrechte in der sozialistischen Republik Rumänien* (Internationale Gesellschaft für Menschenrechte; Frankfurt, 1982).

[9] *Nature*, 295, 89, 544; 1982; 302, 470; 1983.

hesitate to use its powers. By these means, the extended training in research that every scientist must undergo before being entrusted with major personal responsibilities is turned into an instrument for ensuring orthodoxy and conformity.[10] To the extent that this policy discriminates in the matter of education on the ground of political opinion, it constitutes a clear breach of the obligations assumed by the USSR under the relevant provisions of the international code of human rights law.

But ideological discrimination in education is not the monopoly of just one political system: it seems to be closely associated with authoritarian regimes generally. This is evident in the case of Turkey, where a new higher education law[11] was promulgated in November 1981. This forbids any student to belong to any political party, or its attached organizations, or to be involved in any political activity on behalf of such a party. A student is required to obtain written permission from the university rector to be a member of any society—apart from, as the vague wording has it, 'voluntary societies'. Article 54 of the law adds the draconian edict that students involved in a whole range of activities, few of which could be regarded as even mildly criminal, may suffer sanctions ranging from a reprimand to expulsion from the university. To make the consequences of this penalty quite clear, the law adds:

'A decision to expel a student from a higher education institution is reported to all higher education institutions, to the Higher Education Council, to security authorities, and to the relevant enlistment office. Students who have been expelled from a higher education institution are not eligible for admission to any higher education institution.'

Turkey, we should add, has been a party since 1954 to the First Protocol to the European Convention on Human Rights, Article 2 of which provides, without any qualification, that 'No person shall be denied the right to education'. Unfortunately, Turkey is one of the few state parties to that Convention which does not yet allow its citizens to complain about infringements of their rights to the European Commission of Human Rights in Strasbourg.[12] We have no doubt that the application of the law we have just cited con-

[10] Medvedev, Zh., 'From Lysenko to Sakharov', *Times Higher Education Supplement*, 26 March 1982.

[11] Law No. 2547, enacted on 4 November 1981 and published in the *Official Gazette* on 6 November 1981.

[12] The only others are Cyprus, Greece, and Malta.

stitutes as clear a violation of the human right to education as any that we have encountered in our study.

Ethnic or religious discrimination

Educational discrimination on ethnic grounds is widespread in the Soviet Union, despite the fact that this vast country of many nationalities boasts a constitution asserting the equality of all its citizens. Mostly, this discrimination has a geographical basis: the areas of the country inhabited by such minority groups as the Crimean Tartars, the Georgians, and the ethnic Germans do not have adequate educational facilities, so that their young people are at a disadvantage both in competition for entry to such élite institutions as Moscow University, and in the level of the instruction available to them in their local institutions. As we have seen, this is a social and economic problem in other large countries—especially the United States—and is very difficult to disentangle from the effects of straightforward prejudice on ethnic grounds. All we can say is that there is considerable anecdotal evidence of such prejudice in the USSR,[13] and very little sign of any determined action by the authorities to combat it.

But increasing educational discrimination against the 1.8 million Jews still living in the Soviet Union is well documented. In the past the Jewish population of Russia was much larger, but mainly concentrated in certain areas and certain professions. A Great War, a Revolution, a Civil War, and the Nazi invasion during a second Great War have had the effect of dispersing this population much more widely, and opening many more professions to Jews. In particular, they found their way in large numbers into intellectual work, especially science, where they constitute a much larger proportion of researchers and teachers than their numeric proportion of the population as a whole, which is less than 1 per cent. For example, in 1974 14 per cent of all the holders of the senior degree of Doctor of Science were Jews.

This cultural phenomenon, whatever its causes, is familiar in other countries, as is the discriminatory behaviour of some educational authorities in response to it. But the situation in the Soviet Union is extremely serious even by those standards. There is now overwhelming evidence of a systematic policy to deny advanced scientific education to 'ethnic' Jews—that is, to citizens of the

---

[13] Medvedev, Zh., *Soviet Science* (Norton; New York, 1978).

Soviet Union who are identified as Jews in their internal 'pass-ports'. Since this legal status is passed on from parents to children, and has nothing to do with the profession of a religion, it cannot even be escaped by cultural apostasy and voluntary assimilation into the majority group.

The process is well illustrated by the position of Jewish math-ematicians in the Soviet Union.[14] Historically, Jews have been eminent in mathematics throughout the world, and this was as true of Soviet Russia as elsewhere. They made major contributions to the mathematical journals, and held many senior academic posts. The marked decline in the number of these contributions in the last ten years cannot be attributed to declining scientific abilities, but only to a deliberate policy of refusing to publish papers by Jewish authors in the major Russian mathematical journals (see Chapter 6).

Parallel with this, Jewish students of mathematics are being kept out of the major institutions of higher education. A study by two young academics, Senderov and Kanevsky,[15] has shown that Jewish applicants to the mathematical faculties of Moscow Uni-versity have been set impossibly difficult problems in the entry examinations—problems far above the level set to all other ap-plicants—and then failed for not solving them. By this device, the number of successful Jewish applicants has been reduced almost to zero. In 1964, 84 out of 410 entrants to the Moscow University faculty of mathematics and mechanics were Jewish; since 1970, the annual number has ranged from 2 to 4.[16] The authenticity of this evidence is strongly supported by an interview given in November 1980 by Professor V. V. Fedorchuk, chairman of the admissions committee of the mathematics department of Moscow University. He told Professor Walter Rudin, of the University of Wisconsin at Madison, that there was an official policy to discriminate against the children of the intelligentsia in favour of those of workers. He said that the decisive oral examinations were adjusted to the individual—a practice which was not 'ordered', but 'understood'. He then went on to admit that while it was not official policy to give different entrance examinations to Jews as compared with non-Jews, this was in fact done.

[14] Freiman, G., *It seems I am a Jew* (Southern Illinois University Press; Carbondale, 1980).

[15] *Nature*, 299, 7; 1982.

[16] Ibid.

The same discriminatory policy is being applied at later stages of scientific education and research training. Mark Azbel recalls the difficulties and prejudice he had to overcome before he was accepted as a graduate student working for a higher degree.[17] That was in the early 1950s, when Stalin personally launched an anti-semitic campaign in the context of the so-called 'doctors' plot'. After a period when these difficulties were somewhat lessened, the barriers have gone up again, but now to an even higher level. For example, one of the most distinguished institutes of theoretical physics in the Soviet Union had a great deal of trouble in getting permission from the authorities to appoint just one Jewish student/assistant—a young man whose work was already winning international renown in this highly competitive field of science.[18] Jewish scientists have also suffered at the hands of the VAK, which has not allowed them to be awarded the higher degrees for which they have qualified, and has even deprived some of them of the degrees they had previously been awarded (see Chapter 10).

Educational discrimination has thus become a significant disability for the Jewish minority in the Soviet Union, and has strongly contributed to the desire of many of them to emigrate to Israel.[19] But to express this desire publicly by applying for an exit visa is to risk an even more severe loss of rights: the *children* of those who have made such an application and had it refused (the self-styled 'refuseniks') are commonly excluded or expelled from courses of higher education that would lead to the more responsible intellectual professions, and are forced into minor institutions leading only to employment far below their proven abilities. An example of this is Leonid Brailovski, son of Viktor Brailovski.[20] This flagrant violation of a basic human right is evidently a matter of serious concern for world science, which may well be robbed of the contributions of scientific minds of the highest calibre as a consequence.

Discrimination against Jews in the Soviet Union is in fact religious as well as ethnic, in that the opportunities allowed to them for religious education and observance are minute. The open observance of religions other than the Orthodox Church—in-

---

[17] Azbel, M., *Refusenik* (Hamish Hamilton; London, 1982).
[18] Private communication to one of the authors.
[19] Azbel, M., loc. cit.
[20] Private communication to one of the authors.

cluding Islam, which is the religion of a large minority of Soviet citizens—is similarly restricted, although officially tolerated. The many cases where the children of people known to be staunch believers in such religions have suffered severe educational and other disabilities evidently merge with those whose parents have suffered for failing to observe the ideological requirements of the system. In the eyes of some Soviet officials, the difference between actions founded on strong religious belief, and those founded on political dissent, may not always be readily understood.

Educational discrimination against religious groups also occurs in several of the other East European countries. In Czechoslovakia, this applies to the part of the Roman Catholic Church which refuses to follow the 'pacem in terris' group into co-operation with the government, whilst the relatively small numbers of Protestants are also persecuted. In Bulgaria, the main sufferers are minority groups such as Adventists and some Baptists. In Romania, the greater part of the religious community has been drawn into a reluctant compromise with the state, and a professed believer who does not belong to an 'official' church may be unable to obtain the Party certificate required for entry to university. Even in the GDR, where the universities still have theological faculties, the actual profession of faith can be significantly detrimental to a career, unless kept in a very minor public key. In Yugoslavia, which is the most liberal of all the 'socialist' countries of our group, religious belief is formally tolerated, and the churches receive financial support from the state: none the less, known allegiance to a religious denomination can prejudice one's educational opportunities, from primary school onwards.

A different problem arises in Ireland, in the Province of Northern Ireland in the United Kingdom, and in some parts of Canada and of the United States, where there are long established traditions of sectarian education in segregated denominational schools, which may have different priorities and facilities from those maintained by the state.

Gender or colour prejudice

Discriminatory practices in education are often subtle, and deeply rooted in widespread and long-established cultural traditions. This applies particularly to the working of gender prejudice, which has the very obvious effect of reducing the proportion of women among scientists—especially in the senior grades—to a very small fraction of those whom one would expect to have the aptitude for advanced research. Numerous reasons for this are canvassed, but the way it comes about in practice is still far from being completely understood.[21] There are striking differences in the gender effect from country to country, but these do not seem to correlate with any deliberate policies of educational discrimination against women, of the kind which would constitute clear contraventions of the relevant provisions of international human rights law.

As in the case of colour discrimination in the USA (and unlike the case of discrimination against Jews in the USSR), any inherent bias against women in the educational systems of the countries in our group seems to be rooted in local and neighbourhood cultures, rather than in any state policy. For instance, there was even quite recently still not enough public support in the USA to obtain ratification of the Equal Rights Amendment. Recognizing this, the recent UN Convention on the Elimination of All Forms of Discrimination against Women expressly exempts from its definition of discrimination 'special measures aimed at accelerating *de facto* equality between men and women'—generally known nowadays as 'affirmative action'. Indeed, affirmative action in the fields of both colour and gender is now the declared policy of a number of enlightened states in which prejudice against both, and the resultant deprivations, still persist. But that policy too is not without its difficulties, for it can easily be perceived as 'reverse discrimination' against the previously favoured group. Not long ago, the United States Supreme Court had to wrestle inconclusively with this very problem in the *Bakke* case, brought by a white would-be medical student who complained that a black applicant with lower marks than his had been accepted as the result of the university's policy of including a quota of blacks in every intake, so depriving him of his rightful place according to his intellectual merit and capacity. As that example alone shows, the problem is very complex, and presents an important and serious issue for the long-term health of science, and indeed of society as a whole. All we can say about it here is that we have found no evidence of any *official* policy of gender or colour discrimination in the field of science among any of the 35 countries in our survey.

[21] Kelly, A. (ed.), *The Missing Half* (Manchester, 1981).

5

THE RIGHT TO WORK

Freedom of and in employment

Modern scientific research demands time and material resources far beyond those normally available even to a rich amateur. Most scientists nowadays work in groups or teams, sharing the facilities of smaller or larger laboratories. Whether they are engaged to do research on a full-time basis, or whether they also have other duties such as teaching, they are almost all professional employees of governmental, academic or commercial organisations. The progress of science is thus completely dependent on the provision of suitable employment for scientists, and every scientist is entitled, like every other citizen, to the full enjoyment of the rights which the international code seeks to protect in this field of human activity.

Unfortunately, what those rights consist of remains one of the most debateable areas of international human rights law. True, the language of Article 23(1) of the UDHR seems simple enough:

'Everyone has the right to work, to free choice of employment, to just and favourable conditions of work, and to protection against unemployment.'

But the language of the later treaty law, adopted only after years of contentious haggling between East and West, is decidedly more circumspect. Article 6 of the ICESCR says this:

'(1) The States Parties . . . recognize the right to work, which includes the right of everyone to the opportunity to gain his living by work which he freely chooses or accepts, and will take appropriate steps to safeguard this right.
(2) The steps to be taken . . . to achieve the full realization of this right shall include technical and vocational guidance and training programmes, policies and techniques to achieve steady economic, social and cultural development and full and productive employment under conditions safeguarding fundamental political and economic freedoms to the individual.'

Article 7 of that treaty then expands on the UDHR's requirement for 'just and favourable conditions of work', ending with an obligation on its State Parties to ensure:

' . . . equal opportunity for everyone to be promoted in his employment
to an appropriate higher level, subject to no considerations other than
those of seniority and competence.'

On the 'just and favourable conditions', the European Social
Charter too has much to say—as indeed have countless international conventions promoted by the International Labour
Organization, which between them constitute the body of what
one might call international labour law. But on the right to work,
the very first Article of the ESC only says that 'Everyone shall
have the opportunity to earn his living in an occupation freely
entered into.'

All this reflects the fundamental dilemma of political economy
about the organization of work. In the Western liberal tradition,
the worker's individual freedom to choose what work he will do,
and indeed whether he will work at all, is paramount: no human
being should have any right to exact involuntary labour from
another. The socialist will reply that this so-called freedom is quite
illusory in a capitalist economy, in which people are in fact forced
to work through sheer economic necessity, at grossly inadequate
wages, to the profit of their employers. Instead, all work should
be for the benefit of the whole community; the state should be the
sole employer; and the state should guarantee everyone permanent
employment at a living wage. To this, the liberal will object that it
merely transfers the evils of exploitation from many competing
private employers to the bureaucrats of a single monolithic state,
who will be able to use their positions as the only 'official' employers to enforce political conformity, as well as to enhance their
power and to enrich themselves by corruption.

Seeking somehow to reflect both these irreconcileable positions,
the international human rights code declares both a 'right to work'
tout court, and a right for everyone to choose his employment
freely. We shall resist the temptation to speculate whether a society
is thinkable in which both these rights could be satisfied at the
same time. Our concern being only with scientists, we shall just
add one more quotation. It comes from the UNESCO Recommendation on the Status of Scientific Researchers ('the RSSR'),
Article 21(c):

'Member states should draw up . . . policies in respect of employment
which adequately cover the needs of scientific researchers . . . by . . .
considering the provision of the necessary funds for facilities for re-

adaptation and redeployment in respect of the scientific researchers in their permanent employ, as an integral part of scientific research and experimental development planning, especially, but not exclusively, in the case of programmes or projects designed as limited duration activities; and where these facilities are not possible, by providing appropriate compensatory arrangements . . .'

However, despite the shortcomings of the international code in bridging the gap between the liberal and socialist ideologies about the right to work, there is one thing which it makes abundantly plain: in employment, as in education and in every other area which it covers, *there must be no illegitimate discrimination.* This consideration is of the first importance for scientists, for one of the crucial issues for the defence of scientific freedom is how to protect scientific workers from arbitrary dismissal. Scientific work is highly specialized. A scientist who is dismissed at short notice from a responsible research post may have great difficulty in finding comparable employment in the same specialized field; sometimes, he or she may be effectively 'blacklisted' for re-employment in similar posts, and so be excluded both from 'full and productive employment' and from the means to achieve professional advancement as a scientist. The threat of such dismissal is therefore one of the most effective instruments of individual coercion for a scientist, whether the employer is a government or a private corporation.

In some cases, the circumstances of dismissal or demotion may be so clearly discriminatory that they bring the act within the scope of the 'right to work' declared in the international human rights treaties. True, those treaties contain no guarantee of permanent tenure, or of regular promotion, for anyone in any employment. But the dismissal or demotion of an employee could still constitute a breach of the treaty obligations if it was carried out for reasons of an illegitimate discrimination on any one of the grounds prohibited by Article 2(2) of the Covenant, that is 'race, colour, sex, language, religion, political or other opinion, national or social origin, property, birth, or other status', or in order to interfere with the exercise of another human right protected by the code. This would be the case, for example, if the true reason for dismissing a scientist is that he or she has exercised the right to free expression or opinion, or has taken steps towards exercising the right to leave the country, or has engaged in trade union activities. As we shall see later in this chapter, such cases are not uncommon.

Scientists are often trained in research 'on the job': the right to work is not independent of the right to advanced scientific education. The experience gained by foreign travel, the knowledge gained from communication with other scientists, the managerial experience gained by participation in a professional association— these may all contribute to an individual scientist's qualifications for employment or promotion. The right to work is thus closely connected with freedom of movement, freedom of communication, and freedom of association. And the last of these is also an essential 'trade union' right if scientists are to secure 'just and favourable' conditions of work and pay. Although it is more convenient to deal with these other rights in later chapters, we must not forget that they are all closely linked, and that freedom itself is indivisible. Indeed, that last piece of ancient wisdom has the endorsement of the UN General Assembly, which has now several times declared that all human rights are 'interdependent and indivisible'.[1]

General conditions of employment

It is fair to say that the general conditions of employment for scientists in all the 'Helsinki' countries are quite favourable, both by world standards and relative to national standards in each country. We do not observe conditions like those in India, for example, where many competent science graduates are employed as junior clerks, or in China during the cultural revolution, when a large proportion of the skilled scientific workers in the country were forced to work as manual labourers. The open system of higher education in Italy tends to produce a surplus of nominally qualified science graduates who have to take technical jobs below their aspirations, but those who manage to surmount this barrier can thereafter be reasonably assured of 'full and productive employment'.

Indeed, scientific work is a relatively privileged occupation in most of these countries. This is not to say that scientists are immune from the economic and social afflictions of the societies in which they live. In the countries with a large free enterprise sector, scientists working for industrial and commercial firms must live with the risk of redundancy and unemployment—a danger that has now even spread into the governmental and academic sectors of the research world. The lack of assured continuity of employment

---

[1] Most recently in Resolution 32/130 of 16 December 1977.

prevents many scientists from planning their careers and their individual research programmes far in advance, and inhibits the exercise of the personal autonomy traditional in the scientific life.

There is a well-founded belief that permanent individual tenure of academic posts is a major bulwark of scholarly freedom—that only the scholar who cannot be dismissed (except for gross misbehaviour) can afford to criticize publicly the received wisdom of his time, or the powers that be. This view is certainly justified in disciplines such as economics and politics—and even history and literary criticism—which are sensitive to the actions and policies of governments and other powerful institutions. Generally speaking, however, the opinions that natural scientists and technologists express in the pursuit of their academic work are not politically or socially controversial as such, except perhaps in the rare situations where a creed such as 'creationism' is being actively promoted by the holders of political or economic power. In any case, as we have already seen, the international law of human rights does not guarantee any permanency of tenure. The domestic laws of individual countries may of course uphold contracts of employment which include such terms: in the UK, for example, the professors and lecturers of most universities have contracts of this kind, though it is a moot point whether these would be proof against loss of office on the grounds of the 'redundancy' of a certain proportion of the staff of a particular institution or academic department. If it is felt that the traditional form of academic tenure is an essential condition for freedom in science, then action to protect it must concentrate on the terms of academic and governmental employment contracts, rather than rely on the international human rights code.

Apart from this, the conditions of employment of scientific workers in the Western countries of the group are usually well covered by trade union agreements and government regulations, protecting them from dismissal for unjust causes and ensuring adequate compensation for involuntary redundancy. It could be argued that there are still no adequate arrangements for the 'readaptation and redeployment' recommended by Article 21(c) of the RSSR (quoted above) for researchers who become redundant in times of economic depression, as in the past few years. But it is hard to turn this argument into a case for legal action under the human rights code, especially when all productive workers in the country are facing similar hardships. In times of prosperity, scientific and technical workers are certainly in high demand and can earn good salaries, or can even set up on their own as entrepreneurs marketing their professional services. Even in hard times, they are usually in a better position to find jobs than people with fewer qualifications and skills—even if these jobs may not match up to their full abilities, and may only be available on very short contracts.

In the 'socialist' countries of the group, research is a relatively privileged occupation in material terms, especially in the higher ranks of the academic hierarchy. For example, the 250 Academicians and 520 Corresponding Members of the Soviet Academy of Sciences receive, respectively, 700 and 300 roubles a month—in addition to their salaries, of the order of 500 roubles a month, as professors, research directors, etc. A senior scientist may thus earn five or six times the 200 roubles per month of the average worker—not to mention additional perquisites such as preferential housing, medical services, shopping facilities, and personal transport. This system of privileges spreads downwards, so that a scientific worker in a well-established position usually enjoys substantial material benefits beyond the basic salary. Moreover, every worker has, in principle, permanency of employment. The Soviet scientist is not subject to the hazard of involuntary unemployment because a company is losing money, or a research project is being closed down, or a government department is being made to economize. These conditions hold throughout the Eastern group of countries, where scientists continue to be in short supply and there are many employment openings for competent people.

This is the background, on both sides of the ideological divide, against which infringements of the right to work must be judged.

Free choice of employment

All the treaties contain specific provisions outlawing *forced* labour. But the language of 'free choice of employment', 'work which he freely chooses or accepts', and 'occupation freely entered upon' is addressed to the different problem of the *direction* of labour. In times of war, scientists are regularly directed or conscripted into research on behalf of the national war effort, and there are even accounts of scientists in prison camps (under Stalin) being coerced or cajoled to do scientific work.[2] Those were exceptional circumstances, which do not now obtain in this extreme form in any of the Helsinki countries.

Direction of labour does however take place in some of them. For example, the labour laws of Romania provide that everyone of working age should be employed in 'socially useful' work. The interpretation of this law by the central Party organization lays the emphasis on political reliability, and practically precludes the possibility of choosing one's sphere of work. The aim is, apparently, to produce a competent technical work force, without regard for other values. Thus, for example, the first post of a newly qualified doctor, whatever his or her potential for original scientific research, may be in a remote part of the country where this potential cannot easily be realized.[3]

Norway too is apt to send its newly qualified dentists for an initial spell of work in the deprived backwoods, and in the case of *Iverson* v. *Norway* the European Commission of Human Rights held by only a narrow margin that this state practice did not infringe the European Convention's prohibition of forced labour, on the grounds that the service was only for a maximum of two years, provided favourable remuneration, did not involve any diversion from chosen professional work, was only applied in the case of posts not filled after being duly advertised, and did not involve any discriminatory, arbitrary, or punitive application.[4]

In Bulgaria, it has been publicly acknowledged that the system of selection for and direction to scientific work is defective, and contrary to the country's real needs. An editorial in the Party paper[5] says:

' . . . experience gathered in the last few years proves that competitions for the position of junior or senior scientific workers to a large degree do not play a role in which the only objective criterion should be the personal quality of the candidate.'

This apparently means not only that political and ideological

---

[2] Medvedev, Zh., *Soviet Science* (Norton; New York, 1978); the moral issues arising in such situations are perceptively discussed in Solzhenitsyn, A., *The First Circle* (Collins; London, 1968).

[3] *Menschenrechte in der sozialistischen Republik Rumänien* (Internationale Gesellschaft für Menschenrechte; Frankfurt, 1982).

[4] Application No. 1468/62, *Collection of Decisions*, 12, 80.

[5] *Radotnichesko Delo*, 9 September 1980.

considerations may be given undue weight, but also that one is not likely to be successful in applying for the area of work one prefers.

Quite apart from such direct controls, the choice of employment even in the Western countries is often narrowly circumscribed, especially in times of economic depression when there may be very few openings, even for a highly qualified applicant, in scientific work of the kind he or she would prefer. At the present time, for example, the number of posts in institutions of higher education in the UK is extremely limited, so that many scientists who are trained for academic research, and may be very talented in it, are not in fact free to enter this sort of employment. The range of choices available to a particular individual with particular qualifications is inevitably determined by broad considerations of scientific and technological policy, which assigns relative priorities to the various sectors of the research system, or to various fields of research. Nobody can claim a 'right' to be employed in fundamental theoretical physics, say, when the real demand is for aeronautical engineers. It is not for us to debate here whether it is better, or more just, for this demand to be expressed through the competition of private enterprises or as a line item in a state plan: for the individual seeking employment, the options may look just as disheartening, by whatever process they have been generated.

However, what might well count as an infringement of the right to free choice of employment would be a situation in which scientists had no choice but to do research that was morally repugnant to them. This would be the case, for example, if they all had to do military research, regardless of the pacifist principles of some; or if they all had to work for capitalist corporations, regardless of the socialist principles of others. In effect, a scientist in such a situation would be unable to exercise the important right of freedom of conscience and opinion on a matter of grave personal significance.

In practice, this situation does not generally arise in any of the Helsinki countries. In most of them, and in most branches of their science, there is a sufficient diversity of institutions—universities, academic institutes, government establishments for defence research, government establishments for civil research, nuclear weapons laboratories, conventional weapons laboratories, institutes of health, pharmaceutical companies, venture-capital enterprises, etc.—to allow scientists to reject employment that grossly offends their consciences, even though the alternatives may not be very attractive in other ways. Again, there do not seem to be grounds for complaint about the general exercise of this component of the right to work in any of the countries of the group.

Discrimination in employment

It is not enough for posts to be open for suitably qualified applicants; the right to work is seriously infringed if a well-qualified person is denied employment or promotion on extraneous grounds, such as religion, political opinion, race, gender, etc. Regrettably, discriminatory practices in employment are just as widespread as they are in education, and just as indefensible. There is persuasive evidence, for example, that women are still discriminated against in some professions in some countries, and ethnic discrimination has still not been overcome in some national cultures. Depending on the country, Blacks, Catholics, Protestants, Jews, Muslims, Freethinkers, Believers, Communists, Liberals, Turks, Greeks, Welsh, Irish, or Scots may be the victims of prejudice in hiring and firing. Just as in education, such practices are usually very difficult to pin down legally, and almost impossible to eradicate by statutory action.

On the whole, science is more open to merit and less discriminatory in initial employment than most other major professions. There is an ancient tradition of the wandering scholar, who moves from country to country and is offered academic employment wherever he is, on his merits alone. This tradition is still active in the scientific world, although it is often circumscribed by government regulations requiring that suitably qualified 'nationals' must be given preference in such employment. It is noteworthy that the whole area of the European Economic Community is now legally open for employment to all the citizens of all its member countries, and that many scientists do in fact take permanent employment in foreign countries throughout this group, as well as moving freely to and from jobs in the United States and Canada. Relative absence of discrimination against foreigners in the host country is, of course, an essential condition for the freedom to emigrate which we shall discuss in Chapter 8.

Against the traditional background of 'the one world of science', the discrimination against the employment of Jewish scientists in some of the more élite scientific institutions in the Soviet Union is particularly offensive.[6] But so also is the so-called *Berufsverbot* legislation of the German Federal Republic. This was originally intended to protect the newly constituted state from the disloyalty of public servants intending to undermine or overthrow the democratic order, and so to prevent a repetition of the sequence of events that had brought the Nazis to power. The legislation precludes the employment in the public service of anyone whose 'loyalty to the constitution' cannot be assured. Unfortunately, in West Germany the public service constitutes a very wide group, ranging from postmen to professors. The interpretation and application of the law varies somewhat between the different *Länder* of the Federal Republic, but it is said to have been applied against more than 5,000 civil servants in the ten years of its operation, and to have led to the making of two million enquiries, of which 5,000 have concerned scientists (in the wider Continental sense of the term).[7] As all teachers at all levels in the Federal Republic are public servants, teaching has been one of the main professions affected by this law—especially in the secondary schools, where many teachers have been suspended or dismissed from their posts for membership or support of the Communist Party, although the party itself is perfectly legal. So far, the impact of this legislation on academics has been relatively slight, but there have been a few cases such as:

Professor Horst Holzer, a sociologist, dismissed from his post in 1974 by the Bavarian Ministry of Education for membership of the Communist Party;[8]

Professor Jens Scheer, Professor of Nuclear Physics at the University of Bremen, dismissed in 1975 for the same reason;[9]

Dr Heike Flessner, an educationalist at the University of Oldenburg, against whom disciplinary proceedings were started in 1982 both for membership of the CP and for standing as a candidate for that party in the 1981 municipal elections.[10]

The effect of this legislation on scientific freedom in the Federal

---

[6] Azbel, M., *Refusenik* (Hamish Hamilton; London, 1982).

[7] Paper to the Executive Council of the Bund Demokratischer Wissenschaftler; Paris, 1980.

[8] *Nature*, 250, 48; 1974.

[9] *Nature*, 281, 252; 1979.

[10] Paper to the Executive Council of the Bund Demokratischer Wissenschaftler; Paris, 1980.

Republic has evidently not been very significant so far, especially
as it has been the practice to retain in non-tenured posts those
who have been denied permanent employment on these grounds.[11]
None the less, the whole of this practice is highly questionable in
principle, and may well constitute an infringement of the Federal
Republic's obligations under the international code of human
rights law.[12] That question will in due course be determined by
the European Commission (and probably the European Court) of
Human Rights in Strasbourg, where several individual cases about
the *Berufsverbot* are currently pending. Meanwhile, such a policy
seems regrettable, especially in the case of a country which has
maintained a particularly high standard of freedom in science over
the last 35 years.

The provision in Article 7 of the ICESCR relating to promotion
(see above) defines another right which is often infringed as a
result of ethnic, religious or ideological prejudice. It must be
admitted that the notion that promotion in scientific work should
be based solely on 'seniority and competence' expresses an ideal
that is seldom attained, even in the best of circumstances. Professional factionalism, patronage, good connections, and many
other factors (including sometimes outright nepotism) may play a
part in a decision for which it is often difficult to find an objective
measure of 'pure merit'. Nevertheless, there is evidence in some
countries of systematic discrimination against certain groups of
people in their promotion to higher levels of employment.

In the Federal Republic of Germany, for example, the spirit of
the *Berufsverbot* legislation is said to spread into the higher scientific world, where promotion can be prejudiced by the expression
of certain socio-political opinions—now said to go beyond communism to sympathy with other radical movements such as the
environmental or anti-nuclear lobbies. In Turkey, nobody expressing political views of any kind unfavourable to the regime can
expect to be appointed to a significant position in the academic
world:[13] large numbers of academics, including scientists, who
have not conformed to this constraint in the past are thus excluded
from further promotion. In Yugoslavia, any opportunity for ad-

[11] *Nature*, 295, 546; 1982.
[12] See Sieghart, P., in *Rechtsstaat in der Bewährung*, 7, 137 (C. F. Müller; Heidelberg, 1979).
[13] Higher Education Law, No. 2547, November 1981.

vancement as a scientist can be damaged by an open expression of religious belief, or a visible attachment to the cause of one or another of the ethnic minorities in the country.[14] And in all the countries allied with the Soviet Union, membership of the ruling Party is a criterion for promotion to the higher levels that overrides professional excellence or even proven managerial competence. The procedures through which such discrimination is put into practice are of course covert. But where a formal academic qualification is specified for promotion above a certain level—for example, a higher degree—the significant act may be the denial of the degree. In the last chapter we noted a systematic policy of this kind against certain groups of scientists by the VAK, the national committee for the award of higher degrees, in the Soviet Union itself. Any Soviet scientist whose degree of Candidate or Doctor of Science is thus blocked is thereby deprived of any hope of further promotion on merit.

Protection from arbitrary dismissal or demotion

Most advanced countries nowadays have legal or administrative procedures by which a person who has been dismissed from employment may contest the decision on various grounds. These procedures are so diverse that we cannot discuss them in detail here, especially as the grounds vary widely from one country to another. As we have seen, what the international code of human rights law requires is simply that the dismissal should not be based on an illegitimate ground of discrimination, or be calculated to inhibit the exercise of any of the other rights which the code protects.

Our particular concern here is with precisely those cases. As will be apparent throughout this book, many governments and other powerful bodies consider it important to compel their scientific (and other) employees to conform to certain rules of behaviour which may not be easily enforceable. The threat of arbitrary dismissal or humiliating demotion is one of the most powerful weapons available for this purpose, and is often used to prevent the exercise of important human rights. In almost every country in our survey we have met cases where scientists have been subjected to these sanctions for expressing their opinions too freely, or otherwise offending their employers or other authorities.

[14] *Yugoslavia: Freedom to Conform* (Helsinki Watch Committee; New York, 1982).

Most of these cases will be dealt with in the chapters covering the particular rights concerned. Thus, for example, the cases of Dr Morris Baslow and Dr Peter Infante, both of whom were dismissed from their jobs for exercising their rights of freedom of expression and opinion, are discussed in Chapters 6 and 7 respectively. The classic case of Professor Robert Havemann in East Germany will also be recounted in Chapter 7. In fact, arbitrary dismissal from employment is the characteristic fate of dissidents in a number of countries, although this may be only one element in a whole armoury of sanctions, which may include much more severe punishments such as internal exile or imprisonment.

The major threat to scientific freedom is the systematic use of this weapon of oppression against whole groups of people. Policies of this kind are to be observed in all the countries of Eastern Europe, though not with the same degree of intensity in each of them. In Bulgaria, the power to demote or dismiss any scientist exhibiting overt symptoms of nonconformism is available, but apparently seldom used. In Hungary, those who are considered unreliable politically, actually or potentially, may be put on short-term contracts, as a warning that they may be dismissed if they do not reform themselves.[15]

Romanian policy is more severe, though the first step against a dissident is likely to be demotion rather than immediate dismissal. Given the fact that unemployment is there visited with the criminal penalties of 'parasitism', and that all employment is by or through the state, the victim has little choice but to do the same work as before for, perhaps, half the pay—a highly economical means of ensuring conformity, although not obviously conducive to scientific achievement. The worst feature of this policy, however, is that it is often extended to other members of the victim's family, even if they have themselves done nothing to suggest complicity with the supposed offender. This practice is exemplified by a case whose details must be disguised, to protect those concerned. A Romanian university lecturer, having been refused permission to take up a one-year fellowship at an American university, applied to emigrate. The request immediately marked him as politically unreliable: he was sacked from the university and could only find work as a bricklayer. Eventually, under US pressure, the authorities allowed him to emigrate. But then his brother-in-law, a civil engineer and

15 *Index on Censorship*, April 1980, 13.

Communist Party member, was demoted to a junior position at a substantially reduced salary.

We have also noticed already the existence of educational discrimination in Romania on religious grounds. This discrimination too can extend to demotion or dismissal from employment. Thus, for example, the engineer Ion Catana, from Arad, was sacked for belonging to an unlicensed religious organisation; the father of eight children, he had to earn a living as a labourer in an ice factory.[16]

The German Democratic Republic adopts a lower profile than Romania in the use of this instrument of coercion, but as the case of Robert Havemann demonstrates (see Chapter 7), arbitrary dismissal or demotion is not unknown. Another case was that of Siegmar Schmidt, a 29-year-old physicist working in the research department of Carl Zeiss at Jena: in November 1981, he applied to emigrate to West Germany; his request was refused, but he was removed from his research post and reduced to the status of an assembly-line worker.[17] There were more serious troubles for Dr Friedrich Koch, a 50-year-old physician who was medical director and head surgeon of the district hospital in Ebersbach when he sought permission to join his wife who was living in Hamburg, following a visit she had been allowed to make to her gravely ill father there and from which she had not returned. Dr Koch was first accused of insufficient political maturity—witness his not being a member of the ruling SED Party. With refusal of his request to emigrate came dismissal from his hospital post, and revocation of his licence to practise. Later, this was restored and he was given a minor hospital job, but he continued to apply to emigrate. He was then arrested on a charge of 'treacherous instigation', and sentenced to 16 months in prison. As a supplementary punishment, his son and two daughters were forcibly moved to an inferior three-room flat. On his release from prison he renewed his efforts to reunite his family with his wife; in February 1983, he was therefore rearrested, and so this time was his son.

Until December 1981, scientists in Poland were fairly safe from the threat of arbitrary dismissal and other forms of discrimination

---

[16] *Menschenrechte in der sozialistischen Republik Rumänien* (Internationale Gesellschaft für Menschenrechte; Frankfurt, 1982).

[17] Communication from the Internationale Gesellschaft für Menschenrechte; Frankfurt, 1983.

in employment. Since then, the situation has markedly deteriorated. In nearly all cases, the victims have apparently been suspected of sympathy with the Solidarity movement, although precise evidence for this charge is seldom presented. Thus, in late 1982, there was a 'reorganization' at the Swierk nuclear research institute which made 60 scientific staff redundant, nearly all of them senior, up to full professors. All these scientists will now find it difficult, if not impossible, to obtain other scientific employment in Poland.[18] Another case is that of Dr J. Natvjak, head of the neurological department of the Torun military hospital; in late 1982, he was dismissed on the instructions of the authorities, although this was opposed by the hospital management and even by the local Party council. The local reaction was so strong that the decision was later reversed, at least for the time being.[19]

In the Polish universities, the process known as 'verification'— that is, the assessment of political reliability—has resulted in a number of dismissals. It is reckoned that about 5 per cent of the staff concerned have only been given conditional re-employment, and that a further 2 per cent have been shunted into non-teaching posts to protect the receptive minds of students from their influence.[20] Since unemployment is deemed to be non-existent in a socialist society, there is no unemployment benefit in Poland, and a new law passed in October 1982 obliges anyone who is made redundant or dismissed to accept any job offered by the state agency, regardless of his circumstances or qualifications. Refusal to accept this offer can result in enforced military service, as a penalty for 'parasitism'.

The authorities in Czechoslovakia also continue to discriminate in a systematic manner over the right to work. After 1970, employment contracts in the research establishments of the Academy of Sciences were limited to periods of 6-12 months for those who were excluded from the Party. Among the many penalized under this system were the biochemist F. Sorm, the chemist O. Wichterle, and the mathematician Katetova.[21] A notable case was that of the distinguished microbiologist Ivan Malek. An Academician of long standing, a firm Marxist and Lenin Prizewinner, Malek rebelled

[18] *Nature*, 301, 103; 1983.

[19] *Poland News Bulletin*, 11 February 1983, 34.

[20] *Nature*, 299, 570; 1982; *CSCE Digest*, 20 December 1982.

[21] 'Science in the CSSR', *Menschenrechte: Ein Jahrbuch zu Osteuropa* (Rowohlt Taschenbuch Verlag; Hamburg, 1977).

at what he saw as the strait-jacketing of Czechoslovak science by the regime that followed the Russian invasion of 1968. He was deprived of his post as director of the Institute of Microbiology (which he had himself built up), and employed in a junior capacity on limited contracts until his final dismissal in 1973, by which time he was approaching retirement age.[22]

The consequences for scientists dismissed in mid-career can often be extremely grave. In Chapter 8 we detail the case of Karel Culik, who had to find work as a stoker to keep body and soul together. Vaclav Benda, a computer mathematician in his thirties, was dismissed from his scientific post in 1977 for signing Charter-77, and had to work as a labourer until he was arrested on a charge of subversive activities in 1979.[23] Professor B. Paleska, whose case we shall discuss further in Chapter 6, was also dismissed in 1970 from the directorship of the Institute he had created, and later banned from more junior posts and even from clinical practice: by 1974 he was unemployed, totally excluded from science, and effectively unemployable. The theoretical physicist Frantisek Janouch, who suffered similar oppression until he was allowed to emigrate to Sweden, notes that there were thousands of scientists, academics, and other professional workers in Czechoslovakia who were similarly dismissed from their posts and unable to obtain work.[24] It should be noted that this is a country whose official report to the UN Human Rights Committee in 1977 claimed that employment by the state was not subject to any restriction or discrimination on the grounds forbidden by Article 2 of the ICCPR. Moreover, this systematic violation of the right to work is only one element of a more general apparatus of repression, which inflicts even more severe punishments, including imprisonment, on those who dare to exercise their rights to freedom of expression and opinion.

It seems ironic that this kind of violation of the right to work by the state itself should be most prevalent in the 'socialist' countries, where the state is the sole employer precisely because, according to the doctrines of socialism, private employers cannot be trusted not to violate this right. The political reality, of course, is

[22] *Nature*, 251, 181; 252, 187; 1974.
[23] US Commission on Security and Co-operation in Europe (Washington, DC; 1 August 1980).
[24] *Nature*, 251, 181, 1974.

that the authorities in all these countries are merely imitating a system that is fully institutionalized in the Soviet Union. In that country, any recognized scientist who conforms outwardly to the official ideology, who is not an observing Lithuanian Catholic, an Orthodox Jew, or a practising Moslem, and who is not totally incompetent in his or her work, has effectively assured tenure in a permanent institute. But any symptoms of non-conformity are likely to prejudice the prospect of promotion, and may put his or her entire employment in jeopardy. The first sign of disfavour may be a warning to pipe down, followed by orchestrated ostracism from colleagues, professional and personal harassment, and denial of the privileges normally associated with his or her scientific status. The next sanction, actual dismissal from employment, is much more serious, because it is almost automatically coupled with exclusion from any comparable employment in another institute, leading to prosecution for the crime of 'parasitism', whether voluntary or involuntary. If the offender persists in his dissent, more serious criminal charges may be preferred, leading to imprisonment and penal labour, under the most extreme physical conditions, sometimes for years on end.

This is the story of a number of scientists whose names are now well known for their outspoken defiance of their authorities, such as Yuri Orlov, Anatoly Shcharansky, and Alexander Paritsky, whose cases will be discussed in later chapters. But apart from the out-and-out 'dissidents', there are a number of other scientists who have been arbitrarily dismissed for much less extreme expressions of non-conformity.

The most significant group amongst these are the 'refuseniks' who have applied for permission to emigrate from the Soviet Union, and had their applications refused. The largest element among these is constituted by the Jews seeking to go to Israel, but they also include other minorities, notably the ethnic Germans and people from the various Baltic states incorporated into the Soviet Union since the last war. It is now almost a routine procedure to dismiss such persons from their jobs, without appeal, either quite arbitrarily or on the grounds that they were exhibiting a lack of commitment to their work or to the nation. Occasionally they are offered the option of re-employment at a lower grade, but the sanctions are applied more heavily with each repetition of the request for an exit visa and its subsequent refusal. As we shall see in Chapter 8, anyone seeking to emigrate from any country is perfectly within his or her rights under international human rights law, and is committing no offence. The Jewish refuseniks, in particular, go to great lengths to insist that they are not actively opposing the policies of the Soviet state; they simply want to go and live elsewhere.[25]

There can be no question of the scientific competence of those who are thus excluded from scientific work. Many of them have earned an honoured place in the scientific world, and would undoubtedly make further significant contributions to science if they were at least permitted to continue their professional work under normal conditions of employment suited to their experience and standing. The violation of the right of such people to 'full and productive employment' is thus not only an offence against them as individuals; it directly contradicts the avowed Soviet policy of fostering 'the one world of science'.

[25] Azbel, M., *Refusenik* (Hamish Hamilton; London, 1982).

6

FREEDOM OF COMMUNICATION

Professional freedom to communicate

Like all other human beings, scientists need the freedom to communicate. But they need it for two different purposes: a special professional one which is essential for the pursuit of science, and the more general one which everyone needs in ordinary life. In this chapter, we shall deal only with the first, leaving the second to Chapter 7.

Scientific research and discovery is essentially a social activity. Freedom of communication between scientists, and of access to scientific work, is an essential condition for 'the one world of science'. This means that scientists should be able to communicate personally with their colleagues all over the world, by mail, by telephone, and through the printed word; that they should have unrestricted access to libraries and other collections of data; that they should be able to receive and exchange publications; and, in general, that they should be able to exchange information freely about their work on a world-wide basis. This special 'right to communicate' forms one part of the general right to freedom of expression and opinion which we shall consider more fully in Chapter 7. It is also inevitably intertwined with other rights, such as those of movement and of association, with which we shall deal in later chapters.

In studying the implementation of this right in the 'Helsinki' countries, it is instructive to browse through the details of the Final Act itself. On page after page, there are solemn declarations of the value of the exchange of information, and equally solemn undertakings to facilitate 'the freer and wider dissemination of information' on almost every topic by almost every conceivable means. In section 4 (Science and Technology) of Basket II, for instance, these undertakings are specifically directed towards promoting:

'the sharing of information and experience, facilitating the study and transfer of scientific and technological achievements, as well as the access to such achievements on a mutually advantageous basis . . .';

and one of the methods specifically recommended for this is:

'exchange and circulation of books, periodicals and other scientific and technological publications and papers among interested organisations, scientific and technological institutions, enterprises and scientists and technologists . . .'

In section 4(a) (Co-operation and Exchanges in the Field of Education) of Basket III, the participating states express their intention of 'encouraging among persons engaged in education and science direct contacts and communications . . .' Clearly, the Helsinki states are all fully committed to keeping open the public channels by which scientific knowledge is generated, validated, and disseminated.

This commitment is underpinned by the legally binding provisions of the international code of human rights law. In Article 19 of the UDHR, the freedom to 'seek, receive and impart information and ideas through any medium and regardless of frontiers' is declared without qualification: this is the general right from which the particular freedom of scientific communication and of access to scientific information is derived. Nearly the same wording appears in the treaties, such as the ICCPR and the ECHR, and many of the states concerned declare a similar right in their domestic constitutions.

But before we look in detail at violations of this right, we must look carefully at the restrictions and limitations which surround it in the treaty texts. For this right is far from unqualified: its boundaries are circumscribed by a wide variety of public or social interests with which it might otherwise collide. The longest catalogue of limitations on this right in any of the treaties is to be found in the ECHR, where it covers no fewer than twelve distinct items. These deserve to be listed and considered separately. Having declared the general right in its first paragraph, the second paragraph of Article 10 of this treaty goes on to say that the right carries duties and responsibilities, and that it may therefore be subjected to certain formalities, conditions, restrictions, or penalties—but only through *laws* which are *necessary*, in a *democratic* society, in order to protect:

(1) national security;

(2) territorial integrity;

(3) public safety;

(4) prevention of disorder;

(5) prevention of crime;

(6) public health;

(7) public morals;

(8) the rights of others;

(9) the reputation of others;

(10) preventing the disclosure of information received in confidence;

(11) maintaining the authority of the judiciary;

(12) maintaining the impartiality of the judiciary.

The other treaties have similar exceptions, though for rather fewer declared purposes.

To the uninitiated reader, such a catalogue of exceptions will doubtless look formidable; one could be forgiven for thinking on a first reading that it must take away most of what was guaranteed in the first place. But the experienced eye of the lawyer will at once recognize many familiar features of the legal landscape to which these phrases are designed to point. The restriction of free expression in the interests of 'public safety', for example, is a reminder of the obvious proposition that a man who falsely cries 'Fire!' in a crowded theatre, and so causes a panic in which other people may be injured or even killed, cannot be left to go unpunished, or free from any obligation to compensate the victims.[1] 'Preventing the disclosure of information received in confidence' is the familiar limitation on doctors, priests, lawyers, and others from divulging the secrets of their patients, penitents, or clients. The 'protection of the reputation of others' is no more than the well-known law of libel or defamation—and so on. In short, most of the items in this catalogue reduce to nothing more than the restrictions on absolute free speech which have long been known to the domestic legal systems of even the freest countries, and which carry no special risks for professional scientists or anyone else.

But not all these exceptions can be disposed of by reference to such familiar characteristics of civilized life under the rule of law. What about 'national security', for instance, or the 'protection of

---

[1] This was the famous example cited by Supreme Court Justice Oliver Wendell Holmes in *Schenck* v. *United States* 249 US 47.

morals'? At this point, we must remind ourselves again of the fundamental principle of legal interpretation which applies to all such provisos of restriction or limitation: any state party seeking to justify an interference with a protected right on any of these grounds has the burden of proving that nothing less than the steps it has taken was *necessary* to protect the interest concerned. Thus, for example, 'national security' will not serve to justify the suppression of all publications by a scientist who happens—now, or at some time in the past—to be engaged in some piece of research for the military; nor is a defence of 'protection of public morals' likely to pass muster if it is used in an attempt to justify a restriction on the publication of work on the social or sexual behaviour of monkeys by a scientist whose political views happen to offend his government. In short, all such defences must be subjected to objective and critical scrutiny, and will only succeed where the steps taken are no more than proportionate to the protection of one of the public interests specified in the proviso from a clear and specific danger.

All the grounds for restriction of the freedom of expression listed in Article 10(2) of the ECHR have now been much discussed by the Strasbourg institutions which are charged to interpret and apply that Convention. In the course of deciding many individual cases arising under this Article, the European Commission and Court of Human Rights have given authoritative rulings on the precise scope of all the twelve grounds, and have made it abundantly clear that these need to be interpreted very restrictively indeed, and that a state must make out a very clear case before a restriction is judged acceptable.[2] This is a point that scientists and others not familiar with the techniques of the law should particularly note, since unscrupulous authorities often cite these 'exceptions' in order to give some semblance of legality to their oppressive acts.

Only 21 of the 35 Helsinki states are parties to the ECHR. Of the others, the Soviet Union and the seven other East European countries are all parties to the ICCPR. This allows restrictions on the right to freedom of expression only on six of the twelve grounds listed in the ECHR: the rights or reputations of others, national security, public order, public health, and public morals. The Hu-

---

[2] See the decisions collected in Sieghart, P., *The International Law of Human Rights*, § 2. 3. 4. 5 (Oxford, 1983).

man Rights Committee (which has the function of interpreting and applying this treaty) has already said that these restrictions 'may not put in jeopardy the right itself', and reminded states that they must be 'provided by law', and justified as being 'necessary' for one of the listed purposes.[3] It may be that the Committee will also regard the decisions of the Strasbourg institutions as persuasive authority for the meaning of similar words and phrases in 'its' Covenant.

In fact, the East European countries have not yet begun to adapt their domestic legal systems to the Covenant's requirements in this respect. Article 29 of the Romanian Constitution, for instance, states that:

'The freedom of speech, of the press, assembly, meeting and demonstration may not be used for purposes hostile to the Socialist system and to the interests of working people.'

At first sight, it seems difficult to see how such a restriction can be brought within the limitations that the Covenant permits. And all these countries also have in their penal codes, in one form or another, the criminal offence of 'slandering the state', which we shall have occasion to consider in Chapter 7.

The basic functions of scientific communication

Communication between scientists is such a diverse and complex activity that we must try to explain here the variety of functions that it performs, the various steps in the research process that it facilitates, and the multiplicity of channels through which it flows.

The functions fall into three distinct categories. In the first place, a scientist needs *unrestricted access* to all that has been or is being done in his or her field of research: this means more than access to the 'formal' literature of the subject, since this is often years out of date; it must include access to the 'informal' channels by which recent scientific information and ideas are transmitted from scientist to scientist around the world; by mail, telephone, and personal travel. Unless scientists can become acquainted with, and reflect on, the work of others, they cannot address their research to those problems whose solution will advance their field, nor can their own work benefit from the findings of others.

Secondly, it is essential that a scientist should be able to *publish*

---

[3] *Report of the Human Rights Committee to the Thirty-Eighth Session of the UN General Assembly*, 109 (UN Document No. A/38/40).

his or her findings, and give an account of the methods by which they were reached: without that, he or she can neither contribute to the understanding of their colleagues, nor benefit from their independent assessment and criticism. Within the world of science itself, the exercise of this right is subject to only one constraint, namely an objective review of the proposed publication by other well-informed scientists, to be sure that its claims are scientifically tenable and worth publishing. This process of 'refereeing' or 'peer review' helps to maintain the quality and integrity of the work of the scientific community by eliminating research claims that are manifestly trivial or erroneous.

Finally, a scientist must be able to *criticize* the work of a colleague openly—in published articles, or in public assemblies—without fear of recrimination. Naturally, this is subject to the traditional conventions of courtesy and restraint; in any case, critics must take personal responsibility for their comments, in relation perhaps to the effect on their own reputation as disinterested 'searchers after truth'.

Given these premises, let us now describe how communications between scientists are in fact being restricted, and whether the degree of the restrictions is such as to interfere seriously with the performance of their scientific work, or to infringe significantly their individual human rights under the international code.

Communication by mail

Personal correspondence plays a very important part in the advancement of knowledge. In the past, especially before the advent of instantaneous electronic communication and intercontinental air transport, a private letter was the best way to establish informal contact and critical dialogue between scientists working on the same problem in different cities or countries. For example, one of the most famous documents in the history of modern science is the correspondence between Niels Bohr in Copenhagen, and Albert Einstein in Berlin, on the significance of probability in the interpretation of quantum mechanics. Similarly, in *The Double Helix*, James Watson continually refers to the correspondence between Cambridge, England and Pasadena, California, which kept him and Francis Crick informed of the various steps being taken by Linus Pauling towards the solution of the structure of DNA, long before these could have been available in the published literature.

A scientist who is cut off from this elementary contact with the community of other scientists is at a grave disadvantage in research—a reality that is all too evident for many scientists in developing countries where the mails are slow to arrive and expensive to use.

But the excuse of inadequate resources scarcely applies to any of the 'Helsinki' countries. The sanctity of correspondence in accordance with Article 12 of the UDHR is explicitly guaranteed by the human rights treaties ('No one shall be subjected to arbitrary or unlawful interference with his correspondence'), and by the domestic legislation of virtually all these states. All of them are also adherents to the Universal Postal Convention, which likewise assures such security. There are of course a few exceptions, such as the British prohibition of the use of the mails for the transmission of obscene material, but this presumably falls within the exception permitted in the international treaties on the grounds of public morals. And there is the more general condition that printed matter at reduced postal rates must be open to inspection to ensure that the facility is not abused. These limitations are not likely to affect scientific communications.

Nevertheless, there is distinct evidence of systematic interference with the personal correspondence of scientists in a number of countries. In *The Medvedev Papers*,[4] Zhores Medvedev recounts how he kept records in the USSR in the late 1960s which showed suspiciously long delays and significant cases of non-delivery of letters and publications from abroad. By an exercise of scientific inference worthy of any fictional detective, Medvedev was able to reveal clearly the existence of censorship of both incoming and outgoing mail within the Soviet postal system, and was even able to infer some of the haphazard and occasionally ludicrous administrative procedures behind it. A decade later, Professor Leo Peker graphically described the twelve steps, including the two mandatory transits through different sections of the KGB, which any letter from a foreign scholar had to take before it could reach him, several months after its arrival there, at the Institute of Metrology in Leningrad; and the thirteen in reverse before his answer could reach his correspondent. For this reason, he says, Christmas cards for friends in the West have to be posted in the Soviet Union in around May or June. And when some French

[4] Macmillan; London, 1971.

colleagues wrote (in Russian, as a special courtesy to him) to acknowledge the 'warm words' with which he had thanked them for translating some of his lectures and publishing them in France, he was summarily dismissed from his Institute for having 'secret contacts with foreigners'.[5] There seems little doubt that these practices still continue, and that international correspondence to and from Soviet citizens is liable to scrutiny in transit.

A Bulgarian report[6] notes that an incoming letter which has been intercepted by the authorities can be easily identified because it has been re-sealed with a very poor-quality and highly malodorous glue. There is similar, if less obvious, evidence of such interference in all the other countries of Eastern Europe, but it appears to be selective, indicating the probable existence of central blacklists of recipients.

Similar interference with mail doubtless occurs in other states also. For those which are parties to the ECHR, Article 8(2) of that treaty requires that it must be 'in accordance with the law', and limited to what is 'necessary in a democratic society' in the interests of national security and the other protected values. In the United Kingdom, the interception of communications had for many years before 1985 been carried out under the ancient 'Royal prerogative' without being regulated by any statute; on that ground, the European Court of Human Rights found the UK in breach of the Convention in the *Malone* case,[7] and the appropriate legislation, containing elaborate safeguards, has since been brought in.

Since the members of 'the one world of science' need have nothing to hide from their authorities, the scrutiny of their mail may seem little more than an affront to decency, with no more practical consequences than, say, a delay of a few weeks in getting a letter or periodical. But the effects are much more serious when material from such letters—and even the fact that they are written or received—is used against the individual in question, as happened to Leo Peker in the Soviet Union. The general effect of this kind of action by the authorities is what the US Supreme Court calls a 'chilling' one: it severely inhibits the free exercise of this right by the great majority of the people concerned. Whether or

---

[5] Peker, L., 'Com'è difficile la corrispondenza con un collega occidentale', in *La ricerca scientifica nell'Europa dell'Est* (Biennale di Venezia, 1979).

[6] Private communication

[7] Judgment of 1 August 1984.

not they would really be putting themselves at risk, scientists working under such conditions feel reluctant to enter into correspondence with colleagues abroad, and thus cut themselves off from valuable inputs to their research. This concern is reciprocated by foreign scientists, who are often uncertain as to whether they should write to colleagues in the Soviet Union, and in other countries where this practice is thought to be prevalent, in case they should 'get them into trouble with their authorities'. The legal right to privacy of correspondence between individuals is thus an important aspect of freedom for 'the one world of science' under the rule of law, and yet it is widely violated.

Illicit interference with the postal service sometimes goes further: correspondence addressed to, or from, particular individuals is simply not delivered. This has recently been the case, for example, with Andrei Sakharov, who is not receiving the scientific books sent to him from abroad, and is thus prevented from continuing his scientific work.[8]

The extent to which both international and domestic law are being violated in this way is not always easy to determine, but one interesting method was adopted by the Bertrand Russell Peace Foundation. They had noted that correspondence, including materials on human rights matters, was not being delivered to recipients in the Soviet Union. They therefore adopted the device of sending the material by registered post, and requiring advice of delivery. The Universal Postal Convention provides that if a registered letter is not properly accounted for to the sender, he is entitled to a fixed indemnity from the postal authority of the country of despatch. The British Post Office, confident that it had safely delivered the material into the hands of the Soviet postal authority, approached them to reclaim the compensation due. They were informed that this would not be forthcoming, because the person sending the mail was using the service 'for an activity incompatible with the domestic legislation of the USSR'. Under the Universal Postal Convention, this was enough to absolve the British Post Office from responsibility.

But the interesting point is that the Soviet authorities could have had no means of knowing whether the material had any connection with 'an activity incompatible with the domestic legislation of the USSR' unless they had opened the letters and exam-

[8] *Nature*, 287, 384; 1980.

ined their contents. To do so would be in explicit violation of Article 56 of the Soviet Constitution which guarantees privacy of correspondence, and Article 135 of the Penal Code of the RSFSR which makes Departments of State which violate this protection liable to prosecution. Here therefore is a clear case of violation, not only of international law but of Soviet domestic law.

In the USA, until fairly recently, correspondence from certain countries was officially intercepted under the provisions of legislation which prohibited the delivery of what was loosely defined as 'Communist literature'. This legislation, dating from the McCarthy era in American politics, was certainly contrary to the spirit of the Helsinki Accords, and would have been in violation of the ICCPR if the USA had adhered to that Covenant.

In a number of states—almost exclusively those of Eastern Europe—there is also some censorship of outgoing mail, both overt and covert. For example, the GDR in 1979 enacted a law creating (*inter alia*) offences of conveying information damaging GDR interests, defaming the state and, more generally, encouraging harm to the state order or scorn of the communist system. In the case of Romania, testimony to the Trade Sub-Committee of the US Congress Ways and Means Committee noted that 'all correspondence must be checked by at least one member of the directorate of the scientist's institution. Telex or telephone links must be approved at a higher (sometimes Ministerial) level. The international exchange of ideas, so crucial to the practice of science, is thus severely suppressed'. This testimony came from nine distinguished American scientists, including three Nobel Laureates.[9]

Such laws and administrative procedures are used in a number of countries to enforce restrictions on freedom to communicate information which is allegedly critical of the political system of that country. But unless the country concerned can claim a legitimate ground for such restrictions, such as the interests of its national security, these laws and procedures are in breach of its obligations under international human rights law, as well as of the spirit of the Helsinki Accords. In effect, they are being used to discriminate against individuals on the ground of their political opinion, which is explicitly prohibited by the relevant treaties. Yet these very laws and procedures have often been used to inflict savage penalties on those alleged to have contravened them.

[9] *US Congressional Record*, H 12233, 1 October 1976.

Communication by telephone

The 'oneness' of the world of science is epitomized by the use of the telephone. The modern scientist calls up a colleague in Plymouth, or Paris, or Pasadena, or even Pernambuco, to enquire about the results of some experiment, or to get the 'gen' on some piece of equipment, or to argue over a point in some theory, or just to make arrangements for a conference or a collaborative research project. International data links between computer systems have now become commonplace in certain fields of science, whilst access to some of the major archives of scientific information, such as the US National Library of Medicine, is primarily by the international telephone and telex network. Not to have ready entry to this communications system—as is the case for most scientists in most of the less developed countries—is to be excluded from the active frontier of scientific knowledge.

The privacy of telephone communication is safeguarded by the international treaties as part of the privacy of correspondence, and in the domestic legislation of the individual states—for example, in Article 33 of the Romanian Constitution. Classically, the main form of interference with this right has been telephone tapping, which has been used—often extra-legally—in many countries of very different political complexions. In fact, the rules governing violations of this right are a matter of great political sensitivity. In the case of *Klass* v. *Federal Republic of Germany*,[10] the European Court of Human Rights said that there can be circumstances in which such surveillance may be justified, but because of its obvious dangers to freedom a very strong case needs to be made for it; the circumstances in which it may be carried out must be clearly laid down by law; and there must be stringent safeguards against abuse. The Court later reaffirmed these principles in the case of *Malone* v. *United Kingdom*, to which we have already referred.

Whatever the situation in the past, the world-wide telecommunications network has proliferated so explosively in the last two decades that anything like universal identifiable tapping is nowadays impossible. The increasing automation of the telephone system, and particularly the very widespread adoption of subscriber trunk dialling, has so multiplied the ease and use of international telephone communication that, while it is still possible

---

[10] Judgment of 6 September 1978, reported at 2 EHRR 214.

to tap or monitor all the calls that are made from one country to others, there are no conceivable means by which all the parties to all the calls can be identified. In fact, most of the 'underground' information from countries where repression is common now comes—usually in highly allusive form—through the telephone network. But modern technology is making *selective* tapping of telephone circuits progressively easier; where it is known or thought to be practised it may have the 'chilling' effect of inhibiting the use of this means of communication between scientists even for entirely innocent and practical purposes.

An even more serious violation is the disconnection of the personal telephone of an individual citizen who is not guilty of any offence under domestic law. This has been done on a number of occasions in the Soviet Union, usually without any explanation or apology, against persons out of favour with the authorities. A striking example was the disconnection of Andrei Sakharov's telephone in his 'exile' at Gorki. Since he had not been charged with any offence, this administrative action to cut him off from communication by telephone with other people, in his own and in other countries, was—quite apart from international law—a clear violation of Article 56 of the Soviet Constitution, which provides that 'the privacy of citizens, and of their correspondence, telephone conversations, and telegraphic communications is protected by law'.

At an earlier period, Mark Azbel[11] records the frequent disconnection of telephone lines among his own colleagues and community; this device was used, for example, to prevent the transmission of scientific lectures from 'refusenik' scientists in Moscow to audiences in Israel. It is notable that in the middle of 1982 the Soviet authorities 'for technical reasons' severely restricted the number of international lines available from the USSR to the Western world.[12] For all that a great deal of scientific information is transmitted along these lines under official auspices, the failure to protect the rights of *individuals* to communicate by this means is a significant limitation on scientific freedom.

Access to scientific literature
The ability to consult the textual material—books and periodicals—of a subject is an obvious essential for the scientist.

[11] Azbel, M., *Refusenik* (Hamish Hamilton; London, 1982).
[12] *Fifteenth Semiannual Report on Implementation of the Helsinki Final Act: June-November 1983*, 16 (US Department of State; Washington, DC).

There are three ways in which he or she can do this: through access to local libraries; through the purchase of books or personal subscription to scientific periodicals; or through the receipt of 'pre-prints' and 'reprints'. The last of these is one of the important 'informal' procedures by which information about the latest scientific developments is diffused rapidly through the scientific world. Photocopies of original typescripts, proof copies of papers that are still in the press, or reprints of papers that have recently been published and recorded in bibliographic indexes are exchanged by arrangement between scientists who know each other, or between institutes with common interests, or simply on request to the author. All these modes of communication, formal and informal, are recognized by the international treaties, and supported by the provisions on access to scientific and cultural work in the domestic laws of most states where such matters are legally regulated.

Full access to all these channels naturally depends on the availability of personal or institutional resources, such as the means of paying subscriptions in foreign currency, or some standing as an active researcher in a particular field. The exercise of this right is often closely linked with employment as a professional scientist, and is thus one of the aspects of the right to work which we have already discussed in Chapter 5. Pre-prints and reprints are also typical items in the correspondence that scientists exchange with one another by post, as already discussed earlier in this chapter.

Nevertheless, access to the published literature of science must not be regarded as a special privilege for people with Ph.D.s. In almost every country nowadays, and especially in the economically advanced countries of the 'Helsinki' group, there is some sort of National Library where as much as possible of the world's scientific literature is collected for public reference. Some of these libraries are so large—for example, the British Science Reference Library, and the US Library of Congress—that they can be relied on to cover almost every published scientific work that is worth reading. In some other countries the holdings are more limited for the valid, if regrettable, reason of shortage of foreign exchange. Since these collections are a public resource, and all the material in them has already been published openly in one country or another, it is difficult to see why there should be any legal limitation on the general right of every citizen to have access to their contents in an orderly fashion.

This is indeed the policy and practice in most countries. In the UK, for example, it is not necessary to have even a reader's ticket to consult material in the Science Reference Library in London, and copies of all documents held at the British Library Lending Division in Boston Spa are sent to anyone, anywhere in the world, on payment of a modest fee. In some countries, however, few libraries have an open access system comparable to that in the West. Instead, a user must have a recommendation from an institution before he or she is permitted to use the library. This applies, for example, to the libraries of the Academies of Science in most East European countries, which are usually the best provided with foreign scientific books and periodicals. Although this would not normally be a serious disadvantage for the established scientist in good standing, it could be a serious restriction for one who is not so well established. And it can be quite disastrous for scientists who may have fallen from offical grace—or, even worse, have been dismissed from their posts—and as a result are denied the necessary authority because they are now regarded as 'non-scientists' by their institutes. For such a person this means being pushed into an intellectual vacuum where, without other means of access to the books and periodicals needed to keep scientifically alive, the inevitable outcome is scientific atrophy. This is a situation which has become common in the USSR, Czechoslovakia, Bulgaria, Romania and the GDR, but is happily rare in Hungary and Yugoslavia.

In Poland, by March 1985, only relatively few scientists were excluded from professional employment as a consequence of their political activities, though there were growing fears of a major purge in the academic professions.[13] Those that were debarred from employment were, for the time being, still able to use academic libraries, so that at least some of them could continue their theoretical work with the help of stipends provided by the unofficial Social Committee for Science (SKN). However, very stringent controls were imposed under martial law on the use of photocopiers, in effect confining access to them only to persons with a clean bill of political health. Since Poland's endemic shortage of hard currency greatly restricts subscriptions to foreign journals, which often have to be shared by several institutions or colleges in the same city, access to scientific information may be severely

13 *Nature*, 314, 123; 1985.

restricted, not only for scientists debarred from employment, but even for those still in employment whose political attitudes come under any kind of official suspicion.

Even for those who are not subject to the scientific strangulation of being cut off from their country's libraries, there is another difficulty. In the USSR certainly, and to a lesser extent in some of the East European countries, there is the further restriction that portions of libraries have very limited access. These—and this does not apply only, or even mainly, to scientific collections—have reserved sections to which access is only allowed for highly trusted personnel of impeccable 'social' character, in the view of the central authorities. The sanctions for attempting to break these rules can be very severe. An illustrative case is that of the historian A. Roginsky who, in order to obtain access to materials he required, was alleged to have forged a permit to consult the reserved archives. He denied the charge and further maintained that, whether he was guilty of it or not, he had only wished to consult material which should normally be available. His plea failed and he was sentenced to four years' imprisonment.

Access to foreign scientific literature is further restricted in several ways. In East European countries, and more particularly in the USSR, many important foreign scientific periodicals are only generally available in translation. This practice may well be motivated economically, in order to save foreign exchange, and is of course advantageous to science in making material available in a form that may be more intelligible to scientists with a limited ability to read foreign languages. Indeed, the existence of 'cover-to-cover' translations into English of the major Russian scientific journals has played a very important part in bringing Soviet science into its appropriate place in 'the one world of science' in the last 20 years or so. But this procedure can easily be—and is—abused when, for some reason or another, particular papers are omitted from the translated version without comment or explanation.

The most blatant example of this form of restriction on the right of access to scientific information is to be observed in the course of producing editions of certain foreign journals which have not been translated into the national language, but which are ostensibly 'facsimiles' of the original issues. In the Soviet Union an English edition of *Science*, the journal of the American Association for the Advancement of Science, is published regularly and widely distributed in scientific circles. But this is not a straightforward facsimile edition: articles are frequently deleted and blank spaces appear. In a 1979 sample, only 6 out of 20 issues of the facsimile edition were not censored; items deleted included those on Soviet internal affairs, strategic arms limitation, and American–Soviet scientific exchanges. The title-page of one edition compared with the original shows virtually a blank where a series of articles on Chinese science had been deleted.[14] In the similar case of the 'facsimile' edition of the well-known British journal *Nature*, the excision of an article by one of the present authors was even concealed by printing a couple of pages of bogus advertising to fill the gap in the pagination.[15]

Where the issues of the journal are imported directly, rather than reproduced locally, physical excisions are often made, or numbers simply withheld. In Czechoslovakia, all journals are scanned; some are withheld while others may have portions excised. In 1974 no fewer than 14 of the 52 issues of *Nature* were withheld there from distribution.[16]

In the Soviet Union, all foreign scientific journals are subject to censorship. Some to which scientific libraries or individuals subscribe are confiscated before they reach their destination. Specialized journals like *Cancer Research* usually pass through easily, but general periodicals and journals which discuss events in the international scientific community, like *Nature*, *Science*, *New Scientist*, and *The Lancet*, often disappear en route. Any mention of Soviet or East European scientific life is enough for the issue to be confiscated, or buried in the 'special holdings' of libraries. But the offending material may not be so obviously 'political'. Thus, for example, the letters to the editor deleted from the issues of *Science* for 5 May and 16 June 1978 included those dealing with human cloning, tanker safety, solar energy in the year 2000, and paraquat pyrolysis products, as well as those on the Japanese wartime nuclear effort and on the postponement of visits by physicists to the Soviet Union.

Although the matter censored from journals received in the Soviet Union and other countries practising these policies is generally that concerned with the social impact of scientific work or

[14] *Science*, 205, 284; 1979.
[15] Medvedev, Zh., private communication to one of the authors.
[16] *Nature*, 274, 632; 1978.

the politics of the country referred to, this is not the only reason for exclusion. The 1977 Nobel Prize lecture delivered by Sir Nevill Mott was translated into Czech and published in the *Czechoslovak Journal of Physics*. However, this translation omitted all the references Mott had made to the work of two East European scientists, Radu Grigorivici from Bucharest and Jan Tauc from Prague, both of whom had by then fallen out of favour with their respective governments: Grigorivici had been dismissed from his scientific post because his son-in-law had left the country, while Tauc was a refugee living in the United States, having fled from Prague in 1968.[17]

Purely scientific material may be excluded because of a simplistic ruling that what has not gone through the censors for approval must automatically be rejected. For example, when Professor J. Lebowitz of Rutgers University entered the USSR on a recent visit the customs impounded certain scientific papers he was carrying. The authorities attempted to justify this on the ground that he was travelling on a visitor's visa, and therefore not concerned with scientific matters.

Indeed, the attempt to enforce blanket censorship regulations on technical scientific material seems to provoke irrational and illegitimate acts of this kind by frontier officials of every nation. In 1982, five Chinese students who had been working at the Universities of Michigan and Michigan State on an official exchange programme had their luggage searched and items confiscated on their departure from the USA. The articles removed included books, journal articles, slides, and notebooks—all either in the public domain or dealing with their own work which their US scientific hosts confirmed had at no time involved access to classified material. This may not have been simply the act of an overzealous customs official, since the FBI was apparently involved. The articles confiscated were subsequently returned.[18]

Even if they have access to good libraries, most active scientists find it convenient to have personal copies of a certain number of books and periodicals relevant to their research. Given the necessary funds, they should find this a simple matter; as we have seen, the Helsinki Accords, quite apart from the relevant treaties, urge states to facilitate these means for the transfer of scientific in-

---

[17] *Nature*, 284, 301; 1980.
[18] *Science*, 216, 1204; 1982.

formation within and between nations. Yet scientists in most of the countries of Eastern Europe (the exceptions are Hungary, Yugoslavia, and—in principle—Poland) are not normally permitted to subscribe to foreign scientific journals, and the only foreign textbooks they can usually purchase are the few that are available for sale in officially approved bookshops.

Shortage of hard currency to purchase foreign publications is of course a serious constraint on the circulation of scientific literature. In Poland, for instance, only $5 million was allocated for the import of all forms of journals in 1982, being half the quota for 1980 and less than one-fifth of the 1978 amount:[19] considering that a reasonably good library for physics alone would cost at least $35,000 a year, it is not surprising that Western scientific journals are virtually unobtainable in Poland, and that scientific work there is gravely hampered by this lack of contact. In Czechoslovakia, orders for foreign journals are placed through an official agency, and are usually accepted only from major institutions. All that is available for others are the extracts and translations selected and published by the Institute for Scientific, Technical and Economic Information. In Romania, where it is illegal, except in special circumstances, for nationals to hold hard currency, access to Western publications is severely restricted. An order for a foreign scientific journal, whether from an individual Romanian scientist or from an institution, requires the prior approval of Elena Ceausescu, the wife of the President, who controls all scientific activity in the country through her twin offices as Chairman of the National Council on Science and Technology, and Chief of the cadre section of the Romanian Communist Party. But her decisions are not, apparently, based upon strictly scientific considerations, and usually favour only those scientists who are considered to be 'politically reliable'.

Where foreign currency is at a premium, this policy may be economically justifiable. But that this is not the only impediment is shown by the difficulties scientists sometimes have in receiving foreign publications, even if this entails no foreign currency cost. There is no assurance, for example, that free copies of a foreign periodical sent by a foreign colleague will regularly arrive. In some of the Eastern countries, censorship of incoming periodicals addressed to individuals is applied in the same way as it is to those

19 *Nature*, 297, 259; 1982.

going to official institutions within the country—and perhaps even more rigorously.

Freedom to publish

Scientific results can only come to the attention of 'the one world of science' if they are published, and a scientist can only become a member of that 'one world' if his or her results are published to its other members. Now the point where the communication system of science is most easily controlled is where a private typescript is transformed into a public printed page, and the right to publish the results of research is thus of paramount importance for scientists.

But this right is also subject to all the restrictions and limitations allowed by the international human rights treaties. The need for continual vigilance to ensure that these permitted limitations are not exceeded is reflected in a number of declarations which, while not having the force of law, are powerful recommendations to governments and other authorities concerned with the management of science. Thus, the World Federation of Scientific Workers in its 1969 Declaration on the Rights of Scientific Workers demanded that:

'governments should refrain from interference with the freedom to express scientific views, or to publish the results of scientific research, and should take steps to prevent other interference with this freedom.'

The truth of the matter is, however, that a very considerable proportion of the research and development work that is done by scientists nowadays is not really intended to become part of 'the one world of science'. It is done to further the immediate purposes of nations and of commercial organizations, and a great part of its value for those who support it is that its results are *not* made public and available to rivals. This is not the place to argue whether that is a good or a bad thing: it must be accepted as a feature of the real world in which scientists must live and work. It has now become quite normal for a scientific researcher to have to enter into an agreement not to divulge the results of his or her research to unauthorized persons—for example to the employees of a rival commercial corporation. The right to *complete* freedom of communication is thus given up, and cannot be reasserted unilaterally by the individual.

A sensitive awareness of the conflicts of ethical principle that can arise in the exercise of this right is shown in Article 37 of the

Recommendations on the Status of Scientific Researchers adopted by the General Conference of UNESCO in 1974:

'Member States should, in consultation with scientific researchers' organizations and as a matter of standard practice, encourage the employers of scientific researchers, and themselves as employers seek:

(a) to regard it as the norm that scientific researchers be at liberty and encouraged to publish the results of their work;

(b) to minimize the restrictions placed upon scientific researchers' rights to publish their findings, consistent with the public interest and the rights of their employers and fellow workers;

(c) to express as clearly as possible in writing in the terms and conditions of their employment the circumstances in which such restrictions are likely to apply;

(d) similarly, to make clear the procedures by which scientific researchers can ascertain whether the restrictions mentioned in this paragraph apply in a particular case and by which they can appeal.'

In effect, this recommends that those subject to such restrictions on publication should have a prior free choice whether or not they wish to accept them, and ought—economic considerations apart—to be at liberty to refuse employment which imposes such restrictions.

In fact, the legal systems of most countries make it possible to include enforceable obligations of secrecy about the results of scientific research in the contracts of employment which scientists make with their employers. In pursuance of such an obligation, it is reasonable to insist that the results of research undertaken in the course of such employment should not be made public without the permission of the employing organization. Very often, this is no more than a formality: a scientist working in a government research laboratory on a relatively academic scientific problem, for instance, would normally expect to be able to publish papers freely, with no more than 'helpful criticism' from more senior managers. (Indeed, this constraint may be less severe than the extra-legal convention that the work of a graduate student or junior research worker in a university should not be published without the permission of the professor supervising the research—a traditional practice which has produced much anguish to many young scientists in many countries.)

Nevertheless, there are circumstances where this contractual constraint is applied unreasonably, and should be challenged. In some cases, for instance, it can be argued that confidential information *should* be disclosed in order to protect the public interest. But that can often lead to conflicts. One example in the USA in 1980 was the case of Dr Morris Baslow, a marine biologist who published his research findings on the possible adverse effects of power plant operations on the Hudson River environment without first consulting his employer, a firm of private consultants: for this they discharged him, and ultimately tried to sue him for $5.2 million. He eventually obtained a settlement with the help of the Department of Labor, the Federal Energy Regulatory Commission, and the Environmental Protection Agency.[20] More recently, however, the Environmental Protection Agency itself has insisted that in certain areas it will determine whether or not the results of research it has funded can be published. The reason officially given is to assure the adequate standard of the work published; but the sceptical view of many of those involved is that it is designed far more to prevent public opinion being aroused over environmental hazards which, for commercial or other reasons, the administration would prefer not to have made public.[21]

The right of free professional communication here comes close to the issues of freedom of expression and opinion which we shall discuss in the next chapter. But there are also cases where the material to be published is no threat to the employing organization, and there is no suggestion that it is scientifically unsound.

In the countries of Eastern Europe and in the Soviet Union, where there is no general right to freedom of publication, all material, scientific or other, has to go through the official censorship system of the state. Generally speaking, scientific work is not subject to the 'peer review' process customarily employed by the editors of reputable scientific journals in the West—which can be very severe, and bear heavily on work that is regarded unfavourably by referees—but it has to be specifically approved by the institute where the author is employed. There is a good deal of anecdotal evidence indicating that this power is sometimes grossly abused by the directors of institutes and other senior scientists in order to favour work supporting their own scientific views,

[20] See Holden, C., 'Scientist with Unpopular Data loses Job', *Science* 210, 749; 1980; *Science*, 215, 383; 1982.

[21] *Science*, 213, 1345; 1981.

but this sort of restriction on freedom in science is difficult to pin down.

However, in those countries a scientist may also be prevented by his institute from having his work published because he is personally out of favour with the authorities. For instance, Professor Eduard Nadgorny, a founder member of the prestigious Institute for Solid State Physics of the Soviet Academy of Sciences, was esteemed by his colleagues for twenty years as a dedicated and brilliant scientist. Yet in 1981 he was denied access to his own research facilities, and forbidden to publish any further scientific papers, within days of applying for permission to emigrate to Israel.[22] The same happened to Victor Brailovsky, an expert on cybernetics at the Moscow Institute of Radio Engineering Electronics and Automation, whose application for a visa to Israel in 1972 was refused with similar consequences.

A scientist who is unable to publish in the Soviet Union does not have the option of trying to get his or her work published abroad, as would be the case for a scientist working in the West: private individuals are not allowed to send typewritten material abroad. This has to go through an organization, accompanied by a Form 103A, after duly following the multiple procedures prescribed. These require that the paper should first be approved by the academic council of the relevant institute, after taking the views of two experts. It then has to be certified as containing no secret material, approved by the foreign section of the Ministry, and passed by Glavlit, the censorship organization. Thereafter an English translation has to be submitted to the institute for verification that this is identical in content with the Russian text.

These procedures, which involve enormous travel for the typescript, not surprisingly take time. When Zhores Medvedev was invited in 1966 to give a lecture at a meeting in Sheffield of the British Society for Research on Ageing, he determined to send his text well in advance: it eventually arrived in England five days after the session of the symposium at which it was scheduled to be read. He himself was not there to read it, since the even more tortuous process of getting permission to attend in person had failed. Fortunately, the sceptical Medvedev had taken the—undoubtedly illicit—precaution of sending a further copy by the

[22] *News Bulletin of the Scientists' Committee of the Israel Public Council for Soviet Jews*, 31 August 1982.

hand of an English friend who delivered it in time, and it was read on his behalf at the meeting.[23]

Even to send printed matter abroad, the prior permission of the Soviet Ministry of Culture is necessary. Thereafter, parcels containing books are accepted only in the post office nearest to the sender's residence, and on presentation of a passport. The number of books that may be sent by one person cannot exceed three a year.[24] This regulation would evidently curb the efforts of an author to get a foreign publisher for a book that had, perhaps, been briefly published in the Soviet Union and then proscribed.

A certain number of Soviet scientists have in fact defied these regulations, and managed to have their manuscripts taken out of the country and published abroad. But this not only puts them at serious risk of disciplinary action (as in the case of Leo Peker, for example, to which we referred earlier in this chapter); it also means that they are unable to play their part in the interactive processes, involving authors, editors, and referees, by which scientific papers are normally revised and corrected before they appear in print.[25]

In Eastern Europe, generally, publication is dependent on the prior approval of the director of the author's institute and on other bureaucratic authorities. Some of the worst cases of abuse of this power have come from Czechoslovakia. In 1970, Professor B. Paleska, who had 150 scientific papers and two Czech official decorations to his credit, was not only dismissed from his post as director of the Czechoslovak Institute for Electronics and Modelling in Medicine; he was also barred from clinical work and from publishing scientific articles.[26] Professor Karel Culik, who was dismissed from the Mathematical Institute of the Czechoslovak Academy in 1970, has not been allowed to publish either at home or abroad since 1968. A book intended for publication abroad and completed in that year was sent for censorship in March 1973. It was returned eight months later with an interdict on publication, although it was admitted to have no security implications.

The official policy behind such prohibitions is reflected in a bureaucratic directive which it is worth quoting here in full, in the form in which it appeared in 1972 on the notice-boards of the

23 Medvedev, Zh., *The Medvedev Papers* (Macmillan; London, 1971).
24 *USSR News Brief* (Brussels, 16 October 1982).
25 See Ziman, J. M., *Public knowledge* (Cambridge, 1967).
26 *Nature*, 258, 458; 1974.

Faculty of General Medicine of what had once been the respected Charles University in Prague:[27]

'*Circular Ref. No. 3772/72-II-D/III/2-V-5*

The session of the Scientific Council of 27 April 1972 discussed the order of the Minister of Education of the Czech Socialist Republic and the Rector of the University concerning a ban on publication. The Scientific Council decided that heads of departments and of departmental praesidia will be personally responsible for the publications of their members and for the theoretical and political quality of their works.

In his letter of 26 May 1972, Ref. No. 3426/72-C-IX/I, the Rector of the University announced the following: The Ministry of Education of the Czech Socialist Republic, in its letter of 19 May 1972, Ref. No. 11. 838/72-34, authorized Charles University to continue its publishing activities. Attention was drawn to the fact that only those people who meet the moral and political requirements laid down for members of university teaching staffs can have their works published. In particular it is not possible to publish the works of those people who have been expelled from the CPCS, who for political reasons no longer work at the University, or who have emigrated illegally. If an invitation for co-operation is extended to an author outside the University, then the Faculty is obliged to acquire data on his moral and political profile. The aforementioned requirements also hold for the authors of teaching scripts.

The Editorial Boards, Editorial Commissions, and Screening Commissions will be responsible to the Rector or Vice-Rector of Charles University for the theoretical and political level of the published literature. For works not yet published or about to be submitted in accordance with the plan, I request that a statement be submitted to me testifying to their theoretical and politico-ideological standard. This will be signed by the Chairman of the Editorial Board or Editorial Commission, and by the Chairman of the relevant Screening Commission.

Professor Dr V. Balas, C. Sc., Dean of Faculty'

In fact, in Czechoslovakia no scientific work can be published which deviates from the official ideology, or whose author has deviated from official orthodoxy. In 1978, the Director of the Institute of Nuclear Physics, Jaroslav Prochazka, expressed this policy in memorable words:

'I would throw out even Einstein if his political views were not quite in order.' [28]

---

[27] *White Paper on Czechoslovakia* (International Committee for the Support of Charter-77 in Czechoslovakia; Paris, 1977)

[28] *Nature*, 274, 632; 1978.

It is worth observing, in this connection, that Article 20 of the Czechoslovak Constitution guarantees equality to all citizens, and that lawful bans on publication can only be issued by criminal courts under Articles 49 and 50 of the Czechoslovak Penal Code, for a maximum period of five years, against persons convicted of a crime related to the activity to be banned.

In Eastern Europe, as in the Soviet Union, publication *abroad* is even more strictly regulated. In Czechoslovakia, this is, strictly speaking, permitted only if the researcher has previously published papers in a *Soviet* journal—a condition hard to fulfil in view of the lag in Soviet publication schedules. Similar policies are followed in other East European countries: on 29 June 1979, for example, the GDR Parliament amended paragraph 219 of the Criminal Code to make it an offence to seek to have works published abroad without permission.

Although these cases of severe violations of freedom of communication in science have mostly occurred in the Soviet Union and its allies, it must not be thought that every scientist in the West can get into public print with any information that he has a mind to publish. As we have already noted, there is no 'right' to have a paper published in a reputable scientific journal, nor to have a book published by a reputable scientific publisher, except through the narrow and rocky channel of 'peer review'. Many would-be scientific authors are bitterly critical of the processes by which editors and editorial boards select and reject the papers submitted to them, and there is a growing body of evidence[29] that these processes are by no means as fair and intellectually sound as most scientists have been taught to believe.

Of course, in any country where free speech is protected by an effective law, there is nothing to prevent a scientist whose paper has been rejected by a reputable journal submitting it to a less esteemed publication—or even, if the worst comes to the worst, having it printed and distributed at his own expense. Quite a lot of highly unorthodox (not to say cranky) material is eventually published in this way. As far as both domestic and international law is concerned, the 'right to communicate' has been satisfied, and there is little more that can be said. Nevertheless, there is cause for concern in cases such as the 'Velikovsky affair',[30] where

[29] See Harrad, S. (ed.), *Peer Commentary on Peer Review* (Cambridge, 1982).
[30] de Grazia, A. (ed.), *The Velikovsky Affair* (Sidgwick & Jackson; London, 1966).

a major US publishing house was subjected to pressure by certain senior scientists to prevent the publication of an (admittedly downright absurd) book on astronomy by Immanuel Velikovsky. Conversely, many US scientists have been alarmed at the pressures exerted by proponents of 'creationism', who would significantly reduce the publication of scientific information about biological evolution if they had their way (see Chapter 7).[31]

A significant instance of private censorship of a scientific publication in the USA occurred in April 1980, when the Second International Congress on Phosphorus Compounds, organized by the Institut Mondial du Phosphat (IMPHOS), was held in Boston. IMPHOS is an association of phosphorus- and fertilizer-producing countries, based in Morocco and funded mainly by North African and Middle Eastern companies. Its declared purpose is to promote research into, and the use of, phosphorus and its compounds. When the proceedings of the Congress were eventually published, it was found that two excellent contributions by Israeli scientists, Z. Ketsinel and Y. Nathan, had been arbitrarily omitted. Claude Eon, then director of technical research for IMPHOS, who had organized the Congress and who strenuously opposed the censorship of the proceedings, was dismissed from his job. Cases like this show that while laws protecting free speech in general may be the best safeguard for freedom of scientific communication, scientists would be well advised not to take their effectiveness for granted anywhere.

Secrecy and national security

As we have already noted, one of the most serious limitations on the basic right of free communication is in the interests of national security. Although the legally permitted range of this constraint is not often objectively tested, even under the domestic laws of a country where freedom of speech is the norm, there is no doubt that it has a pervasive effect on the communication of scientific information in the modern world. In the Soviet Union, and in the other 'Helsinki' countries with similar political systems, the general principle is that every item of scientific information has to be considered for its possible implications for national security before it can be released for publication. Whether or not this blanket

[31] Nelkin, D., *Science Textbook Controversies and the Politics of Equal Time* (MIT Press; Cambridge, Mass., 1977); Numbers, R. L., 'Creationism in 20th-century America', *Science*, 218, 538; 1982.

application of secrecy is legitimate under the international code of human rights law, it is at least consistent in practice.

In most of the other 'Helsinki' countries, domestic law draws a clear distinction between scientific information that has been produced within the government service or under specific contract to the government, and information that has been produced by private citizens or organizations. Whatever controls the government may exercise over the publication of its 'own' scientific work, it usually does not, in peacetime, have a legal right to interfere on national security grounds with the publication of the results of research undertaken by universities, private companies, or other scientific organizations. Thus, in Britain, the Ministry of Defence 'classifies' its scientific activities according to their relative degrees of secrecy, and extends this system to research and development projects undertaken for it in various industrial laboratories. The Official Secrets Acts also provide a general legal constraint on the publication of any work by a government scientist without formal permission. But there is nothing to prevent a university professor from, say, publishing the chemical formula for a very potent nerve gas that he happens to have discovered, provided that he was not using classified information about such gases to do so.

Until recently, the situation in the United States was considered to be even more liberal from the point of view of 'the one world of science'. The Department of Defense, and all its subsidiary agencies and contractors, do of course operate a sophisticated system of classification to protect their scientific and technological secrets, but there is no general law comparable to the British Official Secrets Acts to cover all federal employees. Indeed, the Freedom of Information Act[32] opens many government activities to outside enquiry, and the First Amendment to the US Constitution has been interpreteted by the US Supreme Court to protect free speech at least as widely as the international code.[33]

In practice, the United States has traditionally had a very open system where, except in regard to classified material, the only real constraint on publication was exercised by journal editors and their referees. Thus, for example, the Department of Defense

---

[32] First enacted in 1966, and revised and extended in 1974.

[33] Among the leading cases in this field are *Street* v. *New York* 394 US 576, *New York Times* v. *Sullivan* 376 US 254, *Roth* v. *United States* 354 US 476, and *Bachellar* v. *Maryland* 397 US 564.

funded a great deal of basic research, with no obvious military applications, whose results were not classified and could normally be published at the discretion of the researcher without having to get permission from the Department. It is a matter of concern, therefore, that recent policies of the US Government seem to be directed towards reversing a thirty-year trend away from wartime secrecy in science, so that national security considerations are beginning to encroach again on the traditional freedom of communication in the private domain.

The explicit instrument of this policy is Executive Order 12356, signed by President Reagan on 2 April 1982.[34] This Order gives unprecedented authority to government officials to intrude, at their discretion, in controlling academic research that depends on federal support. It allows classification to be imposed at any stage of a project, and to be maintained for as long as the officials deem necessary. It stipulates that 'basic research', not clearly related to national security, may not be classified, but it does not define basic research. Whereas previously, if there was any doubt, the material was not to be classified, the new Order puts the onus on the researcher to sit on material for thirty days as if it were classified, so as to enable the authorities to make up their minds whether or not it should be.

An example of this policy in action was the threat of the Department of Defense that many papers to be presented at the August 1982 International Conference of the Society of Photo-Optical Instrumentation Engineers in San Diego could be regarded as within the proscribed zone of information not to be made generally available. Although the government did not seem to have mandatory powers to prevent the presentation of these papers, it could obviously make further research resources difficult to obtain for scientists who ignored this warning. In the event, the conference organizers and the presenters of the papers were reluctantly compelled to withdraw no fewer than 100 out of the 700 papers scheduled to be presented.[35] The argument of the authorities was that foreign scientists attending such a meeting were using the occasion to gather intelligence of scientific developments of military significance: indeed, the National Security Agency had claimed that about 30 per cent of the Soviet Union's intelligence-gathering

[34] *Science*, 216, 276 & 365; 1982.
[35] *Science*, 217, 1207 & 1233; 1982.

was done through US scientists and scientific exchanges,[36] and in January 1982 Admiral Bobby R. Inman, Deputy Director of the Central Intelligence Agency and a past Director of the National Security Agency, had warned that if the scientific community did not start policing itself the government might be compelled to submit their research to censorship before publication.[37]

The question whether all the powers claimed under this Order are legally valid has not yet been tested in the US courts. The US government may well have a right to impose restrictions on the publication of scientific work for which it is managerially, contractually, or financially responsible. But there can be no doubt that this policy contravenes at least the spirit of the Helsinki Accords, which devote much attention to the desirability of exchanging scientific and technological information about many spheres of activity. The American scientific community certainly regards it as a danger to scientific progress. As Donald Kennedy, the president of Stanford University, said in an editorial in *Science* in April 1982:[38]

'We have also emphasised the potential damage to the scientific enterprise from government efforts to restrict its openness—especially when these coincide with efforts of private sponsors to expand secrecy for proprietary reasons. It surely will be difficult to resist the latter if we are forced to accept the former . . . But to apply a burdensome set of regulations to a venture that has gained such great strength by its openness will cost the nation more than it can be worth.'

The present situation in the USA about the right to publish scientific work is rendered even more ominous by the attempts to apply 'national security' constraints on research results obtained *outside* the government sector. This is not an entirely new development. The US Atomic Energy Act states that virtually all information related to nuclear energy or nuclear weapons is 'born secret'—that is, it is automatically classified the moment it comes into existence. Whenever a researcher makes a discovery or invention involving nuclear energy, he or she must report it to the Department of Energy within six months, and the discovery is classified until the Department proclaims it to be otherwise. This notion that privately generated ideas can be automatically classified

---

[36] *Nature*, 296, 693; 1982.
[37] *Science*, 215, 383; 1982.
[38] *Science*, 216, 276 & 365; 1982.

(albeit in the highest national interest) before they are even articulated may well be unconstitutional: it would certainly have been tested if the injunction had been maintained, in 1979, barring *The Progressive* in Wisconsin from publishing an article about hydrogen bombs written by a freelancer who had used information drawn solely from the open literature.[39] Despite this legal uncertainty, there are proposals to extend the regulations under the Act to cover vast amounts of information that have already been published. The consequence could be to take millions of books and documents (including ordinary university textbooks) off the open stacks of libraries and to put them into special collections accessible only to privileged persons. It is unlikely that this extreme policy—which would mirror Soviet practices in respect to the right of access—will be put into effect, but the fact that it has even been officially proposed is decidedly disturbing.

Another legal constraint on the communication of privately obtained research results in the USA is the Invention Secrecy Act,[40] which authorizes the US Patent Office to impose a secrecy order on any patent application if public release of the invention might endanger national security. This is not a trivial matter; at the last count, the Patent Office was sending out such orders on about 350 of the 10,000 patent applications filed annually, and a substantial proportion of these were from inventors with no access to classified material. This practice too has not yet been tested in the courts. In Britain, the government can also prevent the publication of a patent specification on defence grounds.

The danger from these developments is that they cannot easily be given clear and rational limits. If those who now press for them were to achieve all their objectives, the situation in the USA could begin to approach that in the USSR, where all new knowledge is scrutinized for its potential risk to national security, and therefore as a candidate for censorship. This is well illustrated by the case of cryptography. Pure mathematicians in the USA working on the theory of numbers—by almost any criteria, the most useless and irrelevant of all useless and irrelevant academic disciplines—were astonished to be told that certain of their papers should not be published because they might inadvertently compromise the nation's secret codes, as well as its ability to break the codes of

39 See Nelkin, D., *Science as Intellectual Property* (Macmillan; New York, 1984).
40 See *Science*, 213, 1234; 1981.

other nations.[41] This constraint was not applied under any law, but it was effective in that a Public Cryptography Study Group was formed, and researchers began voluntarily to submit research papers potentially relevant to cryptography to the National Security Agency for pre-publication review. If number theory can turn out to be a 'threat to national security'—and we need not doubt that there is some validity in that claim—then it is hard to imagine any other field of pure, academic science which could not turn out, by some mischance, to be equally sensitive and vulnerable to control.

The United States plays such a dominant role in world science, and in the Western group amongst the Helsinki countries, that any trend against freedom of communication there is a particularly sensitive matter for the future of 'the one world of science' under the rule of law. There is little evidence of similar trends in other countries of this group, apart from a notorious case from France concerning the right to send scientific material out of the country. In 1979 Dr R. Dobbertin, a theoretical physicist and a refugee from the GDR who by then had West German citizenship and was employed by the French Science Research Council (the CNRS), was arrested and imprisoned for sending pre-prints of articles of potential interest to his former colleagues in the GDR. This included material which was freely available to scientists working in the same field in France. He was held in custody without trial until, with the abolition of the Court of State Security by the new Mitterand administration, his case was closed—but not before he had spent some three years in prison.[42] But this seems to be an isolated case, unusual for a country with a strong tradition of respect for human rights.

[41] *Science*, 208, 1442; 1980; *Nature*, 287, 2; 1982.
[42] Information supplied by Amnesty International.

7

FREEDOM OF OPINION AND EXPRESSION

Science and politics

Over some matters, scientists are often much better informed than the average person. From their professional knowledge and experience, they are in a position to see not only the benefits that are likely to result from a particular application of science or technology, but also the risks that are inherent in scientific progress.

In his younger days, Andrei Sakharov was engaged in secret work for the defence of his country. As he later explained:

'My social and political views underwent a major evolution over the fifteen years from 1953 to 1968. In particular, my role in the development of thermonuclear weapons from 1953 to 1962, and in the preparation and execution of thermonuclear tests, led to an increased awareness of the moral problems engendered by such activities.'[1]

Accordingly, he began a campaign to halt or limit the testing of nuclear weapons. He helped to promote the 1963 Moscow treaty banning nuclear weapons tests in the atmosphere, in outer space, and under water. He spoke out on problems of biology. He began to agitate for the protection of nature from industrial pollution. And these activities, in the course of time, brought him into conflict with his government.

In 1966, Sakharov began to intervene on behalf of victims of repression. In 1968, he wrote an essay on 'Progress, Coexistence and Intellectual Freedom', which was circulated in samizdat form. It received international acclaim when it was translated and published by the *New York Times*. This was, as he himself says, the turning-point of his life:

'After my essay was published abroad in July 1968, I was barred from secret work and excommunicated from many privileges of the Soviet establishment. The pressure on me, my family and friends increased in

---

[1] Sakharov, A. D., *Sakharov Speaks* (Vintage Books; New York, 1974).

1972, but as I came to learn more about the spreading repressions, I felt obliged to speak out in defence of some victim almost daily.'[2]

He continued to speak out on peace and disarmament, on freedom of contacts, movement, information and opinion, against capital punishment, on the protection of the environment, and on nuclear power plants. Finally, in January 1980, he was taken to the offices of the Procurator General of the USSR and there informed of a decree of the Praesidium of the Supreme Soviet by which he was stripped of his official Soviet awards: the Order of Lenin, the thrice awarded title of Hero of Socialist Labour, the Lenin Prize, and the State Prize for Scientific Achievements. By administrative action he was banished to Gorki, where he has lived ever since, isolated and under surveillance day and night.

The rare combination of high intellectual achievement and high moral integrity exhibited by Andrei Sakharov is a source of inspiration for everyone. Above all, it exemplifies the theme of the present chapter. Let us consider this story first from the point of view of international human rights law. As we have already noted (Chapter 6), the right to freedom of opinion and expression is stated very firmly, both in the UDHR and in the ICCPR, where Article 19 reads as follows:

'(1) Everyone shall have the right to hold opinions without interference.

'(2) Everyone shall have the right to freedom of expression; this right shall include the freedom to seek, receive and impart information and ideas of all kinds, regardless of frontiers, either orally, in writing or in print, in the form of art, or through any other media of his choice.'

We have already seen the force of this Article in protecting freedom of communication. But we have also noted that the freedom of expression (though not that of opinion) which it guarantees is formally bounded by a number of provisos, for the third paragraph of the Article goes on to read as follows:

'(3) The exercise of the right provided for in paragraph 2 of this Article carries with it special duties and responsibilities. It may therefore be subject to certain restrictions, but these shall only be such as are provided by law and are necessary:
(a) for respect of the rights or reputations of others;
(b) for the protection of national security or of public order (*ordre public*), or of public health or morals.'

2 Ibid.

The opinions expressed by Andrei Sakharov clearly do not fall within any of these categories. By what right, then, is he being persecuted in the Soviet Union? The answer lies in two provisions of the Penal Code of one of that nation's constituent states, the Russian Soviet Federative Socialist Republic: Article 70, which prohibits agitation or propaganda 'carried on for the purpose of subverting or weakening the Soviet regime', and the circulation, preparation or possession of 'slanderous fabrications which defame the Soviet state and social system'; and Article 190(1), which makes it an offence to 'circulate anti-Soviet slander'. Both these articles have been freely used in the Soviet Union against scientists who have sought to fulfil their responsibilities to society by expressing their concern about what is going on around them, and similar articles appear in the penal codes of most of the countries of Eastern Europe. If one looks at their language, it is plain that they restrict freedom of expression to a far greater extent than Article 19(3) of the ICCPR allows. All the countries concerned are bound by the provisions of that Covenant, which obliges them 'to respect and to ensure to all individuals' the rights recognized in it. To the extent that they do not—either by their domestic laws, such as the two articles from the RSFSR Penal Code which we have just cited, or by their actions—they are therefore in clear breach of their obligations under international law.

In fact, the punishment meted out to Sakharov is doubly illegitimate, in that no criminal charge has ever been brought against him, even under the articles of the Penal Code which we have cited. The restrictions on him, including his exile to Gorki, have not even been imposed by courts after conviction of some offence, but entirely by administrative *fiat*, so infringing the most fundamental principle of the rule of law.

None the less, there are still some, even in free countries, who argue that such actions are not their concern: they say that, for all they know, the measures taken may be justified because the 'dissidence' of people like Sakharov could well be a danger to the authority of his state. They would make a distinction between freedom to express a 'scientific' opinion—which they would fully support as an issue transcending national frontiers—and the right to express an opinion on a 'political' matter, which they would regard as coming under the jurisdiction of the government of the country concerned, and not something in which 'outsiders' should be involved. The tacit premise of that argument is that sovereign states are entitled to do whatever they wish to their inhabitants in the furtherance of what they perceive to be their national interest, and its logical consequence is that all victims of state oppression must be left to the tender mercies of their oppressors. This is the precise opposite of the fundamental premiss underlying today's code of international human rights law, which accepts no distinction between 'scientific' and 'political' opinions, does not allow the repression of 'dissidence' to be justified in the name of *raison d'état*, and makes the manner in which any state treats its inhabitants a matter of *legitimate* concern for everyone else.

In any case, there can be no continent distinction between 'scientific' and 'political' opinions, because in practice it is not possible to draw any clear boundary between them. Consider again the story of Sakharov. He was always a man with a mind of his own (how else could he have been such an original and creative scientist?), but his first acts of 'dissidence' were entirely within the 'scientific' sphere. Although he was a physicist, he began to read the world literature on the biological effects of radioactive materials, and came to the conclusion that the biologists advising the Soviet authorities were gravely underestimating the dangers of atmospheric tests. But when he discovered that these views were not being heeded on their merits, he tried to convey his concern to the highest circles of government, to which he had access by virtue of his scientific standing. It was only when these rational 'scientific' protests were brushed aside that he came to appreciate that the real issue was the place of science within the framework of power in the Soviet Union, which necessarily led him to consider the nature of that framework. There can be no doubt that his concerns now are primarily in the political and humanitarian sphere, but at what precise point did the transition take place? Was it, as hard-line technocrats might argue, when he started meddling in biology, where he had no expert credentials? Was it later, when he tried to bypass the administrative structure in order to get the ear of Nikita Krushchev for his opinions? Was it when he began to put on paper some rather general thoughts on the problems posed by nuclear weapons in international affairs? Or did he only cross the boundary when he began to take an interest in individual cases of injustice, and to argue for the implementation of the international code of human rights law in the name of peace and humanity?

Any answer to this question can only be arbitrary, but it will also define the position of the respondent in relation to 'freedom under the law'. Only the crassest tyrant or fanatic would doubt the wisdom of allowing free play to dissenting opinions on technical scientific matters. But genuine freedom in that sphere depends, ultimately, on social institutions and legal traditions that protect—and even encourage—a plurality of views in the spheres of ethics and politics. Any boundary drawn between these spheres casts the scientist in the role of a 'household slave', whose range of autonomy and responsibility is limited by his 'owner', rather than by his own capabilities and personal inclinations. In short, this point of view—which is surprisingly often taken by scientists themselves, doubtless hoping to protect their privileges and social status—actually endangers those privileges and undermines their status as citizens. They would do well to remember that the European Court of Human Rights has affirmed more than once[3] that the right to freedom of expression is not confined to information or ideas that are favourably received, or regarded as inoffensive, or as a matter of indifference, but also to those that offend, shock, or disturb the state or any sector of the population. This theme runs through the whole of the present work, but it is nowhere pointed up more clearly than where freedom of opinion and expression is at stake.

Freedom for ideas

The archetypal episode for freedom of scientific opinion is the story of Galileo. From our present vantage point, this can be seen as a violation of the right of a scientist to hold and put forward a genuine scientific idea that happened to be distasteful to the political authorities of his day. This interpretation is, of course, decidedly anachronistic, and the true story was very much more complicated. Nevertheless, it has provided science with an exemplary case for a whole class of similar episodes.

A more recent, and even more persuasive, experience was that of Germany under the Nazis. Again, there is no need to enter at length into the perversions of knowledge and the personal persecutions that crippled science—though not technology—for a

[3] In *Handyside* v. *United Kingdom* 1 EHRR 737, and again in *Sunday Times* v. *United Kingdom* 2 EHRR 245.

generation in that country. This was the extreme case in recent history of the denial of freedom of expression and opinion, and it happened within living memory in one of the most scientifically advanced nations of the world. That is one reason why the whole topic of freedom in science is taken so seriously today by responsible scientific leaders. Freedom for scientific ideas cannot be taken for granted; it has to be defended as an essential condition for scientific progress. (Like all freedoms, it too has its boundaries; but the complex topic of 'the social responsibility of science' is outside the scope of this book.)

Fortunately, the Third Reich was destroyed, along with its apparatus of intellectual tyranny. The parallel story of Lysenkoism in the Soviet Union is also practically over, though it was never terminated officially. From 1937 to 1964, Soviet biology was dominated by the 'new genetics' expounded by Trofim Lysenko, who denied all the principles that had been accepted by geneticists for a whole generation, and condemned the work of many other scientists as fascist, bourgeois-capitalist, and inspired by clerics. Supported by Stalin, and commended by the Communist Party, his was for some years the only form of biology taught in all schools, universities, and agricultural colleges. Few dared to criticize it. The great Russian biologist N. I. Vavilov paid a heavy price for his courage in expressing his honest opinion of the new genetics as 'an outbreak of medieval obscurantism'. After a succession of unwarranted accusations against his own work, he was deprived of his directorship of the Institute of Plant Industry, and died in prison, two years later, in 1942. From then on, for something like twenty years, all opposition to Lysenko's ideas was suppressed within Russia, although they had been thoroughly discredited in the rest of the world. Eventually, with the death of Stalin and other cultural and political changes in the Soviet Union, this stranglehold on scientific opinion was loosened, although the crimes of Lysenko and his collaborators against the human rights of numerous other Soviet scientists have never been officially acknowledged or expiated.[4]

The effect of Lysenkoism was limited, in that it only affected one branch of science. Nevertheless, it did incalculable damage to the Soviet Union, not only in the sphere of knowledge but in its

[4] Medvedev, Zh., *The Rise and Fall of T. D. Lysenko* (Columbia University Press; New York and London, 1969).

practical applications throughout agriculture. And because some
of the conditions for similar perversions of science continue to
exist in that and many other countries, it is an object lesson for
our present study. Is the same sort of thing happening at present
in any of the 'Helsinki' countries?

In recent years, advocates of the fundamentalist religious thesis
of 'creationism' have attempted to persuade several state legislatures in the United States to insist on the teaching of their thesis
in schools, as a scientific theory on all fours with the theory of
biological evolution by natural selection.[5] Many scientists object
strongly to this, on the ground that the 'creationist' thesis, unlike
the theory of evolution, has not been validated by any scientific
evidence—indeed, that the preponderance of the evidence is
against it—and that it is therefore a violation of the rights of both
teachers and pupils if they are forced to teach and learn it as if it
were 'true'. But in the USA, 'truth' is not the test of freedom of
speech under the First Amendment to the Constitution, which is
designed to allow all ideas and information—true, false, or partly
both—to compete with each other for their acceptance or rejection
among members of the public. It could not therefore be unconstitutional in itself to teach creationism, but when the State of
Arkansas tried in 1981 to *enforce* such teaching in the public
schools by a 'Balanced Treatment for Creation-Science and
Evolution-Science Act', the federal courts struck it down as violating the First Amendment.[6]

This seems to be the only major case of an attempt to limit the
freedom to express opinions on a strictly scientific matter (if such
there be) in the Helsinki countries at present. But the situation is
perhaps not quite as happy as this conclusion might suggest. There
may not be many cases of individuals being legally punished or
illegitimately persecuted for openly adopting a dissenting position
on some question of scientific fact or theory, especially where this
is not obviously connected with some controversial practical or
political issue. But total freedom to advocate such a view is often
somewhat limited.

As we have seen, access to the media of publication is normally
restricted to *bona fide* research scientists, who are seldom sym-

5 See, e. g., *Nature* 296, 109; 1982; *Science* 218, 538; 1982.
6 *McLean* v. *Arkansas Board of Education and Others*; the full judgment is published in
Science 215, 934; 1982.

pathetic to the ideas of unqualified 'outsiders'. Within the scientific world itself, there are circles of influence, schools of thought, and groups that are sometimes seen as powerful 'Mafias' with their dominant 'godfathers', who can impede the dissemination of 'unorthodox' opinion. This may happen by a combination of measures that separately fall far short of offending against the code of international human rights law—some prejudicial refereeing, a failure to cite and discuss, the exercise of patronage in employment and preferment, the use of managerial prerogative, a little administrative obfuscation, and so on. But such measures, which are mildly endemic in every scientific community, can proliferate very seriously in any country where scientific influence is linked to bureaucratic authority—that is, where the leading scientists have firm personal control over the projects, publications, and jobs of their juniors.

In this discussion, we are also compelled to take a very restricted definition of 'science', for there are some disciplines which have been labelled in certain countries as ideologically controversial, on which only orthodox opinions may be expressed. Generally speaking, the physical sciences and mathematics are free of such constraints everywhere, although at the height of Stalinism in the USSR there were some attempts to apply them in these fields also. But as one moves into the biological sciences, and beyond into anthropology, psychology, and sociology, the notion of what can be considered 'non-political' becomes more and more limited. Indeed, these notions have been impressed so rigidly on academic life in certain countries that the 'self-censorship' of most intellectuals has become a cultural habit, reinforced by occasional warnings from the authorities at the merest hint of a transgression. Andrei Sakharov, for example, must have been well aware that he would be earning a black mark for himself by taking the side of the opponents of Lysenko, and that he would surely be punished for his later excursions into political theory. Throughout this book, we come across many cases where individuals have been deprived of important rights—to education, to work, to reputation, etc.—for supposed transgressions of this kind which would otherwise seem trivial exercises of the right of free expression.

The elasticity of the boundary between 'science' and 'ideology', even at a very esoteric level, is indicated by the recent attack on the teaching of philosophy in Czechoslovakia (see Chapter 9).

Most people in Anglo-Saxon countries regard philosophy as an entirely academic subject, largely concerned with the precise meanings of words and the logical articulation of general statements about the world—that is, as a highly abstract and rigorous undertaking in a spirit akin to that of the natural sciences. This view of philosophy may well be mistaken; nevertheless, many scientists and other scholars have been surprised and distressed that this particular discipline should have come under such an attack, and that individual philosophers should have been deprived of their basic right to freedom of expression and opinion.

A more direct example of the supposed implications of scientific opinion comes from Turkey. Ismail Besikci, a social scientist, has been jailed for ten years because he referred to the Kurds as a separate ethnic group. He wrote:

'The official ideology in Turkey obstinately continues to deny the existence of a Kurdish people and a Kurdish language . . . An official ideology [denying the existence of the Kurdish people] has been imposed on universities, legal institutions, political parties, the press and media such as radio and television . . . For example, Turkish universities which follow the official ideology give up scientific truth and deny the reality of the Kurdish nation.'

He was convicted of 'making propaganda for communism and separatism' in his seminars, lectures, and published works. This is the third time that Besikci—who is not a Kurd—has been imprisoned for expressing such views in his writings.[7]

Freedom to criticize

In 1981, when more than 400 scientists from around the world convened at the University of Massachusetts for a four-day symposium on indoor pollution, the first international conference on this topic to be held in the United States, they were told, much to their surprise, that the co-chairman of the meeting, David Berg, a senior official of the Environmental Protection Agency (EPA), was unable to attend. In fact, according to sources inside and outside the EPA, Berg had been barred from the conference at the last minute by the EPA, which also denied him annual leave to attend in his own time, because he advocated continued work on indoor

---

[7] *Amnesty International Newsletter* 12, 6; June 1982.

air pollution at a time when the Agency was all but eliminating funding for research on this topic.[8]

In 1982, an issue of *Nature* carried a blank space, from which material had been removed after the page was ready for printing. The reason given for the withdrawal was that the research group from which it had come had requested its retraction after alleged pressure against publication from the UK Medical Research Council. This was the second comment on the same subject which had been made ready for the press, but which had been withdrawn at the request of the authors for the same reason. Both items were replies to correspondence raising ethical questions about the Medical Research Council's plan for a controlled trial of the usefulness of folic acid in the diet of pregnant mothers, to prevent a malformation of the foetus which manifests itself as spina bifida at birth.[9] Apparently what was feared was the way in which the criticisms might be treated in the popular press; whether or not this was justified it is not for us to say, but there can be no doubt that this was another instance of a powerful organization bringing its influence to bear in order to prevent the expression of opinions that might be prejudicial to its operations.

These are just two of a number of such cases. Although the point at issue may not be the truth of some scientific fact or theory, it is evidently related to the special knowledge and concerns of scientists working in a particular area, and touches directly on their right to criticize the actions of public institutions. Even in countries where free speech is highly valued and protected by the law, such cases still occur too often for comfort; happily, they are apt to give rise to considerable public comment when they do.

The rights and wrongs of episodes of this kind are not easily established. The 'right to criticize' is hedged about with provisos that the comment should be fair, not slanderous or libellous, 'in the public interest', and so on. However, many employers try to impose conditions of total loyalty on their employees, which go far beyond the contractual obligation of an employee not to disclose confidential information obtained in the course of his or her employment. When the safety of the public is at stake, scientists must feel free to exercise their responsibility by 'blowing the whistle', without fear that they will suffer undue punishment. In any case

[8] *Science*, 213, 1345; 1981.
[9] *The Times*, 26 November 1982; *Nature*, 300, 302; 1982; 301, 192; 1983.

they are entitled, under the international code itself, to the provision of 'adequate remedies' for infringements of their rights under it.

A notorious case of this kind was that of Drs J. W. Gofman and A. R. Tamplin, who worked in the laboratories of the US Atomic Energy Commission in Livermore, California. They claimed that existing standards for exposure to ionizing radiation were far too tolerant, and would permit a large increase in the number of deaths from cancer if actual exposures rose to these levels. The authorities in the AEC sharply opposed these views, and held them to be unsound. Eventually, the AEC did impose much stricter radiation limits for the workers within its jurisdiction, but not before Gofman and Tamplin had left the Commission after what they claimed to be unreasonable harassment.[10]

Another notable American case involved the Bay Area Rapid Transit system in the San Francisco region. A major feature of this system was to be the automated train control, for which a contract was awarded to the Westinghouse Electric Corporation in 1967. From about April 1969, three of the engineers on the project became increasingly concerned about what they saw as serious defects in the design. They expressed their concern to the management, but drew no significant response except vague warnings not to be 'trouble-makers'. Late in 1971, they decided to take their case to the Board of Directors: this led to a public hearing in February 1972, at which the Board voted 10 to 2 in favour of the management. The management then told the engineers that they could choose between resigning and being fired; they refused to resign and were summarily dismissed. It has since become clear that their criticism of the design was fully justified; it took many years and much additional expense to cure the defects to which they had drawn attention. This is an object lesson to the managements of large organizations when they are tempted to suppress 'disloyal' criticism from their expert employees.[11]

We have already referred (in Chapter 6) to the case of Dr Morris Baslow, who was dismissed from his job as a marine biologist with a private firm of consultants after publishing research findings indicating the possible adverse effects of a proposed power station

[10] See 'Scientific Freedom and Responsibility', *Science*, 188, 687; 1975 for a more detailed discussion.
[11] *Science*, 188, 687; 1975.

on life in the Hudson river.[12] A similar case where the public interest was involved, and where the sanctions proved to be harsh, was that of Peter F. Infante, an epidemiologist at the US Occupational Safety and Health Administration, who wrote a highly critical letter on 12 May 1981 to the director of the International Agency for Research on Cancer, a branch of the World Health Organization. In this letter he contested a recent decision by an Agency panel which had concluded that there was insufficient evidence to prove that formaldehyde was an animal carcinogen: six weeks later, Infante received notice that he was to be fired.[13]

Whatever the precise legal position in such cases, there is general concern in scientific and legal circles about the heavy pressures that a large commercial or governmental organization can exert on its employees to dissuade them from disclosing information—or even expressing opinions—about operations on its part which could well be matters of major and legitimate public concern. In Britain, for example, much publicity was given to the case of Dr Ross Hesketh, who was said to have been harassed by the Central Electricity Generating Board for disclosing information about the use of plutonium from British civilian nuclear reactors in US nuclear weapons. He was a scientist employed by the CEGB under a contract containing a standard confidentiality clause, though his actual work had nothing to do with the information in question, which he apparently derived by inference from public sources. In the end, this disturbing dispute was settled in a manner that was consistent with Dr Hesketh's legal rights.[14]

But perhaps the worst case of this kind was that of Stanley Adams, an Oxford graduate who was working for Hoffman-La Roche, a multinational pharmaceutical company based in Switzerland. In 1973 he reported some of his employers' secret trading practices to the European Commission in Brussels, which thereupon took proceedings against the company under the Free Trade Agreement between Switzerland and the European Economic Community. In the event, the case was not pressed very far, but Adams suffered tragically for his actions. Unfortunately for him, his part in the matter was disclosed to his employers, with the result that he not only lost his job, but was arrested, convicted, and

[12] *Science*, 215, 383; 1982.
[13] *Science*, 213, 630; 1981.
[14] *The Times*, 19 July 1983; *New Scientist*, 3 November 1983, p. 325.

imprisoned under Swiss law for disclosing confidential commercial information. As a consequence, he was financially ruined; his wife committed suicide; and he now lives in London, in poverty and unemployed.[15] There is doubtless another side to this story, but it is a dramatic example of the seriousness of the issues involved in 'whistle-blowing' by scientists or other responsible employees of large organizations, and of the urgent need to establish clear principles and procedures for the just resolution of such matters within a framework of professional freedom and responsibility.[16]

Freedom to dissent

A scientist who tries to communicate information or express an opinion critical of a private corporation in a 'capitalist' society usually risks no more than dismissal from employment or a civil lawsuit: Stanley Adams was a rare exception. But in countries where the state is the only employer, the expression of such opinions is often punished by the criminal law. A critical comment, in public or even in private, against any aspect of policy may be interpreted as 'dissent', and be very severely penalized. Any attempt to exercise the basic right to freedom of expression and opinion guaranteed by the international code of human rights law may, if it involves dissent from the prevalent ideology, lead to long imprisonment, or even such brutal treatment as to cause untimely death.

In this respect, the Soviet Union is the prime offender among the Helsinki countries, followed by its Eastern European allies. Present practices are not as monstrous as they were in Stalin's time, although there has been a noticeable tightening up in the past decade. This is evident from the outline we have already given of the career of Andrei Sakharov, who was emboldened to speak out in the period of the 'thaw' in the 1960s, and has suffered more and more severe restrictions since the middle of the 1970s. Other Soviet scientists such as Yuri Orlov—also a physicist—who were courageous enough to follow Sakharov's example have been victimized even more brutally, and have mostly been so intimidated that public dissent on significant policy issues has been effectively suppressed.

[15] Adams, S., *Roche versus Adams* (Cape; London, 1984).
[16] See Nelkin, D., *Science as Intellectual Property* (Macmillan; New York, 1984).

To illustrate the seriousness of the situation, here are a few cases from many of the same general type:

Iosif Dyadkin, a research scientist in oil geophysics, had a sentence of three years' imprisonment imposed on him in September 1981 for a scientific study which he prepared in 1976, 'An Evaluation of Unnatural Deaths in the Population of the USSR: 1927–1958', and for other articles he had written in recent years. The study, which was based on official Soviet census data and demographic studies, concluded that some 50 million people died during the period under review as a result of collectivization, famine, mass repression, and the second world war. Dyadkin claimed that the methods used to arrive at the official figures had been designed to mask the massive loss of life brought about by government policies.[17]

Viktor Brailovsky had been a prominent activist in the Jewish emigration movement. He holds a doctorate in cybernetics, and is the author of more than thirty scientific articles. Until 1972, he worked at the Moscow Institute for Electronic Machines, and his wife Irina, a mathematician, worked at the Computer Centre of Moscow State University. In that year, the Brailovskys unsuccesfully applied to emigrate to Israel, and lost their jobs in consequence. For several years Viktor Brailovsky was a member of the editorial board of the unofficial journal *Jews in the Soviet Union*, a non-political publication containing information on the history, religion, and culture of Jews, both in the Soviet Union and outside. He also organized regular scientific seminars in his two-roomed apartment for other prospective Jewish emigrants who had lost their jobs. He maintained contacts with foreign journalists and provided them with information on the 'refusenik' movement. On 13 November 1980, two days after he had held a press conference for foreign journalists in his home to announce the beginning of a hunger strike to coincide with the opening of the Helsinki Review Conference in Madrid, he was arrested. On 17 June 1981, he was sentenced to five years' internal exile for 'circulating anti-Soviet slander', and was sent to a remote area of the Kazakh Republic, from which he was permitted to return to Moscow in March 1984.[18] (It should be noted that under Article 190-1 of the RSFSR Penal Code, the maximum sentence of 'deprivation

---

[17] *Clearing House Report*, May 1981.
[18] Committee of Concerned Scientists, *News Release*, 2 August 1984.

of freedom' for this offence is only three years, but apparently defendants are sometimes willing to barter a longer period of exile for a shorter period of imprisonment, or none at all.)

Tatyana Velikanova, a Russian mathematician, was one of the founder members of the 1969 Group for the Defence of Human Rights. In 1974, she was one of three 'dissidents' who announced publicly that they were taking over responsibility for distributing the samizdat human rights journal *A Chronicle of Current Events*. On 11 October 1979, her home was searched by the KGB for six hours and, according to reports, two sacks and one suitcase filled with archival material were confiscated. On 27 August 1980 she was tried by a court in Moscow on a charge of 'anti-Soviet agitation and propaganda' under Article 70 of the RSFSR Penal Code, and sentenced to four years' imprisonment, followed by five years' internal exile. She is serving the first part of her sentence in a corrective labour colony for female political prisoners in the Mordovian complex. Sakharov has described her contribution to the Soviet human rights movement as 'colossal'.[19]

Juri Kukk was a professor of chemistry and a human rights activist from Estonia. He was accused of writing a letter on the Soviet intervention in Afghanistan which he reportedly gave to David Willis, a correspondent of the *Christian Science Monitor*. He was arrested in February 1980, and sentenced on 8 January 1981 to two years in a labour camp for 'distributing anti-Soviet propaganda', an offence punishable under Article 194(1) of the Estonian Penal Code. During his initial detention, he was sent to the notorious Serbsky Institute in Moscow for psychiatric tests. In March 1981, at the age of 40, he died in Vologda while being transferred from a Murmansk transit camp, presumably to the prison camp where he was to serve his sentence. His death is believed to have been the result of forced feeding during a four-month hunger strike.[20]

Sergei Kovalyov holds the equivalent of a Ph. D. in biology. His speciality is the study of mathematical biology, with particular reference to electrical currents in the body, and more than 60 of his scientific articles have been published. He was a senior reseacher at the Moscow State University until 1969, when he joined Sakharov

[19] *Amnesty Release*, 1980.
[20] Taageppera, R., *Softening without Liberalization in the Soviet Union: The Case of Juri Kukk* (University Press of America, 1984).

as a founding member of the Initiative Group for the Defence of Human Rights in the Soviet Union. He signed a number of appeals protesting against conditions in labour camps, the use of psychiatric hospitals to punish dissidents, and the repression of religious minorities. In that year, he was summarily dismissed from his post and transferred to a fish hatchery. On 27 December 1974, Kovalyov joined Sakharov in signing an appeal for the release of prisoners of conscience throughout the world. On the same day, he was arrested and taken to Lithuania, where he was tried in December 1975 on charges relating to his involvement with a samizdat Lithuanian human rights journal called *A Chronicle of the Lithuanian Catholic Church*, as well as with the Moscow *Chronicle of Current Events*. The state prosecutor insisted that Kovalyov was not being tried 'for his views and opinions, but for specific actions, criminal acts, for the violation of laws forbidding anti-Soviet agitation and propaganda. The Soviet Government is indifferent to the opinions of a person if he only keeps them to himself . . . Our state places a prohibition on actions which are alien to its nature.' He was found guilty and sentenced to seven years' imprisonment in a strict regime labour colony, followed by three years in exile. His internal exile is being served in the notoriously harsh physical conditions of the Magadan region, in the extreme north-east of the Russian Republic.[21]

Malva Landa, a graduate of the Moscow Institute of Geology, worked for twenty years as a geological surveyor on sites throughout the USSR, and then for ten years as an editor of geological publications. She retired in 1973, by which time she had become active in the human rights movement in Moscow. In the autumn of 1971, police found samizdat literature in her home and warned her that she was liable to face criminal charges for 'anti-Soviet slander'. In 1972 and 1973 she was again warned that she was suspected of the criminal offence of 'anti-Soviet agitation and propaganda'. In December 1973, anticipating arrest and trial, she wrote an essay entitled 'Instead of a Final Word' in which she analysed Soviet laws restricting freedom of speech, and criticized them as being incompatible with the Soviet Constitution and the UDHR. In June 1974 she publicly associated herself with the *Chronicle of Current Events*, and following the arrest of Sergei Kovalyov in December of that year her home was again searched

[21] *Clearing House Report*, December 1981.

and her typewriter confiscated. Nevertheless, in May 1976 she helped to found the Moscow Group for the Assistance of the Implementation of the Helsinki Agreements in the USSR, and co-authored or signed many of its statements and appeals. In November and December 1976, her 25-year-old son, a physical education teacher, was advised by KGB officers that unless he persuaded his mother to cease her activity in the Helsinki group he might be dismissed from his teaching position. After the arrest of Alexander Ginsburg in February 1977, Malva Landa was among three human rights activists who succeeded him as trustees of the Russian Public Fund for the Assistance of Political Prisoners. But by the autumn of 1977 all three trustees had been forced to leave the fund: Tatyana Khodorovich and Cronid Lubarsky had emigrated from the USSR on being threatened that they would be imprisoned if they did not leave; Malva Landa was accused of being responsible for a fire which had mysteriously broken out in her apartment. She was found guilty of 'negligently causing damage to public property and personal property', and sentenced to two years of internal exile. After eight months in exile in the Soviet Far East, she received an amnesty on the sixtieth anniversary of the October Revolution. On her return home, however, she declared her intention to continue her human rights activities and on 7 March 1980 she was arrested again in Vladimir, during a major crackdown on dissidents throughout the Soviet Union. Three weeks later she was sentenced to five years' internal exile for 'anti-Soviet slander', and is now believed to be in the Dzherkazgansky region of the Kazakhstan Republic.[22]

We have detailed these cases at length in order to demonstrate the degree of victimization that some scientists have had to suffer, their persistence in their attempts to exercise their rights, and the illegitimacy of the charges that have been brought against them. We shall come across many similar cases where this striving for freedom to express their opinions on important matters of practical action or of conscience has put in jeopardy other basic rights, such as the right to work, to professional reputation, to residence, or to travel abroad.

Scientists living and working in other parts of Eastern Europe have been subjected to similar treatment by their governments. For instance, Peter Uhl, a Czech engineer, a member of VONS (the

22 *Amnesty Release*, 1980.

Committee for the Defence of the Unjustly Persecuted), and a signatory of Charter-77, served a five-year sentence in Mirov prison, having been convicted of 'activity directed against the interests of the Czechoslovak State', an offence punishable under Article 98 of the Penal Code of that country.[23] Since his release in May 1984, he has been unable to obtain professional employment, and is now earning his living as a stoker. Several cases have also been reported from Poland where scientists have been imprisoned, or otherwise punished, for critical comments on the regime under which they are trying to live and work.[24]

A classic case from the GDR was that of Professor Robert Havemann, who became Director of the Physical Chemistry Institute of the Humboldt University in East Berlin in 1950. He had a distinguished anti-Nazi record, and had even been sentenced to death by the German authorities during the war, although the sentence was not carried out. In the next thirteen years, he took his place as a leading member of East German society, and was honoured on several occasions by the state. During this period he helped to found the Socialist Unity Party of Germany, the SED. In the early 1960s, however, he began to have doubts about the course that communism was taking in his country, and during his lectures on the philosophy of science in the academic year 1963/4 he announced his opinion that an opposition party was appropriate even under communism. Despite the fact that he remained a convinced Marxist, he was thereupon expelled from the Party and removed from his duties at the university. In 1966, his name was removed from the list of members of the Academy of Sciences. But he did not recant. In 1976, following his protest against the expulsion of Wolf Biermann from East Germany, Havemann was placed under house arrest, which continued until May 1979. He was then rearrested on a charge of illicitly receiving royalties from having a book published in West Germany. He was sentenced again, and remained under strict surveillance and harassment until his death in April 1982 at the age of 72. This story of a distinguished and highly privileged scientist coming to appreciate his social responsibilities, and having the courage to speak out for human rights, parallels that of Andrei Sakharov. It ends with a vicious twist. The authorities issued visas to only four of the many

23 *Entr'Aide et Action*, 15, E8; September 1980.
24 *Science*, 216, 966; 217, 398; 1982.

people who applied from the West to come to his funeral and to honour him as a scientist. Nevertheless, and in spite of official disfavour, some 500 of his fellow citizens attended the funeral.[25]

The difficulty in charting fully the violations of the right we are here considering is that most of them are hidden. For many transgressions, the punishment may never be formally articulated: it may be simply an indication that promotion will be delayed, opportunities for travel refused, or the allocation of a desirable apartment not achieved. It is clear from a wide variety of auto-biographical and journalistic accounts of life in the Soviet Union and its allies that fear of such things can be very effective in preventing scientists from speaking freely about many matters that anyone outside the 'socialist' bloc would only consider 'political' in a marginal sense. People brought up inside this system acquire an instinctive understanding of the boundaries within which some small degree of freedom of opinion is permissible, but those bound-aries are almost impossible to delineate clearly and are far narrower than those set by international human rights law.

In this context, it is instructive to look at the topics that have been deleted from the copies of *Science* and *Nature* that are offici-ally circulated in the Soviet Union.[26] Some of these deletions are obvious enough—for example, all articles and letters relating to human rights, to Soviet-American relations, and to the People's Republic of China. But why should Soviet scientists not be allowed to inform themselves, and thus develop some opinions, on such matters as the British National Health Service, the eradication of smallpox, or even such symptoms of capitalist decadence as ac-counts of an audit of an American university's research grants, and the cutting of science budgets by the US Congress or the UK Parliament?

Criticism of psychiatric abuse

No one concerned about the protection of basic human rights can be unaware of the widespread protests at the compulsory confinement of political dissidents in mental hospitals in the Soviet Union, for political rather than genuine medical reasons. After wide debate, over a period of many years, both in and outside the World Psychiatric Association, and the presentation of detailed

25 *Dutch CSCE Review*, 154, 2; 155, 20; 1982.
26 *Science*, 205, 284; 1979.

evidence from a number of former Soviet citizens who have suffered this treatment, there can be little doubt that these protests are fully justified.[27] The facts speak for themselves: grave offences against the international code of human rights law have been committed, and continue to be committed, by qualified psychiatrists employed by an agency of the Soviet state with the full knowledge and authority of its government at the highest levels. Persons whom any independent expert or layman would judge to be perfectly sane—or, at worst, a little eccentric—have been forcibly detained for long periods, and subjected to extremely distressing and damaging drug regimes, simply because they have expressed opinions differing from the official ones.

The American psychiatrist Dr Walter Reich has argued forcefully[28] that political abuse of psychiatry in the Soviet Union comes about not only because it is an expedient means of silencing dissent, but because the standard diagnostic system employed by Soviet psychiatrists allows a broad interpretation of psychopathology. The founder of this diagnostic system is Andrei V. Snezhnevsky, one of the most powerful figures in Soviet science. Snezhnevsky is the moving force behind what has come to be called the 'Moscow school' of psychiatry, and is head of the Serbsky Institute of Forensic Psychiatry there. In the 1960s, he developed a concept of schizophrenia which included any mental disorder in which a person becomes unable to act or reason in a rational way (often with delusions and withdrawal from social relationships), and defined it in a manner which allows the psychiatrist to label any individual exhibiting eccentric behaviour as suffering from 'mild or sluggish schizophrenia', and hence as mentally ill. Thus the Moscow artist who holds an exhibition of his paintings in his apartment on the horrors of nuclear war may be detained by the KGB, and later examined by a forensic psychiatrist, who will report that the artist is suffering from 'sluggish schizophrenia' and is thus in need of treatment in a psychiatric institution. Reich argues that while the KGB may find psychiatric confinement the most convenient means of handling such an individual, it must also be understood that the psychiatrist probably *believes* that his 'patient' is indeed suffering from some form of mental dysfunction.

[27] Bloch, S. and Reddaway, P., *Russia's Political Hospitals* (Gollancz; London, 1977); *Psychiatric Terror* (Basic Books; New York, 1977); *Soviet Psychiatric Abuse* (Gollancz; London, 1984).

[28] 'The World of Soviet Psychiatry', *New York Times Magazine*, 30 January 1983.

At the other end of the spectrum of psychiatric opinion lie the views of the school associated with the name of Thomas Szasz, which maintains that mental illness is a myth, and that all psychiatrists who assume the authority to confine individuals in mental hospitals without their consent are, in effect, acting unethically as social engineers. Between Szasz and Snezhnevsky there is evidently a vast area for debate about the validity of theories of mental function, the balance between individual impulses and collective norms in social behaviour, the goals of therapeutic practice—and, above all, the ethical responsibilities of the individual expert medical practitioner. These questions go far outside the scope of this book. But what the international code of human rights law requires is that such a debate should take place in the open in every country at every level, so that those who have to take professional responsibilities in this field have an opportunity of informing their professional consciences in the light of all the views expressed. That is why this issue falls into this chapter, because freedom of expression and opinion is at stake.

In fact, the Soviet authorities have taken very strong measures to suppress any such debate in their own country. In January 1977, an unofficial Working Commission to Investigate the Use of Psychiatry for Political Purposes was founded in Moscow. It was affiliated with the (equally unofficial) Moscow Helsinki Monitoring Group, and published more than 20 information bulletins on its investigations into the Soviet practice of declaring dissidents insane, and interning them in psychiatric hospitals. Despite continued harassment, the Commission campaigned for the release of such dissidents, visited them in psychiatric hospitals, and provided moral and material support to their families.

The authorities soon reacted by imprisoning the members of the Commission. One of its founders, Alexander Podrabinek, a medical assistant, was the author of *Punitive Medicine*, a 265-page dossier on psychiatric abuse in the USSR: he is now serving a three-and-a-half-year sentence on the usual charges of 'circulating anti-Soviet slander'. Podrabinek suffers from chronic hepatitis and rheumatic pains in the knees; in April 1982, while serving time in the punishment cell of a prison camp in north-east Siberia, he was also found to be suffering from active tuberculosis.[29] He was released in February 1984.

29 Bloch and Reddaway, loc. cit. 1984.

An even more severe punishment was inflicted on Anatolyi Koryagin, a psychiatrist, who was sentenced to 12 years' imprisonment in June 1981. Before his arrest, Koryagin served as chief consultant to the unofficial Commission. While practising psychiatry in the Soviet Union, he encountered instances where dissidents had been institutionalized by the state for political rather than medical reasons. Deeply shocked at this abuse of medical expertise, he began working with the Commission in 1978, and was the last of its members to be taken into custody. He was incarcerated in Christopol prison, and was reported in 1984 to be 'near death' as a result of a hunger strike.[30] In July 1982, the VAK (see Chapter 5) revoked his higher academic degree in psychiatry (*kandidat nauk*)—presumably in response to the judgment of the court, which ruled at his trial that Koryagin's activities were 'incompatible with the calling of a Soviet scientist'.[31]

The persecutions of Podrabinek and Koryagin are clear violations of the USSR's obligations under international human rights law. It is very proper that Koryagin should have shared with José F. Westerkamp (from Argentina) the 1983 Award for Scientific Freedom and Responsibility of the American Association for the Advancement of Science. The psychiatrist was cited for his 'courageous and responsible defense, at personal and professional cost, of the principle that medical knowledge and skills should under no circumstances be used for the purpose of suppressing political dissent'.

In time, 'the case of Soviet psychiatry' may come to be seen as one of the most instructive episodes in the history of the social relations of science. It is more than a simple example of the misuse of science in the interests of political power. A variety of forces is powerfully combined within the Soviet Union to suppress the criticism and dissent that this inhuman practice abundantly merits. Some of these forces, such as the efforts of the KGB to curb 'dissidents', are quite clearly in the general political sphere. Some, such as the self-preserving instincts of established professional groups and institutions within Soviet psychiatry, belong more to the domain of administration, and are not unaffected by technical considerations derived from the sphere of science. And a major force clearly emanates from a very powerful scientific personality

[30] *Science*, 226, 1058; 1984.
[31] *Nature*, 292, 487; 1981; Bloch and Reddaway, loc. cit. 1984.

immovably entrenched in a theory of which he will admit no criticism. In this case, as in most cases where the right to freedom of expression and opinion is denied to scientists, these forces cannot be disentangled and defeated separately. This right exists for the benefit of *both* science and society, interacting under the rule of law.

8

FREEDOM OF MOVEMENT

The right to come and go

Freedom of movement is an essential right for all human beings, in a wide range of conditions and circumstances. The UDHR, in its Article 13, declares without reservation that:

'(1) Everyone has the right to freedom of movement and residence within the borders of each state.
(2) Everyone has the right to leave any country, including his own, and to return to his country.'

For good measure, the Declaration adds, in Article 9, that 'No one shall be subjected to arbitrary . . . exile.'

As usual, the treaty language is both more cautious and more precise. Article 12 of the ICCPR—imposing, we must recall, absolute and immediate obligations on its state parties—runs as follows:

'(1) Everyone lawfully within the territory of a state shall, within that territory, have the right to liberty of movement and freedom to choose his residence.
(2) Everyone shall be free to leave any country, including his own.
(3) The above-mentioned rights shall not be subject to any restrictions except those which are provided by law, are necessary to protect national security, public order (*ordre public*), public health or morals or the rights and freedoms of others, and are consistent with the other rights recognized in the present Covenant.
(4) No one shall be arbitrarily deprived of the right to enter his own country.'

In other words, people shall be free to come and go within their own countries, and to leave them, subject only to the usual restrictions if these are *necessary* for some of the usual specific purposes, and are *provided by law*; and people shall not be deprived of the right to enter their own countries—that is, not to be exiled from them—on *any* arbitrary ground.

However, it is a notable fact that international law does not recognize any right of entry to a *foreign* country—that is, a country of which one is not a citizen. True, Article 14 of the UDHR affirms a 'right to asylum', which may be invoked for fugitives from political persecution, but not from 'prosecutions genuinely arising from non-political crimes or from acts contrary to the purposes and principles of the United Nations'. A similar right is also recognized by some of the regional treaties, such as the American and African ones. But the UN Covenants say nothing about it. This absence of a 'freedom of entry' in the human rights catalogue is very important for 'the one world of science', and we shall discuss it more fully later in this chapter.

The value of person-to-person communication between scientists, through international travel and exchange visits, is emphasized by the UNESCO Recommendations on the Status of Scientific Researchers. Articles 26 and 27 of that instrument state:

'26. Member States should actively promote the interplay of ideas and information among scientific researchers throughout the world, which is vital to the healthy development of science and technology; and to this end should take all measures necessary to ensure that scientific researchers are enabled, throughout their careers, to participate in international scientific and technological gatherings and to travel abroad.
27. Member States should furthermore see to it that all governmental or quasi-governmental organizations in which or under whose authority scientific research and experimental development are performed, regularly devote a portion of their budget to financing the participation, at such international scientific and technological gatherings, of scientific researchers in their employ.'

These are recommendations about scientists, but they are not seeking to confer any special privilege on them, nor to restrict this supposed privilege to 'official' missions. The fundamental human right to freedom of movement extends to everyone, regardless of employment or office. International human rights law confers no right on the public authorities of any state to require any of its scientists—or indeed anyone else—who is invited to take part in a scientific meeting abroad to ask his or her government for special permission to travel, or to explain or justify the reasons for the journey. As we shall see, the failure of many states to respect this law is one of the principal constraints on freedom of science in the modern world.

Again, it is clear that the right to remove oneself permanently to another country that is willing to have one—that is, to emigrate—is fully protected by the international treaties. This is a right claimed by many people, for a variety of reasons, yet it is widely denied. Scientists, with their international contacts and culture, have been particularly affected by such inhumane and illegitimate denials, which have created an atmosphere of ill-will and distrust between national governments and the international scientific community. It is sometimes argued that this is a 'political' issue, where scientists should fear to tread. But humanitarian, political, and scientific considerations are all inextricably intertwined in such cases. There is no doubt, for example, that the refusal of the Soviet Government to allow Andrei Sakharov to emigrate has caused more damage to international scientific collaboration than can be made up by millions of roubles or dollars poured into official programmes of scientific visits and exchanges.

Freedom of internal movement and residence

In most of the Western 'Helsinki' states, domestic law cannot restrict movement within the country by its own citizens. The extreme example is the United Kingdom, where no one even needs to have any identity documents, or to register their address or any other particulars with any public authority if they do not feel like it—a situation that is virtually unique in Europe. Some other West European countries (like Sweden) have full population registers; most have a legal requirement to register one's address; and many have a requirement to carry some kind of identity document. But only a few have laws that make it possible for a public authority to restrict an individual's movement within the country: in Italy, for example, persons who constitute a social threat to security or to public morality, or have by their actions given reasonable grounds for being treated as persons of delinquent tendencies, may be prohibited from residing in designated communes, or required to reside in a nominated one. Similarly, in Sweden, a person who is on reasonable grounds suspected of having committed an offence punishable by imprisonment may be prohibited from leaving a designated place. In the UK, conditions may be attached to bail in order to prevent an accused person from committing further offences, even though he has not yet been convicted. However, such restrictions, authorized by domestic law, are comparatively rare; their compatibility with the obligations of the states concerned under the international human rights treaties (and particularly the ECHR) is sometimes questionable, and the Strasbourg institutions have shown themselves vigilant to examine that compatibility in any test case that is brought to them.[1] But, broadly speaking, these provisions will at any given time only affect a very small number of individuals on the margins of society, and they do not generally have any pervasive or 'chilling' effect on that society at large.

In the Eastern European countries, much wider restrictions are imposed on residence and internal movement. Thus, in Bulgaria, the individual's right to live in any given place depends on the outcome of a written application for entry in the population register of that place. As the final decision eventually rests with the local Party committee, the outcome is likely to be determined as much by the applicant's reputation for political conformity as by the skills he or she can offer, and the local need for them. This would apply to a scientist, for example, wishing to take up a post in another town. The opinions of the representative of the local Party committee on the management of the relevant institute may thus be given overriding weight in making a scientific appointment. Otherwise, internal movement in Bulgaria is, with the exception of certain frontier zones, effectively free. The same is true of Romania, which proudly notes the great extent of domestic tourism, in which currently almost half the population takes part.

In the GDR, Article 32 of the Constitution guarantees freedom of movement (including residence), but qualifies this by restrictions imposed by the domestic law; these are allegedly for reasons of security, or to protect the health of citizens, or as an additional sentence imposed by a court for an offence (Penal Code, Article 51). It was these procedures which were used for many years to restrict the movements of Professor Havemann because of his 'crimes' against the good of the socialist society (see Chapter 7). Czechoslovakia shares this approach, restricting the freedom of domicile (laid down in Article 31 of the Constitution) by a special provision of the Penal Code (Article 57A) for 'protection against anti-social elements'.

Of all the countries in the Helsinki group, freedom of residence and internal movement is most restricted in the USSR. This constraint is applied both by formal legal processes, and by ad-

[1] e.g. in *Guzzardi* v. *Italy* 3 EHRR 333.

ministrative action. All nationals of the Soviet Union are issued with internal 'passports', which serve in the first place as identity documents. But standard bureaucratic procedures are regularly employed to restrict the residence of an individual passport-holder to the area of his or her normal place of work. This is because the passport is an essential prerequisite for obtaining the residence permit which every adult Soviet citizen must have in order to reside in any urban area. Even a visit to another area requires a temporary permit from the local militia if it extends to more than three days; failure to comply with this requirement can expose the offender to criminal proceedings.

This whole apparatus for controlling the residence and movement of individual citizens, long and fully established within the Soviet Union, clearly violates the international treaty obligations which the Soviet Government has solemnly—and voluntarily— accepted. In fact, it cannot even be justified in terms of domestic law: the regulations governing the issue of passports have never been published in full and are effectively secret, while the reasons for refusing permission for a new place of residence need not be disclosed except in the vaguest terms, such as 'not being in the public interest'.

The effect of these restrictions is to control all movement of Soviet citizens within the territory of the USSR. They have been, and continue to be, used to prevent people from residing in the town of their choice. The effect of this on scientists can be disastrous. It can be used—and it often is—to put them into a situation where they are isolated from contact with professional colleagues, deprived of the opportunity to find appropriate employment, and ultimately exposed not only to penury but to criminal prosecution for 'parasitism'. Although not so physically damaging as imprisonment, 'internal exile' to a remote region of the country can effectively destroy a scientist as a creative researcher and member of 'the one world of science'.

Nevertheless, internal exile is a routine procedure practised on a large scale in the Soviet Union, and on a lower but significant scale in the other East European states. In the Soviet Union it appears to be used for two different purposes. On the one hand, it is applied as a relatively lenient form of punishment for the 'crimes' fathered on dissidents or would-be emigrants; on the other hand, it is a very effective means of isolating such 'anti-social elements' from like-minded colleagues and others they might infect. The threat of internal exile is thus used to deter those contemplating acts of political protest or seeking to exercise the right to emigrate. The effectiveness of the combination of dismissal, internal exile, and imprisonment as a means of suppressing or fragmenting organized dissidence in the Soviet Union is apparent from the winding-up in late 1982 of the Helsinki Monitoring Groups, whose numbers had been reduced, and their cohesion destroyed, by these means.

The prime example of the effect of internal exile on a professional scientist is of course once again Andrei Sakharov. Since 22 January 1980, he has been confined to the town of Gorki in conditions of effective isolation from his colleagues, from the scientific life of his country, and from virtually all the materials he would need to sustain any scientific activity, even in isolation. This constraint has been imposed on him by the actions of the state, although he has never been charged with any offence. It is ironical that he remains a full member of the Soviet Academy of Sciences, one of the most esteemed and privileged groups in the country: there have indeed been attempts to remove him from the Academy, which would have required a secret ballot of its members, but so far these have failed.[2]

Sakharov has earned such world-wide fame, and world-wide support, for his stand on behalf of human rights that the Soviet authorities may well have taken these steps against him, rather than charging him formally and sentencing him to this punishment or worse, in order to minimize the outcry of protest from scientific and humanitarian groups in many countries. But we must not be under any illusions about the illegitimacy of their action, nor its supposed 'leniency'. Although the RSFSR Penal Code makes provision for internal exile as a specific form of punishment for certain crimes, there is no legal authority for the measures which have in fact been taken against Sakharov. Here is a case where it is not even necessary to resort to international human rights law to test the legitimacy of this infringement of a citizen's right to freedom of residence: what has been done to Sakharov is a clear violation of the Constitution of his own country. The fact that he is personally abused in public by various organs of the Soviet government, and is accused of disloyalty, political dissidence, etc.,

[2] *Nature*, 284, 116; 1980.

is beside the point: unless and until he is found guilty, by due process of Soviet law, of a specific crime, none of the punishments which have been inflicted upon him could have been *legitimately* imposed under the laws of his own country. Unfortunately, however, there are no independent and impartial Soviet courts to pronounce on these illegalities: in this sense, the rule of law simply does not operate there.

As for the supposed 'leniency' of this form of treatment, it is worth noting that Sakharov's health is in a poor state, and that he is in need of specialist treatment. This treatment is being systematically denied to him, because it would involve either sending a specialist to examine him in Gorki, or his return to Moscow. Since he is well able to pay for such treatment, or is entitled to it free as a Member of the Academy of Sciences, this is a denial of the human right to health under Article 12 of the ICESCR.

Andrei Sakharov is only one of many Soviet scientists in this plight. In most other cases the action of the authorities is given legal form as the penalty for a specific charge under the Penal Code, but since the court procedures in 'political' cases seldom satisfy the principles of due process required by the international code of human rights law, the loss of the right of movement and residence is as unjust as if it were applied by arbitrary administrative action. For example, Andrei Tverdoklebov, a physicist with an impeccable establishment background, became a friend of Sakharov and was a human rights activist and an early member of the Soviet Amnesty International group (which is not, of course, permitted to function by the Soviet authorities). For these activities he was sentenced to five years' internal exile in 1976 on a charge of 'anti-Soviet fabrications'. Perhaps because he was recognized as being more of a threat in the country than out of it, he was subsequently allowed to emigrate to the USA in 1980.[3] Vladimir Slepak, a radiologist, received a sentence of five years' exile in 1978.[4] Mark Morozov, a mathematician who has been associated with the unofficial Free Interprofessional Union of Workers, not only received a term of exile, but was rearrested before its end and sentenced additionally to eight years' imprisonment for 'anti-Soviet agitation and propaganda'.[5]

[3] US Congressional hearing on 31 January 1980.
[4] *Bulletin*, 20, 18.
[5] *Index on Censorship*, June 1981, 79.

Another typical case is that of Yevgeny Lein, also a mathematician, who had applied for, and been refused, permission to emigrate. He was sentenced to two years' corrective exile in August 1981 for 'resisting arrest and assaulting a policeman' when a cultural seminar he was attending with Jewish colleagues was raided by the police. Evidence at his trial to counter these charges—which in fact indicated that it was the police who had assaulted him rather than the other way round—was disregarded officially, but may have accounted for what was a comparatively lenient sentence under Article 193 of the Penal Code.[6]

These cases are only a small sample of those that are known to have occurred, but they demonstrate the oppressive nature of the device of internal exile. They also hint at the further disabilities that can follow. Restriction of the right of residence, which can be an effective continuation of the initial policy of isolating the victim, is often backed up by the practice of administrative surveillance on release. This can equally restrict rights of residence, but additionally offends against many of the other provisions of the international treaties by, for example, permitting police entry to the home day or night without previous warning, or by prohibiting or restricting exit from the home, or entry to public places of refreshment and entertainment.

The further penalties for failure to observe these arbitrary decisions can be very severe. It is noteworthy that many of those who have served a term of internal exile are resentenced later to a further term or, worse, a term of imprisonment to which is added a second sentence of exile. We have already mentioned (in Chapter 7) the case of Malva Landa, a geologist who had been active in the human rights movement; having been sentenced to one term of exile on a charge of 'negligently damaging public property', she was rearrested on release and sentenced to a further five years.[7] Ivan Kovalyov, son of the physiologist Sergei Kovalyov, was in March 1982 sentenced to five years in a labour camp, to be followed by five years of internal exile.[8] Indeed, the whole of the Kovalyov family have suffered for their championship, by non-criminal methods, of human rights. Sergei, the father, received a sentence of ten years' imprisonment and exile in 1975, while his daughter-

[6] *Soviet Jewry Newsletter*, 5 February 1982.
[7] *Amnesty Release*, 1980.
[8] *Dutch CSCE Review*, 154, 1; April 1982.

in-law Tatiana Osipova, a computer scientist, was sentenced in March 1981 to five years in prison, followed by five years' internal exile, in a trial which on a dispassionate assessment by American human rights lawyers has been shown to be in clear violation of the provisions of the Soviet Penal Code.[9]

The case of Yosif Begun, a middle level electronics engineer and Candidate of Technical Sciences (the equivalent of a Ph. D.) exemplifies the 'cat and mouse' behaviour of the Soviet authorities with persons who try to defy them. In 1971 Begun applied to emigrate, was refused, and later was dismissed from his post in the Moscow State Planning Commission. A year later he was sacked from the labourer's post which was all he was able to find, and thereafter lived by giving private lessons in mathematics and languages. In 1977, he was therefore charged with 'parasitism', sentenced to two years' internal exile, and barred from returning to Moscow on release. When he did return to his home there after his release, he was promptly sentenced to another three years' exile for 'gross passport violation'.[10] On his release after that he remained banned from Moscow—and as a final twist he was rearrested on yet another charge, and sentenced on 14 October 1983 to seven years' imprisonment, to be followed by a further five years' internal exile.[11]

The addition of a substantial period of internal exile at the end of a prison sentence is particularly cruel to scientific workers, who are thus deprived of any opportunity of rehabilitating themselves professionally. There are many other such cases of imprisonment coupled with exile: Tatiana Velikanova, mathematician, four plus five years;[12] V. Skoudis, geologist, seven plus five years;[13] Mart Niklus, biologist, ten plus five years;[14] Robert Nazarian, physicist, five plus two years;[15] A. Marchenko, ten plus five years—at 44, having already spent fifteen years in labour camps.[16] These are just a few of the scientific workers whose supposed offences would not be recognized by the international law of human rights, but

[9] *Clearinghouse Report*, 3; December 1981.
[10] *Jews in the USSR*, 11 November 1982.
[11] Singer, J. E., *The Case of Yosif Begun: Analysis and Documents*, 1979.
[12] *Amnesty Release*, updated to end of 1980.
[13] *Clearinghouse Report*, May 1981.
[14] Ibid.
[15] *Nature*, 291, 184; 1982.
[16] *Bulletin*, 21; July/September 1981.

who have been—and are—made to suffer not only grave personal hardship, separation from their families, and deprivation of the normal circumstances of human society, but are also in effect eradicated as scientists.

In the smaller East European states the device of internal exile is not unknown, but appears not to be practised anywhere on the same scale as in the Soviet Union. This may simply be a matter of geography. In a country like Romania, a scientist who has fallen out of favour may be sent to an insignificant and comparatively remote institute elsewhere in the country, but this can hardly have the same effect in terms of total isolation as condemnation to Siberia, several thousand miles from the heart of the scientific life of the Soviet Union. Another possible reason for the relative rarity of the practice of internal exile in the East European countries is their generally more sophisticated communications systems: these would make the isolation of internal exile less absolute, so that other methods are more effective in bringing about the humiliation and scientific isolation of dissidents.

The right to travel abroad

Once upon a time, so it was said, you could go to Charing Cross, buy a ticket to Vienna or Vladivostok, get on the boat train and go. The passport was then entirely optional, and intended only as a recommendation for the bearer: in the grand words that still appear in current British passports, 'Her Britannic Majesty's Secretary of State Requests and requires in the Name of Her Majesty all those whom it may concern to allow the bearer to pass freely without let or hindrance, and to afford the bearer such assistance and protection as may be necessary'.

But that was at the beginning of our century. In virtually every state of the world, a passport has today become an essential requirement not only for entering and leaving other countries, but the native one too. (This requirement is not always a strictly legal one, and was successfully challenged in Britain as regards exit a few years ago, although it turned out to be much more difficult to get back into the country in this disgracefully undocumented condition.) The ability to obtain a passport is therefore the crucial factor for freedom to travel abroad and to return to one's own country.

In all the Western countries of the 'Helsinki' group other than the UK, this right is formally guaranteed by law for all adult citizens who are not subject to penal detention. In most cases, the only significant administrative proviso is confirmation from a responsible third party that the particulars noted on the application (including, in the UK, 'distinguishing marks') are correct. Accordingly, the formal *laws* of these countries are in compliance with their international obligations, and with the spirit of Helsinki.

The rub comes when one gets down to the actual administrative rules and procedures for issuing passports. In the UK, these are simple, straightforward, and can be very fast—two hours is the record for one of the present authors. In other countries, they may be slower and more cumbersome, and there may be a specific limitation—not allowed for in the international obligations—on the countries for which the passport is valid. This has been a persistent policy of the government of the United States, which refused for a long time to issue passports valid for travel to the People's Republic of China and, until quite recently, to Iran, Libya, and Cuba.

The United States was also notorious, among Western nations, for its policy of refusing passports to a small but significant number of its own citizens who were regarded as 'communists', although not charged with any crime. Several scientists have been victims of this policy, including one of the most famous, the Californian chemist and Nobel Laureate Linus Pauling.[17] Professor Pauling, who has never made any secret of his nonconformist attitudes in politics and science alike, recalled bitterly in a letter to President Carter in 1979 how the State Department had refused to issue him a passport to attend a Royal Society symposium in Britain twenty-five years before.

Since the United States has not ratified the UN Covenants, this policy did not constitute a breach of its international obligations. But the McCarthy-inspired Subversive Activities Control Act under which the State Department denied passports to applicants suspected of communist associations later came under severe criticism within the United States itself, and was eventually declared unconstitutional by the Supreme Court. In the case of *Aptheker* v. *Secretary of State*,[18] the Court pointed out that communism was not a crime; but even if it had been, and even if it could be

---

[17] *Physics Today*, May 1979.

[18] 378 US 500; see also *Kent* v. *Dulles* 357 US 116, and *Zemel* v. *Rusk* 381 US 1, at 23.

argued that travel abroad might increase the risk of illegal events happening, 'so does being alive'. In peacetime, the Court said, there was no way in which the government could prevent a citizen from travelling within or without the country, unless there was actual power to detain him—as, for example, on arrest after the commission of a criminal offence.

In the USA, therefore, the right to leave the country turns out to be adequately protected by the domestic Constitution. In the UK, there is in fact no legal *right* to a passport, but no case is known in which one has been refused on political grounds.[19] If it ever were, it is now probable that the Courts would overrule such an exercise of administrative discretion on an application for judicial review; the ancient writ of *ne exeat regno* is now obsolete. And there is no evidence that this right is being infringed by administrative practice in any of the other countries of the Western group, 13 of which are bound by the Fourth Protocol to the ECHR, Article 2 of which closely follows the wording of Article 12 of the ICCPR.

The situation is quite different in the USSR and the other East European countries. There, although the right to leave and return has been formally accepted in the international treaty obligations, it is systematically circumscribed or denied by applying incompatible domestic legislation, by administrative procedures, or by simple obstructive procrastination. This continues to be the case despite the fact that in 1982, in a case under the Optional Protocol to the ICCPR, the Human Rights Committee found that the denial of a passport constituted a violation of Article 12(2) of the Covenant, in the absence of a justification on one of the grounds allowed by that Article.[20] (It will be recalled that all the Eastern countries in the Helsinki group have been bound by this Covenant ever since it entered into force in March 1976.)

This major form of violation of human rights varies in severity from country to country in this group, but has a very significant effect on scientific life in all of them. A recent case from Czechoslovakia demonstrates how these practices work against both the scientific advancement and the scientific reputation of the country.

---

[19] *Going Abroad* (Justice; London, 1974).
[20] *Lichtensztejn* v. *Uruguay* (Communication No. 77/1980); *Report of the Human Rights Committee to the Thirty-Eighth Session of the General Assembly*, 166 (UN Document No. A/38/40).

Professor J. Kurzweil of the Institute of Mathematics of the Czechoslovak Academy of Sciences was invited to attend the Seventh International Conference on Differential Equations at Dundee in April 1982. This invitation had the formal endorsement of the Royal Society, as an item in their official programme of scientific exchanges with the Academy. The Academy initially agreed, but later (in September 1981) said the matter still remained to be decided. Subsequently, the Academy said they would not allow Kurzweil to come under the exchange agreement, but might let him attend if his local United Kingdom costs were met. The Royal Society agreed to this, only to be told that his fares to and from London would also need to be met; once again the Society agreed but were then told, in February 1982, that he would be unable to come because of 'sudden and unexpected personal troubles'. This message was contradicted by a personal one from Kurzweil to Professor Everitt (who had invited him), saying that he had no personal troubles but would not be allowed to come to Dundee. Further intervention by the President of the Royal Society to the Scientific Secretary of the Academy did not even elicit the courtesy of a reply, and indirect information showed clearly that the Academy took no responsibility for what had happened and had simply opted out of the matter. In other words, his right to travel abroad on legitimate scientific business had been arbitrarily denied through unexplained administrative action by an authority outside the scientific sphere.

This story is typical of many where the offence against the international code of human rights law may not seem so very serious from a humanitarian point of view—in many countries, after all, scientific travel is popularly envied as a touristic perquisite rather than a professional necessity—but is of the gravest consequence for 'the one world of science'. The Royal Society rightly regarded it as a flagrant violation of the 'principle of the free circulation of scientists', which has been strongly affirmed in a succession of Resolutions by the General Assembly of the International Council of Scientific Unions (ICSU), of which the Czechoslovak Academy is of course an active member. Thus, in September 1972, the 14th General Assembly,

'*Observes*, . . . with regret, that scientists are still today sometimes not allowed freely to attend the appropriate scientific meetings organized by the ICSU family either abroad or in their home countries;

Notes that the obstacles encountered in recent years have fallen into the following categories:
i) the refusal of a visa to enter a certain country, or fatal delays in granting visas;
ii) refusal of permission to participate in an appropriate scientific meeting organized by the ICSU family in the country of the scientists in question;
iii) refusal of permission to travel to scientific meetings organized by the ICSU family and held outside the country, and/or excessive payment required for the permission to travel out of the country to such meetings . . .'

The Resolution went on to express a fear that these difficulties 'might endanger the global character of ICSU and its constituent Unions' and reminded its members (including National Academies of Science) to bring such cases to the notice of the ICSU Standing Committee on the Free Circulation of Scientists—about which more will be said in Chapter 13. The first of the categories listed here raises the issue of a 'right of entry', which will be discussed in more detail later in this chapter. The second is related to the right to work, already considered in Chapter 5. But the case of Kurzweil is a clear example of the third category, which is now the commonest obstacle to personal communication between scientists from different countries.

This is a familiar story in the USSR, and in some of the East European countries. It is a byword among organizers of international conferences that the persons who eventually turn up from the Soviet Union to take part in a meeting are likely to be different from those who were invited, or who had applied to attend. The scientific credentials of some of those who do attend are often uncertain, and their contributions to the proceedings do not compare with what could have been expected from those whom they have replaced. Indeed, their behaviour sometimes suggests that they have mainly come for some purpose other than the discussion of scientific matters: the organizers of the annual symposium of the Society of Photo-Optical Instrumentation Engineers at San Diego in August 1982 reported that three of the four Soviet delegates spent most of their time shopping at Nieman-Marcus or visiting Sea World.

The scale of this phenomenon is substantial. One small analysis made in 1981 showed that, in a period of twelve years, only 9 out of 33 Soviet scientists invited to meetings of the International

Union of Pure and Applied Physics actually arrived. This compared with a score of 249 out of the 263 invited from the rest of the world.[21] Official sponsorship by national academies is no safeguard from discourtesy, embarrassment and scientific fiasco. Even at a Soviet/US meeting on Psychology at the University of California in April 1978, sponsored jointly by the US National Academy of Sciences and the Soviet Academy, a telegram arrived five days before the start of the meeting to say that two of the twelve Soviet invitees would not come, and that half the remainder would have to arrive two days late. The American hosts dug in their heels at this and threatened to cancel the meeting: as a result, the Russians did manage to arrive on time, though without the two predicted absentees.[22]

The real reasons for these characteristic 'absences' are seldom given, but a number of factors have been noted. In the case just mentioned, one of the absentees was said to have found it impossible to get together the papers necessary for him to leave the country in time. This may well have been the truth, because this apparently simple administrative procedure has been turned into an obstacle course that would daunt any ordinary scientific worker, unless he already belonged to that small highly trusted group, known as the 'nomenklatura', who have permanent possession of passports valid for travel abroad.

The standard procedure for obtaining a passport, as far as it can be established from those who have gone through it, may be summarized as follows. The request has to be made by the head of the institution; a file is then prepared by the institute, including a detailed *curriculum vitae* of the applicant and details of his family; this goes to the local Communist Party. The local KGB is then consulted. The file then goes on, with KGB comments, to the Central Committee of the Party, where it is examined by an official. The prospective traveller is then called for interview by the central Party organization. A black mark at any stage of this process sterilizes the application.

Travel from the Soviet Union to East European countries is easier than to the rest of the world, and authority for this may rest at a somewhat lower level. But permission can be withdrawn even after the final stage has been successfully reached. For example,

[21] *Science*, 213, 307; 1981.
[22] *Science*, 200, 631; 1978.

Josif Shklovsky, who had signed an appeal for the release of Cronid Lubarsky, was barred from travel at two days' notice when it became known that he was going to a meeting in the US at which Lubarsky himself (who had been forced to emigrate after his release from prison) would be present. The ponderousness of the procedure is demonstrated by the case of a Vladivostok scientist who was to attend a meeting in Japan. In order to obtain permission to make the short journey involved, he had first to make the very much longer journey from Vladivostok to Moscow and back.

Shortage of foreign exchange is sometimes cited as the reason for refusing permission to travel abroad, but this is not a complete explanation. For example, as we saw in Chapter 6, Zhores Medvedev was not allowed to attend the symposium at Sheffield at which his leading paper had to be read *in absentia*; and he was similarly denied permission to attend other meetings in the USA and in Austria—although in none of these cases would there have been any foreign exchange drain on the Soviet reserves, as his hosts were meeting all his expenses. Gregori Margoulis, the eminent Soviet mathematician who was in 1978 awarded the Fields Medal of the International Congress of Mathematicians—the equivalent of the Nobel Prize in the world of mathematics—was not allowed to go to Helsinki to receive it on the grounds that 'his work was not good enough to represent the Soviet Union'—a view hardly shared by his non-Soviet peers who had of course made it clear that they would be footing the bill for his trip.[23]

The fact that Margoulis is Jewish suggests a more sinister motive, which may also explain a number of other cases where travel abroad has been forbidden. For example, there is the case of the two delegates invited to a meeting of the Information Theory Group of the Institute of Electric and Electronic Engineers of the USA in 1978. The two, Mark Pinsker and Roland Dobrushin, had been duly included by the Russians in the group of fourteen invited, but four days before the meeting the organizers were told that they would not be coming. Both were Jewish. Denial of the right to travel may thus become an instrument of religious discrimination, another serious violation of the international human rights code.

Another well-known case involving a very distinguished Soviet scientist was that of Professor Benjamin Levich, the pioneer of the

[23] *Science*, 202, 1167; 1978.

new discipline of physico-chemical hydrodynamics, and a corresponding member of the Soviet Academy, who was not permitted to attend the Oxford conference in honour of his sixtieth birthday in 1977. Since Levich had by then applied for an exit visa to emigrate to Israel, the Russians alleged that this conference was a 'provocation' devoid of scientific value, a view rebutted firmly and factually by the organizers of the meeting—as one of the present authors, who took part, can also attest.[24] In any case, under international human rights law this could never justify the action of the authorities in preventing him from attending.

What these cases clearly demonstrate is that the decision on who may or may not travel outside the Soviet Union for professional scientific purposes is not ultimately governed by criteria of scientific excellence, nor by the contribution that can be made to the advancement of knowledge. As the Charter-77 spokesman said of Czechoslovakia in 1982, these decisions seem to be made by ill-informed bureaucrats motivated primarily by their conception of the ideological orthodoxy of the scientists concerned, and the extent to which they may therefore merit the much-prized reward of foreign travel.[25]

Whether or not access to the outside world is inequitably distributed, it is undoubtedly regarded as a privilege within the gift of the authorities, rather than as an individual's own right to exercise according to his or her interests and means. A personal invitation to a Soviet scientist (and indeed to a scientist in almost any other East European country) is never treated as personal, to be accepted or declined by the recipient. The decision always lies elsewhere, and even a reply from the recipient, if one comes, can only reflect—or sometimes anticipate—that decision. The US National Academy of Sciences reports that invitations to East European scientists to take part in its exchange programmes are always sent through the national academy with which the exchange agreement has been concluded, but copies always go to the individual scientists concerned. The NAS practically never gets a direct response from the scientist himself. In fact, the most revealing response of this kind came from a Soviet scientist invited to Britain under an official British/USSR exchange programme. Paraphrased, it read: 'Thank you very much for your invitation to

[24] *La scienza assediata* (Marsilio Editori; Venice, 1977).
[25] Charter-77 Document No. 26/82 on Scientific Research (Prague, 10 August 1982).

visit Britain for scientific meetings and visits. I would very much like to accept, but unfortunately I shall be ill at that time.'

State control of foreign scientific visits and interchanges is the official policy in all the East European countries. This is true even of Hungary, which is the most open of these countries for travel abroad—and in practice, Hungarians who are personally invited to scientific meetings abroad generally arrive there. But as far back as 1974, an article in *Magyar Hirlap* declared that 'free exchange' was not in the interest of Hungarian science. Instead, there was a centrally planned programme designed to produce the best returns to the state, and in this programme personal professional benefit had to be entirely subordinate to national benefit. In this way too, it was claimed, one could avoid the pitfall of allowing capitalist countries to gain from what was described as the Hungarian scientific researchers' 'national treasures'.[26] Such a policy may have a limited justification in so far as all scientists in these countries are employed by organs of the state, and may need leave of absence from their jobs and other facilities for foreign travel. But the implicit claim that the individual scientist is entirely at the disposal of the national interest is incompatible both with 'the one world of science' and with the letter and spirit of the international human rights code. Most scientists with experience of pluralistic 'liberal' societies would also argue forcibly that such a policy is eventually counter-productive, since it will almost certainly demoralize the better scientists and drive them to emigrate, whenever they can find a suitable opportunity, to another country with a freer academic atmosphere; and that it may thus impoverish the national treasure chest as effectively as did the Nazi persecutions in the German scientific community in the late 1930s.

Romania presents one of the most distressing aspects of this principle of state direction of foreign contact and interchange, with political nepotism as the prime factor. In that country, the overlordship of science and technology effectively rests with Mrs Elena Ceausescu, wife of the President and Secretary General of the Central Committee of the Romanian Communist Party, who was made Chairman of the National Council on Science and Technology (NCST) by her husband in 1979, despite her lack of any known academic qualification in any branch of science. The power of this post was further extended by a State Council decree in

26 *Magyar Hirlap*, 19 January 1974.

March 1980 which effectively removed the last vestiges of the autonomy of the Romanian Academy by putting it under the supervision of the NCST. To complete her domination, Elena Ceausescu is also chief of the cadre section of the Romanian Communist Party which governs not only promotions and nominations of scientists throughout the country, but also decides who is allowed or not allowed to leave the country to attend a congress, or work in a research institute abroad. The Ceausescu family's domination of Romanian science is further reinforced by the occupation of other significant posts in the establishment by their younger son and daughter. As a consequence, decisions that call for scientific knowledge, experience, and judgement are in the hands of persons with no evident capacities of this kind, and the right of every scientist— as indeed of every citizen—to be treated fairly according to his or her personal merits is put in jeopardy.

One case will serve to illustrate the practical effect of this control of movement on those subject to it. Dr M. Sararu, a physicist, was invited by Professor T. Kibble in 1981 to spend a period in his department at Imperial College, London. Her head of department, Professor Ivascu, agreed that, in spite of previous difficulties, she should be able to come in October. A series of telexes and letters then successively postponed her arrival, in spite of a firm intervention by Professor J. Charap, Chairman of the European Physical Society's Advisory Committee on Scientific Freedom, asking why previous assurances that she could come had not been honoured. Ultimately, Dr Sararu did arrive in London at the end of March—only to decide, in the light of this and previous experiences, that she would not return to Romania, but make a new life and career elsewhere.

What can happen further down the line is illustrated by the case of another Bucharest academic, not of science but of the humanities, who, having been refused authorization to take up a one-year visiting fellowship at New York University, applied to emigrate. He was then declared politically unreliable, sacked from the university, and forced to become a bricklayer to survive. Eventually, under strong US pressure, he was allowed to emigrate in 1982, after being stripped of Romanian citizenship and obliged to sell all his property to the state for a derisory sum in non-convertible Romanian currency. Details of this case which might allow the victim to be identified cannot be given, as they might further damage his relatives still in Romania, some of whom have already suffered for his actions. The violation of one basic human right thus engenders further violations of other rights. The Romanian authorities apparently fear that anyone who is not totally reliable politically is susceptible to the germs of 'defection' when they breathe the Ceausescu-free air elsewhere. This is shown clearly by a decree of November 1982 which stipulates that any scholar who fails to return on schedule after having been allowed to travel abroad for study or to attend an international conference will be sued for the cost of his education, to be recovered by confiscation of his assets in Romania.

In Bulgaria the situation is a little less restrictive than in Romania, primarily because the cultural and political framework is looser, and those shrewd enough to develop and exploit the right connections can often get round the administrative problems. The US National Academy, for example, reports little difficulty in filling their small quota of exchange places (12 person-months), and there is a low rate of defection, even though the Bulgarians are sufficiently confident to allow married couples to travel abroad together. In Bulgaria, political conformity to the level of Party membership is not an essential prerequisite for permission to travel abroad; what matters is to have the recommendation of a superior who is politically reliable, which will normally be the case if he occupies a sufficiently senior position to give such authority. But that nepotism can come into such matters is illustrated by the case of the chemist who was awarded a scholarship in 1982 for study in the West: at the last minute his place was taken by another applicant—the nephew of the head of the institute where he worked.

The GDR is a country which controls travel abroad as tightly as any—but with a good deal of skill and subtlety. Permission is given only for each separate visit, and a close relative normally has to be left behind as a hostage. The whole programme of international exchanges in science is directed to areas of application in high technology. The thrust of scientific work is aimed entirely at immediate practical and economic ends calculated to strengthen the power base of Marxism and the state.[27] The means of control are so effective that it is difficult to find evidence from individual case histories of the effect that this has had on the freedom of movement of the GDR's scientists.

[27] See, e. g., *Foreign Affairs Bulletin of the GDR*, 21, 31; 1981.

The situation in Yugoslavia is instructive, since it shows that the freedom to travel is not incompatible with a one-party 'socialist' state. For many years, the basic right to hold a passport valid for a period of years (rather than for a single journey) has been restricted only by such legitimate considerations as liability to military service or court orders. It is true that there have been some further restrictions on people charged with political offences, and there are some notorious cases where foreign travel has been denied to those who have openly crossed swords with the Party. However, only a few exceptional cases are known where this has affected the travel of scientists; indeed it is notable that the central direction of such travel does not preclude free exchange visits by Yugoslav scientists outside the sphere of the official programmes.

Until December 1981, much the same might have been said of Poland, where the Academy had great freedom in organizing and authorizing foreign travel for its scientific members and adherents, and followed a notably enlightened and liberal policy. But this situation changed considerably after the imposition of martial law. Since April 1982, the government has decreed that scientists may only travel abroad for purposes closely aligned to the aims of the foreign policy of the Polish People's Republic, and the socio-economic and scientific policy of the country. All such proposals now have to be subjected to detailed analysis by the director of the applicant's institute or by the rector of the university, who have to take account not only of the cost-effectiveness of the proposal as regards foreign exchange, but also of the extent to which the applicant can be guaranteed 'to represent the political interests of the PPR'. Authority will not be given for those who have 'actively worked to the detriment of the state or who have broken the regulations of the decree on martial law'.[28] Scientists employed by the Academy have to obtain the approval of the 'appropriate Party secretary', thus withering the liberal-minded Academy's hope that it could retain the power to decide what foreign travel by its members and staff was in the best interests of science in Poland.[29]

Freedom to enter a foreign country
Scientific travel to attend international scientific conferences, and for other professional purposes, is also subject to restrictions on

[28] *Nature*, 296, 382; 1982.
[29] *Nature*, 299, 768; 1982.

the *entry* of foreign participants into the country where the meeting is to be held. Such restrictions are obviously as damaging to free scientific communication as those that restrict the movement of scientists *out of* their own countries. As we have already pointed out, the international code of human rights law is silent on this matter. Apart from a declared right (UDHR, Article 14(1)) to 'seek and to enjoy in other countries asylum from persecution', and a requirement (ICCPR, Article 13) for due process of law in the expulsion of aliens, there is no guarantee of any kind for freedom of movement *into* a *foreign* country. Under international human rights law, everyone is entitled (subject to the usual provisos) to an *exit* visa, but no-one is entitled (as of right, even though subject to provisos) to an *entry* visa to any country except his or her own.

The reason is clear to anyone familiar with the politics of immigration; no government is willing to hold its frontiers permanently open to all comers, no matter how many, how poor, or how different in background, culture—or colour—from the native inhabitants. Regrettable though that may seem to many, it must be accepted that international human rights law is no help to the would-be entrant. While a refusal to grant an exit visa, say, to a scientist who wishes to attend a conference abroad—or, indeed, to emigrate permanently—may infringe a fundamental freedom, there is no case in international law for making the same complaint against the country which refuses to admit that (foreign) scientist to attend such a conference—let alone to settle and work there. The nations have been careful to preserve their absolute discretion to admit or reject whom they please—other, that is, than their own nationals. The only exceptions to this rule are regional or local arrangements such as the Treaty of Rome establishing the European Economic Community, under which the nationals of each of the contracting states are freely entitled to travel and settle for work in all those states.

Although this particular aspect of scientific freedom is not protected by any part of the code of human rights law, there is no doubt of its importance in the eyes of the international scientific community. We have already noted that this is the first category of 'obstacles to the free circulation of scientists' referred to in the ICSU Resolution of 1972. We have already quoted the UNESCO document on the Status of Scientific Researchers, indicating the same concern. In a broader context, we may also cite informal agreements between states, where the circulation of scientists is often specifically mentioned. Thus, for example, the Helsinki Accords contain many such clauses:

'The participating States . . . express their intention to remove obstacles to scientific and technological co-operation, in particular through . . . the expeditious implementation and improvement in organization, including programmes, of international visits of scientists and specialists in connection with exchanges, conferences and cooperation . . .'[30]

'The participating States . . . express their view that scientific and technological co-operation should . . . employ . . . exchanges and visits as well as other direct contacts and communications among scientists and technologists, on the basis of mutual agreement and other arrangements, for such purposes as consultations, lecturing and conducting research . . . ; holding of international and national conferences, symposia, seminars, courses and other meetings of a scientific and technological character, which would include the participation of foreign scientists and technologists . . .'[31]

'The participating States intend to facilitate wider travel by their citizens for personal or professional reasons and to this end they intend in particular:
gradually to simplify and to administer flexibly the procedures for exit and entry;
to ease regulations concerning movements of citizens from the other participating States in their territory, with due regard to security requirements;'[32]

'The participating States . . . express their intention . . . to facilitate the dissemination of oral information through the encouragement of lectures and lecture trips by personalities and specialists from the other participating States, as well as exchanges of opinions at round table meetings, seminars, symposia, summer schools, congresses, and other bilateral and multilateral meetings;'[33]

'The participating States . . . express their intention . . . to intensify exchanges among . . . institutions . . . by . . . facilitating travel between the participating States by scholars, teachers and students for purposes of study, teaching and research as well as for improving knowledge of each other's educational, cultural and scientific achievements.'[34]

[30] Basket II, section 4.
[31] Ibid.
[32] Basket III, section 1(d).
[33] Basket III, section 2(a)(i).
[34] Basket III, section 4(b).

What we have seen already must make us very sceptical of the sincerity of some of these statements. They also tend to favour activities carried out under official auspices, which keep scientists firmly under the control of the state rather than recognizing their rights and responsibilities as individual members of 'the one world of science'. Nevertheless, in default of a formal legal treaty covering this matter, the Helsinki Accords set an important standard. In spirit, this is clearly directed at minimizing impediments to free entry when the purposes are benign, and neither subversive in intent nor directed to interference in the internal or external affairs of the state concerned.

As a matter of fact, the record of the Helsinki states is fairly good in this respect. But the situation is far from perfect, and there are certain practices which give cause for concern amongst scientists and others. These are not confined to one pole of the political spectrum; the two major offenders seem to be the super-powers of the Helsinki group, the USA and the USSR, which have both, in their different ways, put serious obstacles in the way of the movement of foreign scientists into their territories for legitimate scientific work.

In the case of the USA, this has lately taken the form of the denial of visas to those whom the administration considers likely to use their visits to obtain information of potential military or economic value. Thus, eight Russians who had been invited to attend the Conference on Lasers and the Topical Meeting on Inertial Confinement Fusion in San Diego in February 1980 were denied visas, while a Soviet co-author of one of the papers pre-sented, V. A. Komofski who was then at the University of Texas on an inter-academy exchange, was not allowed to attend. (Had the USA been a state party to the ICCPR, that last prohibition might have been a breach of Article 12(1), for the right to move freely within a state, subject to the usual provisos, extends to 'everyone lawfully within' the state, and not—as in the case of US domestic law—only to its citizens.) The meeting, it should be added, was supposed to be quite open from a scientific point of view, and there were over 300 non-Soviet scientists present.

The status of such actions under US domestic law is of interest. Of course the Executive has full discretion as to whom it admits to the country, and it is not answerable to any claim from a foreign national whom it chooses to exclude. But in these cases the Executive could also claim that it was obliged to take such action by the notorious McCarran–Walters Act of 1952, passed during the anti-communist McCarthy period in spite of President Truman's attempt to veto it. This was deliberately framed to exclude visitors from communist states, and specified that entry visas should not be given to people who were, or had been, members of the communist party or other allied organizations. A judge of the Supreme Court said in 1979 that this Act violated the Helsinki Accords, but it has neveretheless remained in force. The McGovern Amendment of 1977, which provides discretion for the issue of a visa in cases which were previously excluded, does little in practicc to alleviate the way in which the Act can still be applied. In fact, over the last two or three years it has again been used with increasing severity, in spite of protests from such prestigious bodies as the US National Academy of Sciences and the American Association for the Advancement of Science.[35]

This regressive policy gravely weakens US protests against violations of the Helsinki spirit by the states of the East. As Professor Herman Feschbach, then President of the American Physical Society, said in testimony to a Congressional Committee:

'Points of particular concern are unreasonable restrictions on the freedom to attend scientific conferences . . . and to communicate with other scientists, via normal channels, including international travel.'

Ironically, this was said in testimony describing the activities of the Society on behalf of some 60 physicists suffering repression in the Soviet Union.[36]

The actual denial of an entry visa to the Soviet Union is not, in fact, all that more common than to the USA. There are relatively isolated cases of Western scientists being refused entry—generally when it was believed that they wished to make contacts with dissidents. For example, in September 1981 the Soviet authorities denied entry visas to ten American scientists, including a Nobel Laureate, who planned to participate in one of the Sunday Seminars which had been run by Victor Brailovsky before he was arrested and sentenced to internal exile.[37] But this is not the normal practice even in such circumstances. French scientists, including Professor Kessler of the Académie de France and Pro-

[35] *Helsinki Watch Document*, October 1980.
[36] House Committee on Science and Technology, 31 January 1980.
[37] *Science*, 214, 164; 1981.

fessor Ramcini, have visited the Soviet Union on a number of occasions during which they have met many refuseniks and dissident scientists in Moscow and Leningrad, without suffering any particular problems on entry, during their stay, or on departure. Many Western scientists (including one of the present authors) have attended the Sunday Seminars and International Colloquia organized by the Jewish refuseniks, despite the extreme disfavour in which these meetings were held by the Soviet authorities.

From the standpoint of 'the one world of science', the most significant Soviet malpractice has been the attempt to prevent Israeli scientists from attending international scientific conferences held in the Soviet Union. But even this policy is not carried out very systematically. In 1978, 33 Israeli scientists applied to attend the International Congress of Genetics in Moscow and had their applications duly acknowledged. Ultimately, only 18 of them were issued with visas, and these were qualified by a prohibition against travel outside the immediate area of the conference venue. The Israeli national society for this discipline quite reasonably considered this discriminatory treatment unsatisfactory and insulting, and withdrew from the meeting entirely.[38] The Standing Committee on the Free Circulation of Scientists of ICSU (on which there is a Soviet member), was asked to take this matter up; its representations are always made in private, but in the past they have often sufficed to ensure that such episodes are not repeated (see Chapter 13).

Discrimination against scientists from Israel is not, of course, openly acknowledged by the Soviet authorities. In 1977, when two Israeli scientists were denied visas to attend an International Meeting on Ferro-Electricity in Leningrad, T. S. Zheludev later wrote to *Nature*,[39] endeavouring to defend the Soviet action and claiming that it was the result of unfortunate errors, not all of which were on the Soviet side. He also insisted that there had been and was no future intention to bar Israelis from such meetings in the USSR. These claims were firmly rebutted by the two scientists involved.[40] None the less, there is some encouraging evidence that international scientific pressures against such 'errors' have not been totally ineffective. In 1982, 15 Israeli scientists were given

38 *Physics Today*, April 1978; *Nature*, 271, 605; 1978.
39 *Nature*, 272, 666; 1978.
40 *Nature*, 273, 110; 1978.

visas to attend the International Conference for Research on the Ageing of Man in Moscow—although they did not get their visas until two days before the conference started, and that was only after the Belgian chairman of the international society sponsoring the conference had made it clear that any scientists from abroad attending as members of the society would not participate unless visas were issued without discrimination to all who had applied. It is also encouraging that a group of Israeli scientists who attended the Congress reported on return that they were well treated and in no way discriminated against. This is an example of the influence of international scientific opinion, which is not completely power-less in insisting on the established norms of scientific com-munication and collaboration.

In the remaining countries of the Helsinki group, there are few examples of cases where *bona fide* scientific travellers have been denied entry. Surprisingly, almost the only recent case concerns Canada, a country with an otherwise excellent record of compliance with both its international obligations and the Helsinki Accords. Two Soviet scientists—Dr Pavlichenko of the Soviet Academy and Dr V. Ustinov—were denied visas to attend the 1981 Pugwash Meeting in Banff. Since this was the only known case of such interference with attendance at a Pugwash meeting, anywhere in the world, during the 24 years of its existence as an international forum for science and world affairs, it drew a strong protest from the Canadian delegates and there are good reasons to believe that it will not be a precedent for future Canadian policies in this matter.

Somewhat paradoxically, it appears that here, where we are dealing with a freedom which is *not* guaranteed by legally binding international obligations, the degree of conformity with the spirit of Helsinki is substantially greater than in the case of many other rights which come under the formal rule of international law. But the true function of the international circulation of scientists— that is, face-to-face communication, discussion, disclosure of new results, criticism, experimental collaboration, and other forms of transnational co-operation—can be effectively frustrated by more subtle means than prohibitions on travel or entry. It is in fact more usual for entry to be permitted and then to make it very difficult for particular scientists to meet one another by putting up practical obstacles—such as pleading inconvenience, non-availability of the persons it is desired to meet, and logistic problems of programming. This happens to some extent in countries of every political complexion, but it is made easier where the visits are under an exchange programme operated by a central organization in the host country.

A common mode of restriction is for a visitor to a foreign country to be denied access to certain individuals or departments. This is particularly the case in countries where programmes for scientific visits and exchanges are arranged through one central body—the Ministry of Education, the Ministry of Science, the National Academy of the country, or some other quasi-official body such as the British Council. This body then determines and sets up the programme, and may, for a variety of reasons, exclude meetings or visits which the visitor has requested. There are probably few countries where this sort of restriction does not occur to some degree. From the personal experience of one of the present authors, it can be said that even in the UK there have been occasions when it has been found 'impossible' to arrange a certain visit because of the fear of poaching of technical information of commercial value. Similar diplomatic deceptions are also practised to protect security.

But these practices must not be allowed to extend beyond the bounds of legal freedom—or, indeed, of common courtesy. In some countries, for example, meetings between foreign visitors and certain native scientists have been prevented by various devices because the latter are deemed to be *personae non gratae*, and not for scientific, security, or even commercial reasons. Obstacles of this kind have often been encountered when foreign scientists in the USSR have attempted to make personal contact with people tarred with the brush of dissidence, even if only to discuss open scientific matters with them. Elsewhere, an interesting case is that of the archaeologist Professor G. Ronay, whose projected visit to Hungary was aborted because, although the Hungarians readily provided him with a visa, they said they were unable to arrange for him to meet certain people and discreetly managed to prevent him from making independent arrangements for these encounters.[41] On the other hand, one of the present authors has been able to meet 'disgraced' scientists in both Hungary and Czechoslovakia.

A particularly disturbing recent development for everyone concerned for the freedom of 'the one world of science' has been the more overt exercise of such policies by the government of the

41 *The Times*, 12 January 1980.

United States. These policies are evidently linked with attempts to place arbitrary restrictions on the publication of certain types of result in basic science, to which we have already referred. A notorious case was that of the Bubble Memory Conference, at which the organizers were required to exclude from certain sessions delegates from 'communist' countries. There have been several other cases recently where some agency of the United States government has insisted that a foreign visitor should not have access to *unclassified* academic research. This happened in 1982 in the case of the Soviet robotics expert N. V. Umnov, who was to visit Stanford University.[12]

Freedom to emigrate

So far in this chapter, we have considered freedom of movement out of one's home country only for limited periods, to take part in scientific meetings, to visit foreign scientific institutions, or to undertake research or advanced study. But some scientists feel the need to avail themselves of one of the most important of human rights—the right to leave a particular country permanently, in order to take up residence elsewhere. Freedom to *emigrate* is clearly guaranteed by the international treaties, and solemnly promised by the nations subscribing to the Helsinki Accords: yet the continued violation of this right is one of the most distressing features in the world of today.

This right is of particular concern for scientists because their training and professional expertise, like science itself, is universal: the methods used in research, and the facts and theories being sought, are valid in any country, and may be put to use in any country. A scientist who belongs to 'the one world of science' thus has both the incentive and the capabilities to move from one country to another, and to undertake research under the conditions most conducive to the pursuit of the branch of knowledge to which he or she is committed. Scientific skills are relatively portable, and even where there is no intention to leave one's homeland for ever, scientists frequently wish, or are invited, to work for long periods in other countries. Once there, they may eventually wish to stay permanently. Many scientists from Britain and other European countries, for instance, have migrated to the United States for just this reason, and not so many of them have returned. They draw

[42] *Science*, 215, 1080.

attention to the better research facilities to which they have access there, and they claim, quite justifiably in many instances, that they are thus able to make a more significant contribution to science than if they had remained in poorly funded and understaffed institutions in their home countries. The same plea is also made by numerous scientists from the developing countries, who have taken up permanent scientific posts in all the advanced countries of the 'Helsinki' group.

The cynical observer might also remark that those who have made this move often enjoy a rather higher standard of living than they would have done if they had stayed in their native lands. There is no denying an element of personal self-interest in such a move—but that does not make it illegitimate, or even immoral. The guiding philosophy of the international code of human rights law is that every individual should be free to follow his or her own interests, provided only that these do not violate the rights of others.

This point needs to be emphasized, because there is an argument, adopted by many governments and assented to by some scientists, that a state which has given a scientist financial support for his or her education and research training, and has provided substantial facilities for gaining a reputation in research, is entitled to insist that he or she must remain in that state, and work there for the benefit of that national community, rather than go to work elsewhere for the benefit of some other community—or even the wider community of all men and women. In effect, the argument asserts that scientists are obliged, beyond other citizens, to live and work for the society that has nurtured them, and given them such privileges and opportunities in life.

This argument is nowhere supported by international human rights law, which does not make the exercise of civil and political rights (of which the right to emigrate is one) dependent on any economic considerations. But the argument has some moral weight, which needs at least to be mentioned here because attempts are often made to give it legal force. In a world composed of countries at widely different levels of development, it is understandable that a poor but enlightened country which has devoted its scarce resources to training some of its most talented people will feel that it can ill afford to lose them to rich countries which can offer them better facilities and higher rewards for their work—just as it is understandable that talented scientists, once fully trained, will wish to engage in research on equal terms with colleagues in centres of international excellence which their own country cannot yet afford to provide, rather than risk losing touch with the international community they have worked so hard to join. These are the conflicting considerations that need to be balanced; but the right of decision lies with the individuals concerned, and not with their governments.

There cannot, of course, be any objection to contractual arrangements under which a state provides scientists with the financial means for study or travel abroad in return for a commitment to return to their own country and work there for a specified time. But a necessary condition for such an agreement, if it is to be treated as binding, is that it should be freely entered into, and this can never be the case if the commitment is the unavoidable price for an exit visa which would not otherwise be granted. And no such contract is possible for the scientist who wishes not merely to travel, but to emigrate permanently. Nor can there be any legal or moral justification for the cruel practice of coercing a traveller by holding a spouse, child, or parent as a hostage for his or her eventual return.

So long as economic and other inequalities between nations persist, the 'brain drain' from poor to rich countries will be a matter of political concern. But this is not a problem to be solved by administrative *fiat*. The most that we can do is to echo the sentiments expressed in the UNESCO Recommendations on the Status of Scientific Researchers, Article 9(c):

' . . . with respect for the principle of freedom of movement of scientific researchers, Member States should be concerned to create that general climate, and to provide those specific measures for the moral and material support and encouragement of scientific resarchers as will . . . encourage a situation in which the majority of scientific researchers, or young people who aspire to become scientific researchers, are provided with the necessary incentives to work in the service of their country and to return there if they seek some of their education, training or experience abroad.'

One might point out the converse of this argument, namely that pressure by scientists to avail themselves of the right to emigrate is an indication of malaise in any national scientific community. In a country such as Britain, where this right is freely available, the malaise may not be serious. But in a country such as Poland, where this right is now strongly constrained by the authorities, it is evidence of the very unhappy state of science, and a feeling by many scientists that they are unable to continue their work usefully under such conditions. And not the least of the conditions necessary for the creative pursuit of science is respect for the civil and political rights of researchers, including the right to travel abroad and to emigrate if they have a mind to do so.

In this respect, as in every aspect of our subject, there can be no distinction between scientists and other people. In some of the Helsinki countries, as in many countries in other parts of the world, there are quite large numbers of people who wish to emigrate for a variety of reasons. They may feel strongly that they cannot, in all conscience, come to terms with the social and ideological pattern of the country in which they happen to be living; they may feel that they are denied the opportunity to do the work for which they have the talents and are educated; or they may even feel that they actually belong elsewhere, in the culture of another country. In some cases, the first factor is predominant, as with the dissidents of Czechoslovakia and other East European countries; in a smaller number of cases, the last is the driving force, as with members of ethnic minorities like the Hungarians in Romania. In many cases, as with the Jewish 'refuseniks' and the ethnic Germans of the USSR,[43] all three factors are present.

Whatever the forces driving it, emigration is forbidden or severely restricted by the governments of all the countries of Eastern Europe except Yugoslavia. By virtue of its sheer size, the USSR, with a population including nearly two million Jews and two million ethnic Germans, presents the most massive evidence of violation of this basic human right. Next comes the GDR, where the problem is almost entirely confined to those who wish to move across the border to the other part of Germany. The situation in Czechoslovakia and Romania is also serious.

The case histories are so extensive that we can only give an indication of their scale. In the USSR, the number of Jewish scientists with higher degrees who have been refused permission to emigrate is thought to be between 200 and 300 in Moscow alone.[44] A geographically wider French study, made in 1980, listed some 360 known cases, some of whom had been in this state for ten

---

[43] *Deutsche in der UdSSR* (Gesellschaft für Menschenrechte, 1982).
[44] *Report of World Conference on Soviet Jews*, October 1984.

years. Among ethnic Germans, on the other hand, the number of
scientists involved is relatively small, largely because educational
opportunities have been consistently denied to this group for
longer than they have to the Jewish communities. In Romania, the
overall size of the problem can be gauged from the agreement—
abrogated in November 1982—under which 10,000 ethnic Germans were to be allowed to emigrate each year.[45]

The list of Soviet 'refuseniks' in science reads like the roll-call
of an academic pantheon. Professor Naum Meiman, a 70-year-old
mathematical physicist, 'refused' on grounds of access to secret
materials; Alexander Lerner, another distinguished physicist and
the director of the Institute of Control Sciences until his dismissal
in 1971; Vladimir Kislik, another physicist from Kiev; David Goldfarb, until 1980 director of the Laboratory of Molecular Genetics
of Bacteria of the Academy of Sciences; Alexander Paritsky, of the
Institute of Meteorology in Kharkov; Professor Roal Nezlin, chief
of the Laboratory of Immuno-Chemistry at the Institute of Molecular Biology of the Academy of Sciences: these are just a few.
And lower down the scale of distinction there are many cases of
good second-line researchers who have similarly been refused,
like Liliya Zatuchnaya, formerly of the Ukrainian Polytechnical
College; Mark Kovner of the Faculty of Radio Physics at Gorki;
Semyon Gluzman, a psychiatrist; and many others who could be
named. A full account would also have to reckon the wasted years
of such able and active scientists as Professors Benjamin Levich
and Mark Azbel, who languished in the limbo of 'refusal' for years
before they were allowed to leave the country, and would include
a substantial number of young people whose aspirations to study
science were blighted as a consequence of the measures taken
against them or their parents when they sought to exercise this
right.

Although it is clear that the practice of refusing almost all
applications for an emigration visa is the result of a deliberate
and systematic policy decided at the highest levels of the Soviet
government, it is often rationalized in particular cases by offering
'reasons'. These are wide and diverse, although they are seldom
legally convincing. A common justification for refusing a visa is
that the applicant has had 'access to secret information', implying
that this was a case coming under the proviso in Article 12(3) of

[45] *Deutsche in der UdSSR* (Gesellschaft für Menschenrechte, 1982).

the ICCPR that the right to leave one's country may be denied on grounds of national security. But this denial is legally unjustifiable when no term of years is put on the period for which information is held to be still secret, especially when this is stretched far beyond the period, such as five or ten years, which experience suggests would be reasonable for sensitive scientific knowledge. Nevertheless, this was the stated objection in two well-known cases — Alexander Lerner, the distinguished cyberneticist, who was not permitted to leave although he had had no access to classified material since 1971,[46] and (even more preposterously) Naum Meiman, whose exposure to any confidential matters ended in 1955.

There are also gross discrepancies in the interpretation of what constitutes 'secret work'. Soviet domestic law is so broad on this point that it can be applied to the mere fact of having done military service, which would include virtually every adult male Soviet citizen. A civil engineer, Lev Elbert, was 'refused' on the grounds of having had access to classified information while serving in the Army; as he pointed out in his appeal, he spent the whole time digging trenches for a swimming pool. Most often, this pretext seems to be plucked out of the air simply to provide administrative cause for a refusal for which no other rationalization is conveniently at hand. Thus, Mark Kovner's application was refused on the grounds of secrecy, while that of his wife, who worked in the same institute and was privy to the same information, was allowed. Following this refusal, his next application was refused on the grounds that 'he knew those with access to secrets'; the only reply to his third application was that 'there was no reason to review his case'.[47] (We return to the question of secrecy in Chapter 13.)

Another reason often given for refusal is that a close relative has raised an objection. This could be made the basis for a legally valid justification in some cases if it could be shown that the exercise of the right to emigrate would damage the rights of others — for example, by depriving a spouse of contact with children, or a parent of support from a child, both of which can be claimed and enforced in the USSR. There are certainly cases where parents have refused to agree, most often from fear of the likely repercussions on the remaining family of a known emigrant, who

---

[46] *Abacus*, Spring 1984.
[47] *Jews in the USSR*, 4; 7 October 1982.

in Soviet official eyes would be seen as an anti-patriot. But this justification fails if it is stretched beyond the bounds of credulity or reason, as in the case of Mrs Zatuchnaya, whose application was rejected on the grounds that there was an objection from her husband—whom she had divorced in 1966 and with whom she had had no contact in the intervening sixteen years.[48]

The most unjust of all the reasons given for refusing permission to emigrate is the accusation that the applicant is guilty of some social or political offence through the very fact of having applied for an exit visa. It is not uncommon to prosecute applicants on charges under certain articles of the RSFSR Penal Code, most commonly Articles 70 and 190(1). Article 70 deals with anti-Soviet agitation and propaganda, amongst which it includes 'slanderous fabrications which defame the Soviet state and social system'. Article 190(1) is similar, but is distinguished from Article 70 by 'the absence in the guilty person of the goal of undermining or weakening the Soviet regime, or the purpose of committing any particular, especially dangerous, crimes against the state'—that is, it requires a lower level of premeditation and intent in the offender. Soviet legal doctrine can discover these 'crimes' in the mere fact of wishing to quit the homeland; the offence is held to be gravely compounded by taking part in any public campaign for respect for that right. Such a doctrine can have no standing in international human rights law, yet it has been and continues to be used to frustrate the emigration of thousands of Soviet Jews and others in a similar situation, such as ethnic Germans.

The practice is first to sentence the would-be emigrant to imprisonment or internal exile, and then to obstruct any subsequent application on the grounds of a criminal record. This has been the fate of many applicants, including Alexander Paritsky, who had earlier been dismissed, subjected to harassment, and stripped of his degree;[49] Alexander Till, an ethnic German who was sentenced to two-and-a-half years' imprisonment in 1982;[50] and Yosif Begun, whom we have already mentioned. Sometimes charges are laid under other Articles of the Penal Code. Alexander Bolonkin, an aviation engineer and lecturer at the Moscow faculty of higher mathematics, who had already served a sentence under Article 70,

48 *News Bulletin*, 30 September 1982.
49 *Nature*, 292, 789; 294, 394; 1981.
50 *Dutch CSCE Review*, April/May 1982; *USSR News Brief*, 15 May 1984.

was charged on his release with 'stealing state property'; following his release after serving a sentence for this charge, he applied to emigrate and was charged once again under Article 70.[51] The curious sequel to this charge was that shortly thereafter, in April 1982, he appeared on TV to recant, to dissociate himself from his former dissident colleagues, to deny as slanderous all allegations that dissidents were detained in psychiatric hospitals, and to thank his investigators for the humane treatment he had received. But the spontaneity of his statement was suspect, because it was read very falteringly from a script, and it is known that he had been undergoing 'investigation' in an isolation cell in Ulan-Ude in October 1981.[52]

Other charges that are used at times are those of 'parasitism' and 'hooliganism'. Vladimir Maier, a construction engineer born in 1936 and an ethnic German, was sacked in 1975 for applying to emigrate to West Germany. Effectively unemployed since then except for casual labour, he was arrested in Omsk in late 1981, charged with 'parasitism' and sentenced to two years in a prison camp. He now seems to have little chance of escaping a 'Catch 22' situation in which he is not permitted to emigrate because of his criminal record, cannot get work because he has applied for a visa, and is punished under the Penal Code for being out of work.[53] 'Malicious hooliganism' was the charge in the case of Vladimir Kislik (see above), when he was arrested in 1981 after an earlier arrest on a charge of 'violation of authors' and inventors' rights' i.e. plagiarism.[54]

It is true that a certain number of Jews have been permitted to leave the Soviet Union during the past ten years or so. It seems, however, that this policy is now out of favour, and the stream of emigrants has been reduced to an insignificant trickle. The prospects for the numerous refuseniks that remain—including many scientists—are thus sad indeed: they can have little hope of solving the problems of personal privation and professional decline.[55]

In Czechoslovakia, official policies and practices are very similar to those in the USSR. The story of Karel Culik will serve as an example. He held a professorship at the Institute of Mathematics

[51] *USSR News Brief*, 6–2, 1982.
[52] *Dutch CSCE Review*, 154, 3; 1982.
[53] *USSR News Brief*, 5; 5/1982.
[54] *Nature*, 286, 549; 1981.
[55] *The Times*, 22 September 1982.

of the Czechoslovak Academy, and had a considerable reputation in the field of computer science. But he was dismissed from this post in 1970 because of a marginal involvement in, and a strong suspicion of sympathy for, the events of the 1968 'Prague Spring'. Permitted in 1971 to work in a more junior capacity at the Research Institute for Mathematical Machines, he was, with one exception in 1971, consistently refused permission to accept invitations to visit and attend conferences abroad. These included an invitation to a year's visiting professorship at New York University in 1972, when he was finally forbidden to go at one day's notice, after having made all preparations to leave. In 1973, he was even forbidden to attend an international conference in his own field in Slovakia. These restrictions had the effect of alienating him from scientific work in Czechoslovakia. When he was dismissed from his more junior job in 1973, he finally decided to attempt to emigrate to Canada, as he saw no professional future in Czechoslovakia and felt that in his field he was rapidly declining as a result of scientific isolation. He records that he did not want to emigrate, and would have much preferred to remain in and serve the scientific interests of his own country, paying only short visits abroad for strictly professional purposes; but as he was denied the possibility of working in his field, forbidden to lecture, to publish, or to participate in any way in the scientific life of his country, he considered that emigration was the only hope of avoiding professional atrophy. His request was refused, as had been his earlier requests to visit abroad, on the ground that it was 'not in the interests of the state'—and every attempt to discover just what these interests were failed completely. From this time on, the pressure on him increased severely; he became unemployed and had to find ill-paid casual employment as a stoker and labourer to keep his family alive; from February 1974, he was even deprived of the right to social security benefits. His wife, a former faculty member of the Department of Philosophy and Sociology at the University of Brno, had been dismissed in 1970, also after twenty years' service. Refusal followed refusal, until finally, in 1976, he took the advice of a Party official, reluctantly agreed to renounce his Czech citizenship, and was at last allowed to emigrate.[56]

The main difference in this respect between Czechoslovakia and the USSR is that there are relatively few Czechs who actually wish

[56] Dossier of correspondence privately communicated to Dr Tahourdin.

to leave their country, except as a last resort. Czech culture is fairly coherent, and most of those who are dissatisfied with life there wish to remain, and to try to reform their own social and political system. All they wish to do is to exercise their fundamental right to freedom of expression and opinion, as guaranteed by the Czechoslovak Constitution, by the ICCPR to which that country has adhered (indeed it was Czechoslovakia's ratification which brought it into force), and by the domestic law by which the Covenant was made part of the national law of Czechoslovakia. This is fundamentally the attitude of the Charter-77 adherents,[57] and it is for this activity that they are being penalized. It is only when Czech scientists are deprived of the opportunities to work in their profession and are faced with scientific extinction that they apply to emigrate to save their professional careers. This was the case, for example, with Frantisek Janouch, now in Sweden, who had been dismissed from his post as a theoretical physicist and totally excluded from the scientific life of his country before he was allowed—reluctantly—to leave it.

'Reasons of state' are often invoked by authoritarian governments to justify the suppression of overt dissidence, especially among influential intellectuals. But it is hard to accept that 'political realism' can justify a policy of deliberately humiliating a useful, productive person for years on end, before allowing him to recreate a professional life elsewhere. A country that practises such a systematic denial of basic human rights is as much the loser as the individual concerned. It reflects a state of affairs where, as a recent Charter-77 paper notes,

'. . . political criteria are more important than scientific qualifications and ability. The whole system is unjust and harmful and the principle of stagnation is already included in the directives for screening.'[58]

The effect of this policy is to be seen in the declining status of Czechoslovak science—a decline that is evident in its contributions to international conferences and in the literature of many fields in which this small country was previously held in high esteem.[59]

We have already referred to the recent Romanian decree which

---

[57] *Human Rights in Czechoslovakia* (Commission on Security and Co-operation in Europe of the US Congress; Washington, DC, 1982).

[58] *Letter to the Government and the Central Council of the Trade Unions on the fulfilment of ILO Convention No. 111* (Charter-77 Document No. 17/82; Prague, 17 May 1982).

[59] Janouch, F., 'Science under siege in Czechoslovakia', *Bulletin of the Atomic Scientists*, 6; April 1976.

abrogated the agreement to allow 10,000 ethnic Germans to leave each year—an agreement that had been given in exchange for the valuable economic benefits of 'most favoured nation status' accorded to Romania by the USA.[60] It was this sort of pressure which allowed Professor Mihail Gavrila, former professor of theoretical physics at Bucharest University, who had managed to quit Romania for the Netherlands in 1975, to be joined later by the two children he had then had to leave behind. Generally speaking, however, no Romanian citizen, whether a scientist or not, and whether for ethnic, cultural, political, or professional reasons, is legally allowed to emigrate to another country.

The GDR is another country which profits financially from traffic in emigrants. Those principally involved are people who wish to go to the FRG: it is reported that, in effect, the FRG pays about 70,000 DM for each East German emigrant permitted to exercise the basic right to 'leave any country, including his own'. But even those for whom this ransom money can be put up may have to go through a hard and humiliating experience before they eventually succeed in leaving. In 1980, Dr Jürgen Langer, a gynaecologist, was denied his request to emigrate, and was told that any subsequent application would simply end in the waste paper basket. To underline his sin of asking, his wife was dismissed from her post as a teacher, and their 16-year-old daughter was publicly humiliated by expulsion from the National Youth Organization. A few months later, in September 1980, both Dr Langer and his wife were arrested and sentenced to 16 and 10 months' imprisonment respectively for 'activity damaging to the state or social system'. After serving part of these sentences, they were released in May 1981 and *expelled* to the FRG—presumably against payment of the ransom.[61]

But the outcome is not always even as relatively satisfactory as this. A particularly sad case is that of a young chemist, Dr Gisela Mauritz. Under severe psychological pressure, she attempted in 1974 to flee to West Germany with her four-year-old son. She was arrested and sentenced to four-and-a-half years' imprisonment, while her son was removed from her and put into care. In June 1977, she was given the option of leaving the country—provided she gave up her child. This she refused to do. In December 1978,

[60] *Nature*, 300, 307; 1982.
[61] Information supplied by the American Association for the Advancement of Science.

she was released from prison in a seriously disturbed psychological state, and confined to the small town of Dobeln. She was forbidden to travel to Berlin to see her son, and was denied information about his condition. In her then seriously disturbed state, she finally agreed to his anonymous adoption; in return for that, she was to be allowed to leave East Germany. But this promise was not fulfilled: in December 1980 she was again arrested and, after six months of investigation, she was sentenced to two years' and two months' further imprisonment as 'an enemy of the state'.[62] This is one of those tragic personal stories whose full significance cannot be unravelled without much more information; nevertheless, Gisela Mauritz was deprived of her child, her freedom, and her professional life simply for trying to exercise one of the rights confirmed by the Helsinki Accords—which the GDR claims to realize 'not only in the letter but also in the spirit'.

Even Hungary, which is often regarded as one of the most liberal and tolerant of the East European states, and which has specifically incorporated the freedom of movement into its domestic law, hedges this around by giving the Ministry of the Interior the power to decide on the issue of passports and travel permits. It is true that, comparatively speaking, large numbers of Hungarians do travel abroad; yet according to official statistics, some 4–5 per cent of those wishing to visit non-socialist countries are denied this facility—which adds up to some 12,000 to 15,000 individual refusals a year, not counting the general restriction to one such journey in approximately every three years, on the grounds of shortage of foreign currency.

Some of the grounds for denying this right are purely political, such as a charge that a person 'during a former foreign stay behaved in a way offending the interests of the Hungarian People's Republic'. Another provision condemns anyone who has ever been subject to more than a year's imprisonment to virtually indefinite denial—unless a court decides otherwise. This, inevitably, penalizes those who were involved in the events of 1956, although many of them later had their sentences much reduced.

The harsh consequences of this provision, and another which denies the right to travel to anyone who intends to join someone illegally abroad (including a spouse or a child), are evident in the case of Sandor Lichtenstein, a 54-year-old engineer. He was an

[62] Ditto.

active participant in the events of 1956, for which he was then condemned to death; this sentence was later commuted to life imprisonment, and still later ended by the 1963 general amnesty. His wife and two children left Hungary on tourist visas in 1979, sought and received political asylum in West Germany because of his previous political activities, and in 1980 emigrated to Canada. Lichtenstein, who has not been in any trouble with the authorities since his release, applied in 1980 for a passport to join them, having been assured by the Canadian government that it would accept him. In spite of satisfactory references from his then employer who supported his request to leave, he was refused on the grounds that 'your going to live abroad, on account of the illegal remaining abroad of your wife and two children for a time less than five years, would be against the public interest'. On appeal, he was refused in exactly the same terms; and this has been repeated several times since. He remains alone in Hungary. It should be noted that this action by the Hungarian authorities also contravenes the emphasis on family reunification which figures so prominently in the Helsinki Accords.

In Lichtenstein's case, the domestic regulations can be challenged for their illegitimacy under international human rights law. But the indifference of the Hungarian authorities even to their own law is illustrated by the story of Dr Tibor Pakh—not a scientist, but a lawyer and human rights activist. He was arrested at the Hungarian frontier in October 1981 when attempting to travel to Poland, although his passport was valid for such a journey. The passport was confiscated, he was returned to Budapest and later forcibly detained in a psychiatric hospital. Only courageous protests on the part of a considerable group of scholars induced the authorities to release him after three weeks.[63]

Just occasionally, the standard Soviet policy of closing its frontiers on its own citizens is reversed, and someone is forced to emigrate against his or her will. The medieval practice of external exile died out long ago in the Western countries of the Helsinki group (though not yet in Latin America), but it is used from time to time by the East Europeans to get rid of some of the troublesome, or those who are 'bought out' by other countries. In some cases it is offered as an alternative to further punishment within the country; for example, when Cronid Lubarsky, a Russian astro-

[63] *Nature*, 294, 7; 1981.

physicist who had formerly been at the Institute of Solid State Physics, was released from a five-year prison sentence, he was offered these alternatives, and was thus effectively forced to emigrate.[64] Another case was that of Tatiana Manonova, the Leningrad chemist (and feminist), who was expelled from the Soviet Union in 1980 after suggesting that women should advise their sons to go to prison rather than to fight in Afghanistan. Other such cases could be quoted from Romania and Czechoslovakia, where, for example, Karel Culik was deprived of his citizenship as a condition of being allowed to emigrate. The best-known case, of course, is that of Alexander Solzhenitsyn, who had no desire to leave the Soviet Union but was unceremoniously bundled on to an aeroplane to the West, while at the same time having his Soviet citizenship withdrawn. In a sense, this procedure shows a legalistic desire to abide by the provisions of the ICCPR: if everyone is to have the right to 'enter his own country', the only way that the Soviet authorities can keep out undesirable or inconvenient citizens is to deprive them of their citizenship. In the same tradition, a person who has gone abroad, expecting to return, is sometimes told to hand in his or her passport and is then denied the right of re-entry. This happened, for example, to Zhores Medvedev, who was allowed to make a scientific visit of several months to Britain: a few weeks after his arrival, he was called to the Soviet Embassy in London, and was informed that he had been deprived of his citizenship and would not be allowed to return home.[65] His wife, on the other hand, who is also in England, has kept her passport so that she can, and does, travel to the USSR.

In fact, where such cases relate to citizens who have fallen out with their governments on political grounds, they do involve a violation of the code of international human rights law, since Article 12(4) of the ICCPR says that 'No one shall be *arbitrarily* deprived of his right to enter his own country', and that paragraph is *not* subject to any of the standard provisos. (Article 15(2) of the UDHR also declares that 'No one shall be arbitrarily deprived of his nationality', but the Covenant does not repeat this provision.)

Finally, it may be noted that Article 83 of the Penal Code of the RSFSR makes it an offence punishable by imprisonment for one to three years to cross the national border and go abroad

[64] *Science*, 193, 863; 1976.
[65] *Nature*, 244, 380; 1973.

without the appropriate passport or permission of the Soviet authorities. Experience shows that this sentence can be substantially increased by substituting or adding other charges, such as that of treason (Article 64), which can include the crime of 'flight abroad'. It was under this Article that Tcherepanov was sentenced to a total of 15 years in a labour camp—which was of course less than the maximum of the capital sentence which this 'crime' can carry. Tcherepanov, who was not a scientist, had wished to join his fiancée in the West.[66] This case is very close to the situation of a number of Soviet scientists who wish to emigrate to join their close relatives—spouses, parents, children—outside the USSR. Many of them have been refused, and continue to be refused' that permission. Tcherepanov's case shows what might happen if, in desperation, they attempted the ultimate measure of fleeing the country.

[66] *Nature*, 244, 380; 1973.

9

FREEDOM OF ASSOCIATION AND ASSEMBLY

The right to meet and act together

Like other people, scientists need to meet together in small or large groups, and to act collectively in the pursuit of their calling. The legal aspect of this is usually expressed in the form of two distinct rights, which are both protected by the international instruments. Of these, the right of *assembly* is essentially material; it implies the presence in the same place and at the same time of a number of people engaged in a common, lawful and peaceable pursuit. The right of *association* is symbolic rather than material; it implies membership of some body or collection of people sharing a common interest. Thus, to belong to a trade union or a learned society involves the exercise of the right of association; to attend its meetings involves the exercise of the right of assembly.

The general character and function of scientific associations is indicated by the UNESCO Recommendations on the Status of the Scientific Researcher, Article 42:

'Member States should recognize it as wholly legitimate, and indeed desirable, that scientific researchers should associate to protect and promote their individual and collective interests, in bodies such as trade unions, professional associations and learned societies, in accordance with the rights of workers in general . . . In all cases where it is necessary to protect the rights of scientific researchers, these organizations should have the right to support the justified claims of such researchers.'

Since science is a collective human activity involving interpersonal communication and co-operation, these rights are crucial for scientists. Without membership of a learned society, a scientist is deprived of essential professional and intellectual contacts. Without membership of a trade union, he or she may be deprived of equally essential material benefits. And every scientific conference, however informal, constitutes an assembly.

Both these rights enjoy full protection in international human rights law. As usual, the UDHR (Article 20 (1)) affirms this without qualification:

'Everyone has the right to freedom of peaceful assembly and association.'

Again, as usual, the various treaties repeat these guarantees in substance, adding specific protection for the right to form and join trade unions, but with the now familiar provisos of exception and limitation. But the assemblies and associations in which scientists would wish to take part in the pursuit of their calling are scarcely likely to pose a threat to national security, public safety, health or morals, nor to promote disorder or crime, nor to interfere with the rights or freedoms of others. A state which sought to restrict the freedom of scientists to associate or to assemble would, in all but the most exceptional circumstances, be doing so in violation of the internationally accepted standards of human rights law.

That law does not distinguish between national and international associations or assemblies. While the refusal to allow a scientist to attend a conference outside his own country will prima facie infringe his freedom of movement (see Chapter 8), the refusal to allow him to attend one in his own country will primarily be an infringement of his right to freedom of assembly. Nor do the treaties make any distinction between what might be called a 'learned society'—that is, an association devoted to the advancement of knowledge in a particular sphere—and a 'professional association' or 'trade union', whose main concern might be the welfare of its individual members. Although any association may choose to limit itself to one or other function, this limitation does not put it into a special category from the point of view of the human rights code. Thus, for example, a scientific society may claim as much protection for meetings to discuss the career prospects of scientists as for the discussion of new scientific theories.

Indeed, in an era when so many technical decisions are being made which vitally affect the welfare of society, the scientific community can no longer remain aloof from the conflicts to which these give rise. A scientific association may thus feel obliged to intervene on behalf of the public interest, for instance by setting up committees of inquiry into cases which have aroused the conscience of scientists, by publicizing the results of such inquiries in professional journals and in the news media, and by calling such matters to the attention of governmental authorities. On the other hand, the role of a professional association of scientists need not be altogether defensive in relation to the actions of employers or governmental authorities. Freedom of association also legitimates the procedures indicated in Article 7 of the UNESCO Recommendations on the Status of Scientific Researchers:

'Member States should cultivate opportunities for scientific researchers to participate in the outlining of national scientific research and experimental development policy. In particular, each Member State should ensure that these processes are supported by appropriate institutional mechanisms enjoying adequate advice and assistance from scientific researchers and their professional organizations.'

Scientific associations

In all the Western countries of our survey, associations of scientists proliferate. Some are highly specialized and narrowly defined learned societies, whose sole activity is to organize conferences and publish learned journals. Some are professional organizations whose main business is to protect the interests of their members as salaried employees or as licensed practitioners. Some are public interest groups, trying to influence a parliament or a congress. Some are entirely voluntary, depending only on the individual enthusiasm of their members. Some are semi-official, giving their members certain privileges and responsibilities under a state charter. Some are small and local, others are nation-wide, or even international, with thousands of members and budgets of millions of pounds, dollars, francs, marks, kroner, lire, guilders or pesetas. It is almost impossible to list them all, or even to divide them into distinct categories. They are the structural components of the 'scientific community'.

Apart from Turkey, we have found only one case of any present restrictions on freedom of association amongst scientists in any countries of the Western group, or any constraints on the activities they may undertake other than the normal obligations of any corporate body under domestic law. The exceptional case is the decision of the British Government, in 1984, to ban normal trade union membership among the 5,000 staff of the Government Communication Headquarters (GCHQ) at Cheltenham, on the grounds that this was prejudical to national security. Since many of them are scientists, this highly contentious decision comes within the scope of this book and calls for comment. However, at the time of writing the whole matter is still *sub judice*; the House of Lords, the highest domestic court of law in the UK, has found in the government's favour, but proceedings are pending on the international plane at the International Labour Organization, and may eventually also reach the European Court of Human Rights.

There are two important decisions of that Court in the field of freedom of association, both in fact concerned with compulsion to belong to an association, rather than with the prohibition of associations. The first[1] concerned the existence in some European states of institutions established by law, such as the *ordre des médecins* in Belgium, which persons who wish to practise a profession are compelled to join, and to the jurisdiction of whose disciplinary bodies they then become subject. The Court held that such a compulsion does not derogate from freedom of association, so long as other *voluntary* associations formed to protect professional interests are permitted to exist and function, which members of the profession concerned are free to join or not. In the other case,[2] the Court decided that the freedom of association protected by Article 11 of the ECHR *was* infringed where the management of an entire national industry (British Railways) had agreed with one of its dominant trade unions to operate a 'closed shop', so that someone who had worked there before the agreement was made was thereupon forced either to join the union concerned, or to lose his job.

In Turkey, the current state of affairs is giving grave cause for concern. In a recent incident, Dr Yeter Göksü-Ögelman, a lecturer in physics at the Cukorova University who helped to organize a women's rights group, 'The Progressive Women's Organization', was dismissed from her post and charged under Article 141 of the Turkish Criminal Code with having 'administered a society with the purpose of establishing domination of a social class or overthrowing any of the basic economic or social orders', an offence punishable by imprisonment from 8 to 15 years.[3] On the face of it, in the absence of clear evidence that the society concerned used, or intended to use, violent means to achieve its objectives, this would seem to have been a flagrant violation of Dr Göksü-

---

[1] *Le Compte, van Leuwen and de Meyere* v. *Belgium* 2 EHRR 433
[2] *Young, James and Webster* v. *United Kingdom* 4 EHRR 38
[3] *Nature*, 296, 186 & 260; 1982.

Ögelman's right to freedom of association protected by Article 11 of the ECHR, to which Turkey has been a state party since 1954— though, regrettably, she does not yet allow her inhabitants the right of individual petition to Strasbourg.

The situation in 'closed' societies such as the Soviet Union and its allies is entirely different. Broadly speaking, one may say that there is no general right of association at all. Organizations that are not formally permitted are effectively forbidden. For example, trade union activity, in the sense in which that term is understood in the human rights instruments, is virtually non-existent—as the poignant events in Poland in the last few years have demonstrated.

Within this political context, scientists appear to have a fair amount of liberty, provided that the activities of their permitted associations are kept rigorously within the technical realm. For example, every large city in the USSR has its own local math-ematical society. The largest and most important of these is the Moscow Mathematical Society, founded in 1864, which meets weekly at Moscow State University. The meetings last two hours, with a short break. There are usually one or two talks, dealing with some important new development in the field of mathematics, presented in a form intelligible to a wide audience. Interesting talks sometimes attract as many as 200 mathematicians, most of whom are undergraduate students. To be elected to the Society, one has to be a working mathematician, and to be recommended by a member. The Board of the Society, which arranges the meetings, invites speakers, and is headed by a President and two Vice-Presidents, is also elected. The Society has the right to nominate its own candidates for Membership of the Academy of Sciences of the USSR, and for Lenin or State Prizes, although it has no control and little influence over the final selections for these honours. In a word, this is a traditional learned society, of a kind that might equally be found in London or Berlin, Toronto or Milan, which runs its own affairs with little outside interference.

But when a mathematician, Mark Morozov, allowed an unofficial group, the 'Free Inter-Professional Association of Workers', to hold an inaugural news conference in his Moscow flat, he was arrested. He was later charged with 'anti-Soviet agitation and propaganda', and at a closed trial in June 1978 he was sentenced to 5 years' internal exile: he was last reported to be imprisoned in a strict regime corrective labour colony in the Perm region.[4]

[4] *Index on Censorship*, June 1981, p. 79.

The position of the Academies of Science

In the USSR and in each of the other countries of Eastern Europe, a special position is occupied by the national Academy of Sciences. These institutions have no direct counterpart in the UK or the USA, since they combine the honorific and advisory functions of the UK Royal Society or the US National Academy with the direct administrative functions of bodies such as the Science and Engineering Research Council in the UK or the National Science Foundation in the USA. Thus, to be elected an Academician or Corresponding Member of such an Academy is not only one of the highest honours that a scientist can aspire to: it may also place him in direct command of one or more of the many scientific institutes within the Academy system. (The exception is the Romanian Academy which, although remodelled on the Soviet pattern in 1948, was stripped of its institutes in 1970-71: see below). In most of the 'socialist' countries, scientists employed within the Academy network may also hold university teaching posts. (Here, the exception is Poland where the two structures are kept formally separate, ostensibly in the interests of full employment. This meant that many scholars who lost their university posts in the purges of March 1968 were able to find employment in institutes of the Polish Academy of Sciences, where, since they would have no direct contact with students, their non-conforming political views were considered to be less dangerous.) Since a large proportion of the best scientists in the country is employed in these institutes and universities, the Academy system is therefore a major sector of the scientific effort of the country.

In the Soviet Union, in spite of the claim of the Party to exert its authority over all aspects of scientific life, the Academy has, until recently, been generally regarded as the most independent of all the leading institutions. At its 250th anniversary celebrations in 1975, the audience of academic and senior scientific officials listening to Chairman Brezhnev's speech included Dr Andrei Sakharov, then as now the Soviet Union's leading dissident.[5] By long tradition, election to the Academy is by a secret ballot of the 245 Members, who thus form the only organized group in the Soviet Union enjoying this degree of autonomy. Moreover, Academicians

[5] *Caris*, 55/75 (London; BBC, 1975).

are elected for life, and there is no precedent for their removal except by a decision of the Academy's Praesidium. The Academicians themselves have good reason to guard their positions jealously, and are careful not to offer any occasions for external interference. Membership of the Academy brings with it a salary for life, and a whole range of perquisites and privileges, from access to special shops to a chauffeur-driven car. They thus constitute a very powerful and privileged élite within the scientific community, and in the country as a whole.

It seems, however, that this independence is now being whittled away. Evidence of the change came with the election of a new President to replace Mstislav Keldysh, who retired in 1975 on grounds of ill-health. The election itself was delayed for six months, apparently because the Kremlin and the scientists could not agree on the choice of a successor. When, eventually, the choice fell on a 72-year-old nuclear physicist and member of the Party's Central Committee, Dr Anatoly Alexandrov, this was considered at the time to represent a compromise between the more independently-minded scientists and the forces favouring firmer Communist Party control. But many observers saw the election of a Central Committee member to this distinguished office as a sign of the curtailment of the traditional autonomy of the Academy. This was underlined by the fact that Alexandrov's name was proposed by Mikhail Suslov, the Party's chief ideologist, rather than by a leading scholar, suggesting that the Party leadership had had the final say in the election.[6]

In Czechoslovakia, the Soviet tanks and troops that appeared on the streets of Prague to put an end to the 'Dubcek Spring' took particular care to seize the building of the Czechoslovak Academy of Sciences. This temporary physical occupation of the Academy was followed by administrative measures curtailing its freedom. As part of the post-1968 'normalization', new statutes were imposed on the Academy, depriving it of much of its former autonomy and reducing the scholarly qualifications required of its leading officers. The chairman, Dr Frantisek Sorm, was dismissed, and replaced by one of the vice-chairmen, Jaroslav Kozesnik. Two new vice-chairmen were nominated by the government, and a new General Secretary, Karel Friml, was appointed, even though he did not hold a postgraduate degree. Ideological conformity was emphasized

6 *Nature*, 258, 377; 1975.

above academic achievement: in 1971 all Academy members had to execute an affidavit relating not only to their own political reliability but also to the reliability of their relatives.[7] A similar process seems to be taking place in Poland, where the Academy of Sciences had been able to maintain a substantial degree of freedom in its scientific activities until it was brought to heel by the martial law regime in 1982.

The most demeaning action suffered by any learned society in Eastern Europe in recent years occurred in Romania. The Romanian Academy, which was founded in 1866, was regarded as the leading scientific and cultural institution in that country. Until 1948, when it was reorganized on more political lines, it had included among its members the most prominent scientists, artists, and cultural leaders of Romania. The loss of its research institutes in 1970-1, which were placed under the supervision of the National Council for Science and Technology, and the subsequent liquidation of some of them, considerably reduced the competence of the Academy, whose role became largely one of representing Romania in international scientific fora, engaging in co-operation agreements, and encouraging scientific achievement by means of prizes and other incentives at its disposal.[8] In 1977, upon the death of its Chairman Dr Theodor Burghele, a well-known surgeon, it was widely rumoured that Elena Ceausescu, the wife of the President, entertained ambitions of succeeding to this position. However, in March 1980, Gheorghe Mihoc, a mathematician, was elected by a two-thirds majority—a degree of support that Mrs Ceausescu would probably not have received in a secret ballot. But she got her way in the end. By a State Council decree of the same month, the Romanian Academy itself was placed under the supervision of the National Council of Science and Technology, presided over by none other than Elena Ceausescu.

From these episodes it is clear that there is very little genuine freedom of association for scientists in the countries of Eastern Europe. The smaller, more local, more specialized learned societies are able to manage their own affairs without overt interference, but the major associations representing the scientific community as

---

[7] Janouch, F., 'Science in the CSSR', in *Menschenrechte: Ein Jahrbuch zu Osteuropa* (Rowohlt Taschenbuch Verlag; Hamburg, 1977).

[8] Mihoc, G., *The Academy of the Socialist Republic of Romania* (Editura Académiei Republicii Socialiste Romania; Bucharest, 1981).

a whole are now closely controlled by the government and Party apparatus. This is not solely a matter for concern among the scientists in each particular country. The national academies and their more specialized sectional organizations claim to represent the scientific communities of their respective nations in all international scientific activities, such as those undertaken by the International Council of Scientific Unions (ICSU) and its affiliates. The fact that this claim is not based only upon the free and spontaneous expression of the opinions of the scientists in those countries needs to be continually kept in mind by the leaders of other national scientific communities which enjoy this right. The constraints that are thus applied to freedom of *international* association amongst scientists gravely compromise the tradition of 'the one world of science'.

Freedom of assembly

It is not unusual for a scientist to be prevented from attending a conference in a foreign country; many such cases of infringement of the freedom of movement have already been noted in Chapter 8. But when he or she is prevented from attending a meeting in their own country, that constitutes primarily an infringement of the right of assembly. Such cases are relatively rare, but they have happened several times to Jewish 'refuseniks' in the Soviet Union. When the International Conference on Magnetism was scheduled to be held in Moscow in August 1973, three Soviet scientists of international repute, Professors Azbel, Giterman and Voronel, were invited by the international organizing committee to take part; nevertheless, their attendance was prevented by the local Russian committee arranging the Conference.[9] A few years later, another refusenik scientist of even greater eminence, Professor Benjamin Levich, was not sent an invitation to attend an international meeting held in the Soviet Union on his very own subject—Heat and Mass Transfer. It was only after protests from abroad that he was allowed to attend.

The most striking violations of the right of assembly as defined in international human rights law also involve the refusenik scientists in the Soviet Union. The story of the 'Moscow Sunday Seminar' raises such important issues for the freedom of the scientific enterprise throughout the world that it needs to be told at

[9] M. Azbel, *Refusenik* (Hamish Hamilton; London, 1982).

some length. Mark Azbel's account of the founding and subsequent history of this imaginative institution is particularly instructive and moving.[10]

Let us first make it clear that there is a long tradition in science of very small, highly informal, and unofficial meetings where one of those present gives a paper which is then discussed by the other participants. Such a seminar may well be arranged to take place periodically, but can scarcely be called an association. For example, the Moscow Mathematical Society, under the chairmanship of Professor I. M. Gelfand, ran a regular 'Monday Seminar' at the University to discuss topical subjects. It attracted a number of participants, including foreign guest mathematicians who would be asked to talk to Gelfand's seminar before addressing the Society more formally the next day. At the seminar, the speaker would often be interrupted by Gelfand or his associates, and it is reported that the discussion or remarks following after that were sometimes more interesting than the main talk.

This was the model followed in the Sunday Seminars, organized by the Jewish scientists in Moscow who had been excluded from their libraries, laboratories, and lecture rooms because they had applied to emigrate to Israel. The first of these was started in 1972 by Alexander Voronel, and met every Sunday at noon in his apartment. The purpose was to keep the refusenik scientists in touch with each other and with the progress of their subjects, and the meetings were devoted solely to the reading of scientific papers and the discussion of scientific ideas. At first, only eight or nine people would attend them, but in the course of time these numbers increased considerably, and many scientists who were not refuseniks—some even, like Sakharov, who were not Jews, and some Western scientists who happened to be in Moscow—would also take part. During the International Conference on Magnetism held in Moscow in August 1973, some forty foreign physicists, learning that three refuseniks had been forbidden to give papers at the Conference, crowded into Voronel's apartment and listened to their presentations there.[11]

The original seminar founded by Voronel was on 'Collective Phenomena', which covers a wide range of fields—from mathematics, physics, and astronomy to materials science, engineering,

[10] M. Azbel, loc. cit.
[11] M. Azbel, loc. cit.

and physical chemistry. It served as the prototype for other seminars, in Moscow and in other cities. For example, Alexander Lerner organized one in Moscow on cybernetics and control theory, while the Leningrad Seminar, held in the apartment of Dr Aba Taratuta, covered pure mathematics as well as the application of mathematics to biology. In Kharkhov, Dr Alexander Paritsky founded a seminar concentrating on engineering, designed especially to teach young refuseniks and those who had been refused permission to enter university. In Kiev, Dr Vladimir Kislik opened a seminar in physics and engineering.[12]

Inspired by the participation of foreign scientists in these seminars, especially during the Magnetism Conference, the idea arose of arranging an international session of the Seminar on Collective Phenomena in Moscow. This was planned for July 1974, and was organized by a committee including Voronel and two Western scientists, one from the University of Sheffield and another from the University of Washington in Seattle. Some seventy papers were prepared for this meeting by authors from the USSR, the USA, Israel, the UK, and many other European countries.

The Soviet authorities reacted to these preparations by arresting the Soviet organizers of the meeting and removing them from Moscow, and preventing other Soviet participants from leaving their apartments. Western scientists intending to take part were refused entry visas. These actions against the would-be participants, and especially against their legitimate right of peaceful assembly, gave more publicity to the Seminar than it would in all likelihood have received had it been allowed to take place. Perhaps for this reason, the next international meeting of the Seminar, scheduled for its fifth anniversary in April 1977, was treated more temperately by the Soviet authorities. Alexander Voronel had been permitted to emigrate, and the new chairman of the Seminar, Mark Azbel, was at first denounced in *Izvestia* as being in the pay of the CIA, and then allowed to go ahead with his arrangements for a special jubilee meeting to which scientists from abroad were invited. The KGB insisted that the Seminar be 'confined to matters of scientific interest' (which it always had been, anyway) and sought to ensure that it was so by a display of electronic surveillance devices inside, and an equally dramatic display of KGB agents outside, Azbel's apartment where the meeting was held.[13]

---

[12] *Nature*, 282, 435; 1979; 286, 549; 1981.
[13] M. Azbel, loc. cit.

The Third International Conference on Collective Phenomena took place in the Moscow apartment of Dr Victor Brailovsky, who had by then taken over from Azbel. This meeting was sponsored by the New York Academy of Sciences, and was attended by about thirty Soviet scientists, seven from France, three from the USA, and one from the UK. Five other Americans who had planned to attend had their visas to the Soviet Union revoked shortly before the meeting, and several Soviet scientists living outside Moscow were prevented from coming. Nevertheless, this meeting took place without any disruption.[14]

But the political climate was changing. Three days before the scheduled opening of the Fourth International Conference in this series, in April 1980, KGB agents broke down the door of the Brailovskys' apartment, and arrested Victor Brailovsky. After interrogating him for five hours and warning him against allowing the conference to take place, they released him; but Brailovsky refused to cancel the meeting, which went ahead as scheduled. It was sponsored by the New York Academy of Sciences, the British Institute of Physics, the French Physical Society, and the French Institute of Chemistry. Some forty Soviet scientists were joined by five from Scandinavia, four from the USA, nine from France, and three from the UK; several other French and US scientists who had planned to attend were refused visas. Among the scientific papers presented two were read *in absentia*: one contributed by Yuri Orlov and the other by Andrei Sakharov.[15]

The Fifth International Conference on Collective Phenomena was planned for September 1981. In the absence of Victor Brailovsky, who was arrested in November 1980 (see Chapter 7), the leadership of the Seminar had passed to a group of refuseniks, including Irina Brailovsky, Dr Alexander Ioffe, Professor Ya'akov Alpert, Professor Solomon Alber and Dr Alexander Golfand. A week before the opening date, all these scientists were warned by the KGB that they would be charged with anti-Soviet activity, and would experience Brailovsky's fate, if the meeting went ahead. They were also put under house arrest. In the light of the treatment that other refuseniks had received in the previous few months, the organizers of the Conference were clear that these were not empty

[14] *Physics Today*, June 1979.
[15] *Science*, 211, 904; 1981.

threats; the Fifth International Conference, which was to have been attended by some sixty foreign scientists, was called off.[16]

The same threats have also forced the closure of the regular Sunday Seminar in Moscow, and other unofficial seminars, none of which has met regularly since the summer of 1981. In Kiev, Vladimir Kislik, who had been stopped from going to Moscow in April 1980 to attend the Fourth International Conference and warned about his continued participation in these unofficial activities, was imprisoned in July 1980 on charges of 'hooliganism'. He went on hunger strike and was removed to a hospital for the mentally disturbed, but was released after two weeks following protests from the West. Eight months later, however, he was once again arrested on charges of 'malicious hooliganism', and in May 1981 he was sentenced to three years in a labour camp. In Kharkov, Alexander Paritsky was arrested in September 1981, and was sentenced to three years in a labour camp for 'disseminating anti-Soviet propaganda'.

The wavering attitude of the Soviet authorities to these activities, and the firm measures that were eventually taken to close them down completely, show how closely they touch upon the theme of this book. Nobody really supposes that the proceedings at these seminars and conferences were in any way subversive, or a threat to the national security of the USSR. The organizers have always stressed, most emphatically, that they are not 'dissidents', and are not in the least concerned with the policies of a state which they are making every effort to leave. One of the present authors can attest, from personal observation, that the atmosphere in the seminar, although physically cramped, was at a very high level of scientific competence, and that the discussion was comparable to the best one would expect at a first-rate university or institute of advanced study. Those taking part were obviously gaining considerably from the experience, and there was a clear benefit to science itself through the exchange of information and opinion. To prevent such peaceable assemblies not only offends against a legitimate human right, as protected unequivocally by international law; it is also a gross affront to the tradition of science as we know it, where talking, teaching, and discussing in small informal groups has always been an essential means of progress.

This the Soviet authorities must know. But the open exercise of

16 *Science*, 214, 164; 1981.

this right in these seminars could not, in the end, be tolerated, for it symbolized an independence of mind and spirit that is not consistent with a totalitarian system of government. Even at the cost of making nonsense of all their claims to value the pursuit of scientific knowledge, they have felt bound to crack down on any open manifestation of such independence. If there is to be science, they are saying, then it must be official science, owned by the state, and no other. This point of view, which shows also in attacks on the 'cosmopolitanism' of certain scientists, is obviously completely inimical to the concept of 'the one world of science' which is held by most scientists in the West—and many, surely, in the East. Nobody who has looked into the matter can be unaware of the political and social barbed wire in which the Jewish citizens of the Soviet Union are now entrapped: nevertheless, through their Sunday Seminars they had shown the way for the whole world of free science.

Similar manifestations of intellectual freedom have been shown in other countries, in a more general academic context. In the years following the Soviet occupation of Czechoslovakia, professional scholars and writers who were not allowed to practise their calling there met together and developed a programme of teaching for young people excluded from higher education for political reasons. Starting in the autumn of 1977, several regular courses were given in Prague by philosophers such as Milan Machovec, Julius Tomin, and Ladislav Hejdanek; and in Brno by Jan Simsa, Milan Uhde, Jaroslav Meznik, and Zdenek Vasicek. Although both lecturers and students were subjected to police harassment, the courses continued, with interruptions, until 1978, and were resumed in the autumn of that year. The philosophy seminar of Julius Tomin later became the centre of intense police harassment and international publicity.[17] In response to an invitation from Tomin, a number of foreign scholars came regularly to Prague and took part in the seminar. Two of them, the Master of Balliol College and a Norwegian scholar, were actually taken into custody during their seminar, and unceremoniously expelled from the country. When harassment of this kind persisted, Dr Tomin sought and secured permission to leave the country temporarily, and accepted an invitation from Oxford University. In June 1981, he and his wife

[17] *Times Higher Education Supplement*, 6 June 1980.

Zdena were deprived of their Czechoslovak citizenship, and thus prevented from returning home.[18]

After the departure of Tomin, Professor Ladislav Hejdanek began to organize regular working seminars on various philosophical subjects in his apartment, where guest speakers from abroad would attend from time to time. Over a period of eighteen months, the police intervened four or five times, and the lecture meetings were twice cancelled. The position changed abruptly, however, with the military take-over in Poland. Immediately after martial law was declared there on 13 December 1981, the police interrupted the philosophy seminar in Prague and detained all those present. On 28 December a lecturer from France, Dr Jacques Derrida, was detained at the airport and charged with possession of hallucinatory drugs; only after the intervention of the French ambassador was he allowed to leave the country. But it is believed that this seminar has now resumed, and continues to meet.[19]

In Poland itself, workers' protests against price rises in June 1976, and the subsequent police repressions, led to the establishment of an unofficial 'Workers' Defence Committee' (KOR). This, in its turn, led to a whole wave of further independent activities, including the establishment, at the beginning of 1978, of the unofficial 'Society for Academic Courses' (TKN), which endeavoured to fill the gaps in the state higher education syllabuses. Structured courses for undergraduates were established in what became popularly known as the 'Flying University' (after a similar movement in the late nineteenth century which boasted the future Madame Curie among its alumni). Although the courses were primarily in the arts and humanities—the fields in which the official syllabuses left the most serious gaps—the 58 founding members of TKN included a large proportion of mathematicians, physicists, chemists, biologists, and other natural scientists, whose subjects could be adequately represented within the official university system, but who wished to add their weight to the moral and social responsibility for the initiative. The unofficial 'dean' of the whole undertaking was Dr Jan Kielanowski, an eminent expert on animal nutrition and a member of the Polish Academy of Sciences.

From the beginning, the Flying University was subjected to

police harassment. Initially, this took the form of prosecuting the apartment-holders who offered their premises for the lectures, for allegedly contravening health and safety by-laws; selectively stopping some of the students as they were leaving the lectures and noting their names and addresses, in the hope of frightening off those lucky enough to have been missed the first time; and arresting at the railway stations lecturers attempting to travel from Warsaw to lecture in other university cities. The second phase, in the spring of 1979, included the physical beating-up of lecturers and participants by 'unknown hooligans', police harassment of organizers and their families, and threats of dismissal from work. The third stage, in November 1979, was the arrest of Dr Kielanowski. Following police interference with the inaugural lecture of the 1979–80 session (although the venue, a church crypt, was formally outside police jurisdiction) and the subsequent fine, equivalent to a month's academic salary, imposed on the lecturer Dr Wladyslaw Bartoszewski, the courses broke up into small seminars which observed strict security of venue and tried to avoid contacts with visiting foreign academics.

In September 1980, with the foundation of Solidarity, the Flying University briefly re-emerged into the open, with large public lectures in the Great Hall of Warsaw University. During the sixteen months of liberalization, many hitherto banned subjects were quietly reabsorbed into the regular university syllabuses, and no formal Flying University activities were planned for 1981–2. Then, during the martial law regime, some four fifths of the active TKN lecturers were interned or imprisoned—and promptly began organizing lectures for their fellow inmates. At the same time, small 'self-education circles' sprang up throughout Poland, among both students and industrial workers. More recently, a new organization, the 'Social Committee for Learning (SKN) has been established as part of the 'alternative society' advocated by underground Solidarity leaders. This has the dual aim of providing textbooks for self-education courses, and stipends for scholars excluded from the official academic milieux for political reasons. Unlike TKN, the membership of SKN is a closely guarded secret, but it is believed that at least some of the original TKN members participate in its work.[20]

[20] *Index on Censorship*, No. 6, 1978, 57–9; No. 6, 1979, 19–22; No. 2, 1985, 22–3, 36; *Times Higher Education Supplement*, 6 June 1980; 26 April 1985.

In Yugoslavia, a somewhat similar initiative—an independent sociology seminar—gradually grew up out of some informal get-togethers towards the end of the 1970s. This group, consisting of a nucleus of some fifty 'regulars' and perhaps twice that number of 'casual' members, met at approximately fortnightly intervals—without, at first, apparently attracting the attentions of the security police. However, on 20 April 1984 the police raided the seminar and took its participants into temporary custody. Six of them were subsequently charged with 'conspiracy against the Yugoslav state system', but after a prolonged trial the charges were dropped against one defendant, reduced against three more, and suspended on health grounds against the fifth—so apparently leaving the sixth charged with conspiring with himself. Underlying the case, which attracted considerable attention in the international academic community, was the unspoken 'Catch 22' thesis that non-academics had no business to take part in such activities, and genuine academics should know better.[21]

[21] *Times Higher Education Supplement*, 4 May 1984, 18 May 1984, 22 June 1984, 29 June 1984, 11 January 1985, 8 February 1985, 15 March 1985.

10

RESPECT FOR HONOUR, REPUTATION, AND INTELLECTUAL ACHIEVEMENT

Recognition of scientific achievement

Deep personal involvement is an essential driving force in those who hope to advance scientific knowledge. Recognition of the achievements of individual researchers, or of identifiable teams of researchers, often working in competition with one another, compensates for the losses in other directions which single-minded dedication entails, and is as vital for the progress of science as any of the freedoms we have hitherto discussed. Without the prospect of such personal recognition, many scientists would be unlikely to maintain the concentration of purpose, the enthusiasm, and the high standards of investigation and critical assessment which are required in contemporary science. There is no substitute for the freely given recognition of achievement by one's scientific peers— whether informally, through the citation of published work or invitations to address international scientific conferences, or (more officially) through the award of public prizes, or election to membership of a national academy. Interference with these incentives to scientific excellence can be as damaging as more direct restrictions on research, or on the communication of scientific results.

Although most scientists are employed by governments or other large organizations, they have well-established *personal* rights in relation to the results of their research. This applies, in particular, to publications in the form of books, and articles in learned journals, of which they may be sole or joint authors. The material benefits of such authorship are of course protected by the usual laws of copyright. But scientific authors are seldom paid directly in money for such publications: the real return comes through the enhanced reputation and respect that they may earn among their colleagues, especially internationally. The functioning of the scientific community depends heavily on the reliability with which such publications may be attributed to their authors. This is clearly recognized in the UNESCO Recommendations on the Status of Scientific Researchers, Article 35:

'Member States should encourage and facilitate publication of the results obtained by scientific researchers, with a view to assist them to acquire the reputation which they want . . .'

Considerations such as these were evidently at the forefront of the minds of the draftsmen of the international code of human rights law. Article 12 of the UDHR declares that:

'No one shall be subjected . . . to attacks upon his honour and reputation',

and Article 27(2) goes on to say that:

'Everyone has the right to the protection of the moral and material interests resulting from any scientific, literary or artistic production of which he is the author.'

The former words are repeated in Article 17 of the ICCPR, and the latter in Article 15(1)(c) of the ICESCR, in both cases without any of the familiar provisos. These provisions therefore now establish the international law in this field.

They are firmly phrased rights, with a variety of applications. They give legal reinforcement to the recommendations of Article 36 of the UNESCO Recommendations, which says that:

'Member States should ensure that the scientific and technological writings of scientific researchers enjoy appropriate legal protection, and in particular the protection afforded by copyright law'

They also provide a motive for Article 40(a), which recommends:

' . . . written provisions to be included in the terms and conditions of employment of scientific researchers, stating clearly what rights (if any) belong to them . . . in respect of any discovery, invention or improvement in technical know-how which may arise in the course of the scientific research and experimental development which these researchers undertake.'

In the defence of scientific freedom, moreover, it must be appreciated that a scientist's personal reputation is often his or her most precious asset. In all fields of 'public' science—that is, where the results of research are normally intended to be published—this is the key factor in gaining employment or winning preferment. Universities and other institutions devoted to academic research rely almost entirely on the *curriculum vitae* of a candidate for appointment or promotion, carefully scrutinizing lists of publications, noting attendances at major conferences, taking account of communal responsibilities such as the editorship of learned journals, and above all estimating the standing of the candidate in the scientific world from the comments of expert referees. The right to personal protection in all such interests thus applies with particular force in the circumstances envisaged in Article 28 of the UNESCO Recommendations:

' . . . decisions as to access by scientific researchers . . . to positions of greater responsibility and correspondingly higher rewards should be formulated essentially on the basis of fair and realistic appraisal of the capacities of the persons concerned, as evidenced by their current or recent performances, as well as on the basis of formal or academic evidence of knowledge acquired or skills demonstrated by them.'

Respect for honour and reputation

In the Western states of the Helsinki group, people have the right to protect their personal honour and reputation through the civil or criminal law. Provided that those who seek the protection of the law when they are libelled, or slandered, or otherwise wronged are able to obtain an effective remedy before an impartial and independent tribunal, their state will have performed its obligations under international human rights law. Cases of this kind involving scientists are not unknown—and are sometimes very instructive about the *mores* of the scientific life.

The situation is somewhat different in the 'socialist' countries, where legal actions of this kind between individuals, or between an individual and a state organization, are not customary. The individual scientist thus has no direct redress against an attack on his or her reputation by the authorities, and is extremely vulnerable to arbitrary action by the powers that be. Nevertheless, honour and reputation play just as large a part in the scientific life there as they do in other countries. For example, public scientific achievement is normally the means of winning membership of the national Academy of Sciences, with all the privileges that this can bring both scientifically and materially. The title of Member, or Corresponding Member, of the Academy is itself an honour, comparable with other forms of recognition dispensed by the state, such as Meritorious Worker of Science and Technology, the Lenin Prize, Hero of Socialist Work, etc., bringing with them various other attributes of rank and social standing. The same applies at lower levels, where the title of Professor, or Doctor of Science, or *kandidat*, carries with it, almost automatically, certain attributes of social influence and success. Although these titles are conferred by organizations such as universities that are under the authority of the state, they are not posts in a managerial hierarchy but are supposed to be earned by individual achievement, as assessed by specialists in each scientific field. They are both the fruits and the outward symbols of scientific reputation and honour, just as they are in Western countries.

Until fairly recently, this right was reasonably well protected in the USSR—at least as long as a person was alive and at liberty: anyone convicted (however unjustly) of a crime against the state is scarcely in a position to defend their 'honour and reputation' or their 'moral and material interests resulting from any scientific, literary or artistic production'; such a loss may be the least of their sufferings. But the Soviet authorities have recently developed a practice of deliberately trying to destroy the professional reputation of scientists or other intellectual workers who have fallen out of official favour, even if they have not been formally charged with any criminal offence.

This policy has been applied, for example, to Andrei Sakharov, who was stripped of all his formal honours, except membership of the Academy, before being sent into internal exile by 'administrative action'. All that he had achieved as a scientist, whether secretly for the defence of his country in his earlier days, or openly in his published papers, was thus officially set at nought—and will presumably now be obliterated from the internal historical record of his country. Sakharov's international reputation is so great, as a scientist and a humanitarian, that such an action by the authorities rather adds to than subtracts from it. But the same cannot be said of lesser fry, who are very dependent on recognition of their personal achievements.

Many 'refusenik' scientists, for example, have suffered severely from this practice. An application by a Jewish scientist to emigrate to Israel marks the beginning of a period in which he or she is subjected to a host of humiliating punitive actions. As we have seen in Chapter 5, loss of employment is almost inevitable; the applicant is brought under great pressure to resign, and will be certain to be dismissed if he or she does not. In the case of Professor

Alexander Lerner, as soon as he was dismissed from his position as director of the Department of Large Scale Systems at the Institute of Control Sciences, the lecture he was giving was actually interrupted and his students were forced to leave the auditorium. He was also expelled from the editorial board of the *Journal of Automation and Telemechanics*, and from the public office of chairman of the Scientific and Technical Committee of the University of Moscow. Even medical aid at the polyclinic of the Academy of Sciences was immediately discontinued. To compound the humiliation, his daughter Sonya and his son were expelled from their institutes. Sonya had been one of the youngest university students in the USSR, and had received a degree in mathematics at the age of 15 under the supervision of Academician Gelfand.

But direct loss of employment, of official posts, and of the privileges that go with them is not the only reprisal taken against refusenik or dissident scientists. They may, in addition, be excluded altogether from the world of science. Refusenik scientists obviously have no opportunity to take part in scientific meetings abroad; they may (as we saw in Chapter 9) be prevented from attending scientific conferences in the Soviet Union itself, even when they have earned an invitation by their international reputation. They are likely to be shut out from technical libraries, and not permitted to attend lectures or seminars in their former institutes. Their work is not accepted by the Soviet journals, and they are forbidden to send it abroad for publication.

The final step in making a scientist a non-person in the scientific world is to withdraw their books, and to delete all citations to their work in scientific papers. Books by Mark Azbel and by Alexander Lerner, which were already in the course of publication at the time of their applications for exit visas, were taken out of production— even though Lerner's book, *The Beginning of Cybernetics*, had sold 40,000 copies in five days when it was first published.[1] An article in the American *Journal of the Chemical Society*—'Theory of Electron Transfer Reactions in Solution', by Parbury P. Schmidt—was reproduced and circulated in the USSR with the name of Professor Levich deleted wherever it appeared in the original text. The book *Optimal Heating of Metals*, of which Lerner was the scientific editor and one of the authors, was published in 1972 by the 'Metallurgy' publishing house without his name being mentioned

[1] *Nature*, 282, 554; 1979.

and without any reference to the fundamental contributions that he had made to this subject.

In many ways, the most serious breach of this basic right to enjoy the honour due for honest work is the recent Soviet practice of 'revoking' higher degrees. The sanctity of academic degrees is a fundamental principle of academic life throughout the world. Once earned and granted in recognition of scholarly achievement, they cannot be taken away. This new Soviet practice is thus a grave affront to the whole academic world, and deserves to be fully documented.

The facts are as follows.[2] The titles of 'Candidate of Science', (which is roughly equivalent to a British or American Ph.D.), and of 'Doctor of Science', (which normally requires a further ten years of advanced research), are awarded by a special All-Union body, the Higher Attestation Commission, usually referred to by its Russian initials VAK. This body originally came under the Ministry of Higher and Specialized Education, but in 1974 a resolution of the Central Committee of the Communist Party brought it under the direct control of the Council of Ministers. This involved what the Chairman of VAK, Professor V. G. Kirillov-Ugryumov, described as 'qualitative changes'. In particular, a new regulation came into force on 1 January 1976, requiring postulants for higher degrees to 'combine a profound professional knowledge with a mastery of Marxist-Leninist theory and with the convictions of an active builder of communist society'. In the case of Jewish scientists who have applied to emigrate to Israel, this action itself has been cited as evidence of a lack of such 'convictions', and might be used to 'legitimate' a decision not to award a degree in the first place. But the regulation can scarcely be interpreted as a ground for depriving scientists of the higher degrees *which they had already been awarded*.

Nevertheless, since the spring of 1980, the following scientists have been officially stripped of their academic titles: Yury Medvedkov, Candidate of Geographical Science; Olga Medvedkova, Candidate of Geographical Science; Victor Kipnis, Candidate of Economic Science, Mathematical Statistics and Forecasting Methods; Valery Soifer, Candidate of Biology and Science; Alexander Paritsky, Candidate of Technical Science (design of high-precision ultrasonic devices); Mikhail Fuks Rabinovich, Candidate of Phys-

---

[2] *News Bulletin*, 4; 30 April 1982.

ics and Mathematics (hydrodynamics applied to meteorology); Semion Katz, Doctor of Physics and Mathematics; Leonid Stonov, Candidate of Agricultural Sciences; Yevgeny Gilbo, Candidate of Applied Probability (specializing in control theory); Vladimir Melamed, Doctor of Science. The typical procedure in such cases is described in the following open letter,[3] addressed by Victor Kipnis 'to all scientists in the world who are concerned about the situation of scientists in the Soviet Union':

'In 1971, I graduated from Moscow University with a degree in mathematics. Since August 1971, I have been working in the Scientific Research Institute TSSU of the USSR, where I work on matters connected with applied mathematical statistics and econometrics. In January 1979, I defended my thesis [i.e. was awarded the degree of Candidate]. In March 1980, together with my family, I applied to the Soviet authorities for permission to leave the country and emigrate to Israel to join my (step)sister. As soon as my desire to emigrate became known in the scientific research institute where I work, they began to torment me, in an attempt to force me to resign from my post. After my refusal to leave work "of my own free will", on 19 March 1980 they established a Scientific Council in the institute where it was unanimously agreed to apply to the Supreme Examination Board [i.e. the VAK] with the proposal to deprive me of my degree of Candidate of Sciences because of my request to be allowed to emigrate to Israel. As far as I can find out, the VAK at first refused to confirm this decision until my family and I had left the USSR. But in December 1980 the VAK confirmed the decision of the Scientific Council of my Institute regarding the removal of my degree.

'I was transferred to a considerably lower position with less than half the salary. I am not allowed to partake of any scientific work; my articles are not published in scientific journals or papers. I am prevented from taking part in scientific seminars and conferences, etc. In February 1981, I appealed to the XXVI Conference of the CPSU for the matter to be straightened out. But several months later I received a reply stating that all that had happened was in accordance with Soviet legality.'

In December 1981, Leonid D. Stonov received this one-paragraph letter which nullified years of study and research:[4]

'The VAK of the USSR informs you that following the request of the Scientific-Technical Council of the All-Union Research Institute on

---

[3] Kipnis, V., 'Open letter to scientists of the world', 3 March 1982; republished by the Medical and Scientific Committee for Soviet Jewry, 30 March 1982.
[4] *Science*, 216, 360; 1982.

Chemical Means of Plant Protection addressed to the VAK of the USSR on the 28th January 1981 (Protocol No. 6-1), it deprives you of the academic degree of Candidate of Agricultural Sciences and the academic title of scientific worker. The diploma of the Candidate of Agricultural Sciences No. MSKh 003289 and the certificate of senior scientific worker No. MSNO 27299 are declared to be invalid and should be returned to the offices of the VAK of the USSR at the following address: Moscow, No. 12, Griboyedova St.

Deputy Chief Academic Secretary, (Signed) V. V. Davydov.'

The deprivation of a degree of course affects more than the self-esteem of a scientist. In fact, he ceases to be recognized as a scientific worker. If he still retains some form of employment, he finds himself subordinate to people he had previously supervised. He is denied access to scientific libraries and laboratories. He is deprived of the work stimulus that all scientists need. He is humiliated and may be ostracized by his academic peers. He will eventually face charges of 'parasitism' and may be condemned to a labour camp. These may be the consequences of losing the protection guaranteed by this right.

Respect for 'intellectual property'

Article 27(2) of the UDHR refers not only to the 'moral', but also to the 'material' interests resulting from scientific production. This last is a reference to the rights of 'property' that authors, including scientists, have in their original work. Even in 'capitalist' societies, where the concept of property is familiar enough to the law, the notion of 'intellectual property' is not easily defined: to say that it is 'an aggregate of rights in the results of creative efforts of the mind' does not really take one very far. In practice, what is meant are the rights of copyright, patents, trade marks, and know-how which are protected by the domestic laws of most countries, and about which several international treaties now also exist. These are fertile fields for litigation between individuals and commercial corporations, but they seldom involve basic human rights issues. Here again, the obligation of states under the ICESCR is simply to have such domestic laws in place, and to give their inhabitants effective remedies for any infringement of them.

Even in 'capitalist' countries such as the United States, the intellectual products of individual scientists are sometimes in danger of being 'expropriated' by the state. The fact that much modern scientific research is financed directly or indirectly by governments has raised several controversial questions concerning the 'ownership' of research results. To whom do the data from state-funded research belong: the scientist who does the research or the government agency that pays for it? At what point in the research process are the data to be made available to interested citizens, competing scientists or industrial firms? Should ideas or raw data be publicly available in their tentative stages? Is the public interest best served by withholding data until after peer review of the findings? What obligations of confidentiality does a researcher have to his subjects when personal information is gathered? Does the state have a 'right to know' if it sponsored the research? None of these questions can be answered simply by reference to the international human rights treaties, which do not elaborate on the simple phrase 'moral and material interests'.

For this reason, it is difficult to assess the performance of the Western Helsinki countries in the area of respect for intellectual property. Essentially, this depends on the extent to which 'due process' is available to adjudicate conflicts over ownership, especially where the state itself is involved. Nevertheless, there are important aspects of scientific freedom at issue here. The complexity of these issues can be gauged by examining some of the actual disputes of recent times in the United States.[5]

In 1978, Milo Shannon-Thornberry completed data collection on the socio-economic factors affecting infant feeding practices and the relative effects of bottle and breast feeding on morbidity and mortality rates. A group of non-profit church organizations had sponsored the research. Lacking the resources to convert the data to computer records, Thornberry enlisted the facilities of the Department of Health, Education and Welfare's Centre for Disease Control (CDC) to help in the tabulation. He agreed in return to make the survey material available to the federal agency. In September 1979, two manufacturers of infant-formula powdered milk, Mead-Johnson and Abbott Laboratories, requested the raw data. Thornberry objected. He had collected them with private financing and claimed prior rights to analyse and publish them. He feared that the intent of the request was 'industrial sabotage' of research threatening to corporate interests. In fact, a division of Abbott later circulated to physicians a letter seeking to undermine the

[5] See Nelkin, D., *Science as Intellectual Property* (Macmillan; New York, 1984).

credibility of the research. In April 1980, a Federal District Court held that CDC's possession of the data and its involvement in the project defined the data as 'agency records', and therefore generally accessible. Although CDC's role in the research was mostly clerical, the court considered disclosure to be proper.

James Allen, of the University of Wisconsin, had been working on a long-term, federally funded study of the effect of dioxin on rhesus monkeys. In 1979, he presented preliminary results as testimony during a hearing by the Environmental Protection Agency (EPA) on the dioxin content of commercial herbicides. After the hearing, Dow Chemical Company tried to obtain all the data from Allen's study, arguing that if the results were made public the background data should be available as well. Allen objected, on the ground that the work was not completed or properly analysed, and that the testimony was only a preliminary progress report. An EPA admininstrative law judge granted Dow's request and issued a subpoena, but Allen refused to comply, on the principle of the scientist's right to autonomy. Following this reasoning, a US District Court overturned the ruling, agreeing that disclosure of data to a company with vested interests could jeopardize a costly study, and that the public interest was better served by withholding the data until after peer review. This decision was upheld by a Federal Appeals Court in 1982.

The Department of Health, Education and Welfare (HEW) funded a study by a private research organization to evaluate the accuracy of its project ratings. When interviewing the scientists who had rated the projects, the researchers promised not to reveal their identity. HEW, however, asked for the computer tapes, which contained the names of the respondents. The researchers objected, on ethical grounds, but HEW insisted that a researcher could not promise confidentiality without first obtaining written agency permission. Eventually the researchers released the tapes.

In 1977, a man with leukaemia donated a sample of cancerous cells from his bone marrow to research haematologists at the University of California School of Medicine. The scientists succeeded in establishing a new cell line that could be used to study leukaemia. They sent a sample to a colleague, who discovered that the cell line produced interferon, an important natural regulatory protein with anti-viral properties. That scientist sent his sample to another colleague, who worked at the Roche Institute of Molecular

Biology, funded by the pharmaceutical firm Hoffmann-La Roche. He, in turn, used the sample to develop an optimal medium for the production of interferon. The biotechnology firm Genentech, under contract to Hoffmann-La Roche, then used the cells to manufacture interferon genes, creating the potential for a very profitable enterprise. There followed a dispute between the University of California and Hoffmann-La Roche over the ownership of the genes. The University claimed ownership and the right to future royalties, as the institutional base of the scientists who had created the cell line. Hoffmann-La Roche contested this, and filed a patent application covering both the interferon and the gene-splicing manufacturing process. Lawyers from the University protested, arguing that the firm had made unauthorized use of the material, taking commercial advantage of the open exchange of information and material among academic scientists.

In the summer of 1980, a computer scientist at the Massachusetts Institute of Technology wrote a proposal to work on the mathematical basis for developing computer techniques that would be impervious to code breaking. He applied for a grant from the National Science Foundation (NSF), which has routinely supported cryptography research in the United States. Since 1977, NSF has sent such proposals to the National Security Agency (NSA) for technical review because of their potential significance for intelligence activities. That agency is responsible for the collection of intelligence information, does most of its own research, and has been increasingly uneasy about studies relating to its concerns but outside its control. This particular project was the first basic research of this kind to attract serious attention, and NSA wanted to assume part of the funding so that it could require review for military sensitivity before publication. Mathematicians working in this area were appalled at the idea that their work might be classified as unpublishable, and therefore unavailable for public use—and also would not appear in their personal lists of publications. As we saw in Chapter 6, they negotiated a system of voluntary restraints on publication in exchange for an advisory role in such decisions.

In 'capitalist' countries such as the United States, the right to intellectual property is not absolute, and appears to be circumscribed by a number of other considerations. A researcher's employer may simply own the results of the research under the

contract of employment, so that even scientific findings or hypotheses may not be at the disposal of the person who discovered
them, with the right to disclose them to others or to use them for
his or her own profit. A scientist may contract to turn over the
results of a particular piece of research to the government, a university, or a commercial undertaking, in exchange for sponsorship
or financial or technical support without which the research project
could not have been undertaken or completed: this contract may
then prevent him or her from discussing, publishing, or otherwise
profiting from the research without the employer's consent. On
the other hand, the US Freedom of Information Act—which is
designed to give open access to government information, and so
enhance democratic control of government agencies—may entail
the enforced and early publication of scientific results, and so also
prevent the scientist who made the discovery from using it for his
exclusive advantage. Finally, the government's power to classify
research on grounds of national security or law enforcement can
severely restrict the opportunities for scientists to exploit their
intellectual stock-in-trade.

In the 'socialist' countries of the East, no rights to 'intellectual
property' are acknowledged in domestic law. There are no patents,
trade marks, or copyright. Officially, scientific work can only be
carried out in government institutes and institutions. Plans for
scientific research, as well as its funding, have to be submitted to
and approved by the Academy or the appropriate Ministry in the
context of the general plan laid down by the Party, and funds are
only released by decision of official bodies after confirmation of
the plans by higher authorities. There, it is impossible even in
principle for a scientist to pursue a particular line of research,
using his or her own resources; the laboratories and apparatus
needed for scientific research cannot be sold or hired out to individuals in their own names or to private corporations. Moreover,
under the law relating to 'parasitism', a scientist must work exclusively in a government institution, and may not employ others
as research assistants.

In practice, however, the courtesies of recognition of individual
scientific discovery are generally respected, and scientists of high
status, such as Academicians, can muster very powerful forces to
obtain the facilities which they need, and to defend their 'material
interests' in their intellectual products (see Chapter 7), even

though this form of 'property' is not recognized in the laws of 'socialist' countries.

11

A GENERAL SURVEY

Scientific freedom in the Helsinki countries

In the last seven chapters, we have considered in detail, and in separate categories, the observance and violations in the Helsinki countries of the different rights and freedoms especially important for scientists. We must now try to bring these threads together.

The Helsinki Accords were signed by all the major advanced scientific countries of the world, apart from Japan. Some of the smaller countries in the group—Finland and Austria, for example—have a proportion of scientists in their populations comparable to the larger countries. Some of the medium-sized countries, such as Greece, Turkey, Romania, and Bulgaria, have relatively small scientific communities, but are fully committed to the expansion of their scientific and technological capabilities as a major factor in national economic development. Throughout the region, science is highly respected as an integral part of national and international culture, and scientists have a high standing in society. These are not countries like India or Nigeria, where scientific activity, although of high quality in its own sphere, is swamped by the traditional non-scientific culture of a vast rural society; nor like Bolivia, say, or Papua New Guinea, where the local scientific communities are too small to sustain significant research.

Our investigations have occasionally picked up whispers of crude contempt for personal scientific achievement—the Czechoslovak scientific administrator, for example, who said that he would 'throw out even Einstein if his political views were not quite in order' (see Chapter 6)—but we have found nothing in the countries of our group that is comparable to the Chinese 'cultural revolution', when science itself was officially reviled, and a large proportion of the nation's trained scientists were made to work as unskilled agricultural labourers. The Lysenko episode in the Soviet Union (Chapter 7) is now over, and in no country of the group is there an official ban on the presentation of any scientific theory which does not impinge directly on politics. Indeed, the loudest attack on the free expression of opinion on a broad scientific topic is in the United States, where some Christian fundamentalists are still very active in their campaigns to enforce the teaching of 'creationism' as a science in the public schools of a number of states (Chapters 6 and 7).

Science and technology are not only respected in the Helsinki countries: they are also lavishly supported by governments and private corporations. In the most economically advanced countries of the group, the official indicators show that a significant proportion of the national income—typically, between 1 and 2 per cent—is devoted to research and development. Even in the present period of financial stringency, science in general is a prosperous activity which is not fettered by sheer lack of resources. In some countries, science is suffering from lack of foreign exchange to buy journals and other items which have to be paid for in hard currency. This is particularly so in Poland, but there it is only part of a grave crisis in the economy and polity of the nation as a whole. In some of the 'capitalist' countries of the group, such as the USA and Britain, there is concern about the lack of suitable employment opportunities for trained scientists, but the actual rates of unemployment in the relevant occupational groups remain much below the average for the rest of the population. In these countries, there is much more risk than there was ten or twenty years ago that a scientist might lose his or her right to continue working at a particular job in a particular institution or enterprise, but it seems that a high proportion of those who are thus declared 'redundant' are finding employment elsewhere, though not always in science.

Nevertheless, the material freedom of scientists in the Helsinki countries does not mean that they are also free to follow their scientific bent. In both the 'capitalist' and the 'communist' countries of the Helsinki group, a high proportion of the spending on science goes to military research and development, which is beneficial neither to 'the one world of science' nor to the one world of humankind. Estimates of the proportion vary, but this unproductive activity now involves something like one third of the world's scientific community, whether directly as state employees or indirectly as employees of industrial companies.[1] However

[1] Thee, M., in Rotblat, J., (ed.), *Scientists, the Arms Race and Disarmament*, 51 (Taylor and Francis; London, 1982).

necessary it may be for political reasons, even in a democratic nation such as Britain, science that is so closely linked with the military power of the state can scarcely be considered free.

This linkage between science and war has two significant effects on the individual rights of scientists. One is that it reduces their freedom in the choice of their work (Chapter 5). A science graduate who has conscientious objections to taking part in warlike activity has much less choice of alternative employment than, say, someone with similar views but with medical, legal, or managerial training. A scientist who has worked for a long period in military research and development often finds it very difficult to transfer to another type of scientific work—more difficult, indeed, than the retired soldier with more general skills. This issue is not widely canvassed, even in Western countries where it may be discussed freely, but it certainly affects a number of morally scrupulous people. As the story of Andrei Sakharov and Solzhenitsyn's novel *The First Circle* indicate, it is a serious matter indeed in countries like the Soviet Union, where scientists involved in military research usually have many material privileges, but are firmly segregated from their colleagues in other fields of science.[2]

Secrecy in science

The other effect is to throw a veil of secrecy over a wide range of scientific work. As we saw in Chapter 6, the world of modern science is traversed by vast and impenetrable barriers against the flow of certain types of scientific information. These walls are thicker and higher in the Eastern than in the Western countries, but a similar secretiveness infects all the countries of the Helsinki group, including countries such as Britain and the United States which take pride in being 'open societies'. It is ironical that 'national security' justifies the imposition of constraints on freedom of scientific communication—a freedom that must be part of the very regime of security and co-operation envisaged by the Helsinki Accords.

What our study shows is that the effects of this obsession with secrecy are not confined simply to the communication of scientific information. In the Soviet Union, and in other countries with similar types of government, 'national security' is a blanket phrase used indiscriminately by the authorities to justify a variety of

[2] Medvedev, Zh., *Soviet Science*, (Norton; New York, 1978).

constraints on individual liberty. Almost all the rights of importance to science are thus affected—the right to work, freedom of movement, freedom of opinion and expression, and the rights of association and assembly. It is even used, disingenuously, as an excuse for not permitting elderly scientists to emigrate (Chapter 8), on the pretext that twenty years earlier they were involved in secret research. In these countries, indeed, any communication of information can be regarded officially as a potential threat to 'national security', so that the result of every research project, however innocent in purpose, is considered initially as a state secret which may only be divulged with specific permission.

The penalty for such a breach can be severe. For example, in January 1984 the Praesidium of the USSR Supreme Soviet added to the law concerning criminal responsibility for crimes against the state a new decree, which prescribes punishment of up to 3 years' deprivation of liberty, or up to 2 years' corrective labour, for 'passing to foreign organizations or to their representatives, or compiling for this purpose, economic, scientific, technical, or other information containing official secrets by a person to whom this information has been entrusted for official reasons or at work, or to whom this information became known by some other means'.

Unfortunately, a similar attitude is common in governmental circles in the NATO bloc. The words of the Soviet decree are not dissimilar from those of the Civil Service Pay and Conditions of Service Code in Britain, of which paragraph 9904 states that 'under the Official Secrets Acts 1911 and 1920, it is an offence for any officer to disclose to an unauthorized person, either orally or in writing, any information he has acquired through his official duties unless he has received official permission'. The Code further points out that 'the Official Secrets Acts cover material published in speech, lecture, radio or television broadcast, in press or in book form; they cover non-secret as well as secret information, and apply not only during an officer's employment but also when he has retired or left the service'. Many people regard the British Official Secrets Act 1911 as much too wide in its scope, although any effect it might have in practice on normal scientific communication are difficult to assess. In a country where all scientists are state employees, in the absence of any clear definition of 'official secret' and of a policy of systematic declassification, the 1984 Praesidium decree could result in further inhibition of exchange of information and ideas between scientists in the Soviet Union and the rest of the world.

The latest policies of the US Department of Defence in relation to scientific meetings (Chapter 9) and publications are very significant symptoms of the same trend. There, an attack is being mounted on the fundamental principle that scientific information may be—indeed ought to be—freely published, unless this right has been specifically abrogated before the research is undertaken. The American scientific community is fully alive to this threat to scientific freedom,[3] but the short-sighted doctrine of absolute priority for 'national security' in a strictly military sense is part and parcel of the international insecurity of the modern world.

Commercial secrecy is another constraint on scientific freedom. This effect is not, of course, confined to industrial undertakings in the private sector of 'capitalist' economies: the state industries of 'socialist' countries are also involved in international commerce, and usually classify all their research activities in the first instance as 'state secrets'. Since at least half the scientists in the economically advanced countries are employed in industrial research and development, this can scarcely be a negligible factor, but the actual incidence of commercial secrecy on the advancement of science, as distinct from its technological application, is difficult to assess.

The patent system favours early disclosure of scientific and technological developments, but the temporary monopoly which it confers in return for that disclosure can often be circumvented by competitors who 'design round' the patent. Applying for patents is also expensive, and the cost spirals if one seeks to obtain their protection in more than a few countries. Instead, therefore, manufacturing corporations increasingly try to maintain the exclusivity of new inventions by keeping them secret, and exacting strict obligations of confidentiality from their employees.

In fact, it may well be the case that short-term protection for trade secrets, including the results of proprietary scientific research, is an essential ingredient of a market economy, and that this sort of economy is capable of generating more scientific knowledge, in the long run, than a hypothetical society in which all

[3] Chalk, R., 'Security and scientific communication', *Bulletin of the Atomic Scientists*, August/September 1983; *Science*, Editorial Report on Annual Meeting of the AAAS, 27 July 1984.

scientific information is immediately made public to all and sundry. Whether or not that is so, commercial secrecy is a striking feature of modern science, and is strongly protected by the domestic laws of all the countries in the Helsinki group. There is a growing tendency, even among academic scientists, to hold back publication of discoveries which might be exploited commercially, until after the commercial advantage has been assessed or taken. This trend derives from intensive national competition in world trade and the successes of science itself in creating new industries, such as micro-electronics and biotechnology. The growing number of scientists who become commercial entrepreneurs in such fields may well benefit personally from this, but a number of cases in our study illustrate the pressures it can exert against the individual rights of other scientists.

A scientist employed by a large corporation—whether in the public or the private sector—may put his job at risk if he discloses information, or even expresses technical opinions that are at variance with corporate policy. Such action in support of proprietary secrecy may well be sanctioned by national law, but as several of our cases suggest it is sometimes the means by which dangerous operations or policies are concealed. One of the most serious weaknesses of the state capitalism practised in the 'socialist' countries is that it defines the 'whistle-blower' as a criminal, and thus stifles criticism of what may be ill-advised or incompetently performed projects even when they are on a vast scale. It would be tragic if a similar trend were to manifest itself in the countries which have traditionally protected freedom of expression and opinion.

In some radical circles it is held that science in 'capitalist' countries is not free at all, since it is designed to serve the interests of the bourgeois ruling class. In some conservative circles the same charge is made against 'communist' countries, where science is held to be under the control of the ruling Party. Assessing the validity of either of these views would entail a broad discussion of the rival political ideologies whose mutual hostility is the prime cause of our present troubles. But it is significant that both sides agree that science should *not* be entirely under the control of a particular ruling group in a particular society, but should serve the broader interests of humanity. This is certainly the view that we take ourselves, consistently with our view that international law, serving the same universal interests, must take primacy over sectional interests and ideologies in the matter of human rights.

The most disturbing feature of the present situation is that science in *all* the Helsinki countries is coming more and more under the control of the very large bureaucratic organizations which hold the purse-strings—government departments, 'quasi-non- governmental organizations' such as research councils and state-controlled academies, and commercial firms—and is thus in danger of losing its traditional social function as an independent source of original or critical ideas. This increasing 'collectivization' of science[4] is probably an inevitable result of its increasing technical sophistication, and of the increasing complexity of modern society. Science is no longer a profession where individual researchers may follow their own bent, without regard for the foreseeable social consequences: research nowadays is so expensive that it has to be planned and budgeted for on a large scale, and must therefore be rendered accountable for its actions.

As we shall see in the next chapter, there are great benefits to be won from the direction of scientific effort towards humanitarian and pacific goals. This is where the state-controlled scientific institutions of the 'socialist' countries may have an advantage. In principle (though not always in practice) they are in a position to apply very large resources to projects of general social value, and to push them through without regard to immediate costs. For the very reason that such projects are on so large a scale, their objectives and execution require special scrutiny by knowledgeable persons who have no vested interest in them. However conscientious the planners, they may make mistakes, which will be magnified manifold. This makes it all the more important that the schemes be open to public criticism and review. In practice (whatever may be argued in principle) there is no substitute for openness and democratic accountability in the application of scientific research, as in all the serious business of society. This should be a precondition for the application of science—but one that is far from satisfied in many of the countries of the Helsinki group.

Freedom for scientists in the Helsinki countries
The extent to which scientists can exercise their rights and responsibilities depends on the extent to which science itself is free.

[4] Ziman, J. M., *An Introduction to Science Studies*, Ch. 11 (Cambridge, 1984).

Conversely, freedom for science in any country depends on the freedom allowed to scientists as individuals. This in turn depends on the extent to which their fellow citizens are also free. We have found no evidence to suggest that *scientists* in any of the Helsinki countries are systematically denied rights that are generally available to other people. Indeed, in some of the countries where those rights are severely curtailed for the mass of the population, scientists could even be regarded as relatively privileged in their access to foreign communication and travel, and as having more licence than most to express, within their own technical communities, mildly dissenting opinions on practical matters.

It is of course common knowledge that the Helsinki countries vary widely in the rights that are actually available to their citizens, and that these variations are correlated with differences of political ideology, economic organization, and cultural tradition. It need scarcely be said, for example, that any Soviet citizen seeking to travel abroad will face bureaucratic obstacles which would be regarded as quite intolerable to a citizen of the UK, but which have been practised by Russian rulers for centuries in the name of 'national security'. Similarly, the high cost of medical treatment in the United States, which most UK citizens might regard as a serious limitation on the right to health, is a tradition there, justified by reference to the hallowed principle of private enterprise, and the rooted objection to any form of state regulation of private affairs, which permeate American society. Another contributing factor is the very high level of damages awarded by US juries (to which, under the Seventh Amendment to the Constitution, every civil claimant for more than $20 is entitled) in medical malpractice suits, which in turn inflate both the physicians' insurance premiums and the batteries of expensive tests to which they feel bound to submit their patients if they are not later to be accused of negligence. These are facts of contemporary life which are broadly familiar, often deplored, and fiercely debated, nationally and internationally. It would take us far beyond our present study to survey these variations country by country, or to attempt to explain or justify them by reference to larger issues of principle.

However, it is at least clear that we are not dealing here with any manifestly pathological condition. None of the Helsinki countries is currently in the grip of a tyranny so insane and bloodthirsty as obtained under Adolf Hitler or Josef Stalin. In none of them does the government currently use its army or police to torture and murder its suspected opponents on a truly massive scale. It cannot be said of any of the Helsinki countries that the civil and political rights of its scientists are so grossly and consistently violated that serious and sincere scientific work there has become quite impossible, as has from time to time been the case in some of the world's countries. The era of McCarthyism in the United States, when a number of honest citizens, including a number of scientists, were hounded from their jobs,[5] is also long past.

On the other hand, a number of the countries of the group—all the members of the Warsaw Pact, together with Yugoslavia and Turkey—are ruled by a Party or Junta which brooks no organized public criticism or opposition. This control is exercised systematically through a number of channels, to the extent that any individual who challenges it on sensitive issues faces very severe penalties, legal or extra-legal. These penalties, as we have seen, range from loss of employment, through exile and imprisonment, to cruel forced labour or the abuse of psychiatry. The number of people directly suffering such punishments is not accurately known and varies greatly from one country to another, but judging from what is known about named scientists it seems that no more than a small fraction of the population is directly affected in any country of the group. Generally speaking, public expression of critical opinion (other than by selectively published letters to the newspapers) is cowed by making an example of a few outstanding dissidents, without trying to control private comment in detail. What is especially liable to lead to repression is attempting to organize protest, or sending critical comments abroad. But policies and practices vary from country to country, being modified by cultural factors such as the position of the Catholic Church in Poland, or the corruption that has been endemic for centuries in Bulgaria and Romania.

Suppression of civil and political rights occurs when a country's rulers do not trust, or cannot rely on the support of, those whom they govern. This is most likely to happen when there is a single ruling party, and no opposition to act as a watchdog, and is of course wholly inconsistent with international human rights law. Its general political effects are too well known to be spelled out here. From our point of view, the most significant of these effects

5 See Edsall, J. T., 'Government and the Freedom of Science', *Science* 121, 615; 1955.

is to compromise the role of science as an independent factor in public affairs, and to strip scientists of the sense of personal responsibility for the social consequences of their work. Without the means to make public their informed concern on such matters as environmental pollution, biomedical ethics, or nuclear weapons, they tend to become uncaring and cynical, and an important component of their professional expertise is lost to society. As we have already noted, the sort of science that is done in such conditions cannot always be assumed to be the best that might be done for a nation or for humanity, and scientists subject to these constraints are sometimes hard put to it to make a genuine contribution to 'the one world of science' on those occasions when these social concerns come up for discussion.

In practice, however, normal scientific work seldom involves scientists individually in politically sensitive issues. Unlike, say, journalists and lawyers, they are not usually directly affected professionally by general constraints on their civil and political rights. From the evidence available to us, it does seem that most of them, in most countries, simply accept and conform to the political and social conditions under which they live, and try to get on with their research. Their discontents are directed primarily at practical deficiencies in the research environment—inadequate apparatus and other technical resources, incompetent management, excessive bureaucracy, poor access to information, unfair promotion practices, and so on. Such deficiencies, and the discontents to which they give rise, are to be found everywhere, and are not the monopoly of any particular political system. As we have indicated, many of them are due simply to poverty: countries such as Greece and Turkey, or Romania and Bulgaria, simply do not have the economic resources to endow science at the same level as East or West Germany.

Some of these deficiencies are also connected, indirectly, with national policies towards the rights of individuals. It is quite clear from our studies that the retrogression of basic biology in Czechoslovakia, for example, is due to government practices that are deliberately designed to obstruct communication between Czechoslovak scientists and their colleagues in the West. In fact, there is direct quantitative evidence that scientific activity has declined significantly in that country since 1968, almost certainly because of political constraints on scientists and other intellectuals.[6] By contrast, in Hungary, where people in general are much freer to express their opinions and to travel abroad, scientists have less cause to complain about this feature of their working conditions. As we have already noticed, there is much international concern about the Polish lack of foreign exchange for scientific journals: the effects on Polish science of recent drastic changes of government policy on fundamental freedoms of expression and association are much more difficult for an outsider to assess.

Generally speaking, therefore, the scientific community in the region covered by the Helsinki Accords is not in a violent ferment about the individual rights of its members. In all the 'capitalist' countries except Turkey, most of the rights covered by international law are reasonably well respected, and the means exist—through the legal system, the press, or the normal processes of democratic government—to take up cases of injustice or to reform unjust policies. On the other hand, in all the 'communist' countries except perhaps Yugoslavia, most scientists take care not to test openly the actual limitations on their rights, knowing that persistent overt dissent will be severely punished. Where these limitations have been questioned on a large scale, as in Czechoslovakia in the 'Prague Spring' of 1968 and in Poland before the imposition of Martial Law on 13 December 1981, the movement has not originated in the scientific community, although as our case studies have shown individual scientists have played an important part in events, for which some have paid dearly. Just a few very brave scientists—notably Andrei Sakharov, Yuri Orlov, and Alexander Shcharansky in the Soviet Union, and Robert Havemann in the GDR—have stood up for the general human rights Articles of the Helsinki Accords: most of the rest have kept their heads down—perhaps prudently, considering what has happened to the overt dissidents—and got on with their work. Their discontents are expressed in such a piecemeal and sporadic fashion that it is very difficult to say whether they are broadly satisfied with the situation, or whether they merely accept it in silence as a grim reality.

In recent years, this quietism has been significantly disturbed by only two human rights issues involving scientists. The first of

---

[6] Janouch, F., 'Science under siege in Czechoslovakia', *Bulletin of the Atomic Scientists*, April 1976.

these is sharply localized, but very nasty—the deliberate abuse of psychiatric facilities and procedures against perfectly sane people accused of political dissent. As we saw in Chapter 7, a small number of Soviet scientists came to appreciate the enormity of this activity, and spoke up against it. The harsh treatment they received is not only a grave offence against their own freedom of responsible expression: it also suggests that the Soviet authorities are aware of the disquiet felt by many members of their own scientific and medical communities on this subject, and are concerned to stamp out any internal criticism of a practice that has now become deeply institutionalized in their political system, and seems to be founded on the assumption that only someone sick in mind would wish to suffer the penalties incurred by systematic criticism of that political system. As we shall see in Chapter 13, the history of the international campaign against these abuses of psychiatry illustrates the strengths and weaknesses of action in support of international human rights law when the formal machinery of that law fails to redress a manifest wrong. (It is also worth recalling, in this general survey of the situation, that a narrow-minded official tendency to treat outright non-conformists as if they were slightly mad is not confined to 'communist' countries: the essential point is that in an open society any such tendency can be kept in check by public exposure and the rule of law.)

The other serious human rights issue affecting scientists directly is much broader and less specific: it is racial, religious, cultural, and political discrimination in education and employment. Here again, we touch upon a matter that seems to affect all human societies. The most extreme example at the present time is obviously South Africa, where a young black or 'coloured' person has practically no chance of getting a proper scientific training, however gifted he or she may be. If we had been writing only twenty or thirty years ago, we would have had to deplore a similar situation in the southern United States. Even now, in the United States and in Britain, racial prejudices and stereotypes create significant disadvantages for black students entering higher education, even though sincere efforts are made officially to combat them.

Educational discrimination against Jewish students is a feature of another ancient tradition of European culture, namely the anti-semitism which culminated in the horrors of Nazism. For reasons that are often debated but still not well understood, a disproportionate number of Jews seem to have an aptitude for science, or at least seek scientific careers, so that the effects of discrimination against them are often serious for science itself. At the present time, the only country in the Helsinki group that discriminates systematically against Jews in higher education and scientific research seems to be the Soviet Union (Chapter 4). As a consequence, Jews living in that country have a strong incentive to leave it; and many have sought to emigrate, in order to retain their Jewish traditions in an intellectual climate which they can respect, as for example in Israel. The Soviet authorities interpret this as a criticism of all aspects of their society, which it only very rarely is— though the victims of discrimination can often see more clearly than others what is wrong with the system in which they all live. There is a large number of Jews in the Soviet Union which includes many professional scientists, so that the exodus of this whole group would be a more serious matter for the Soviet authorities than the emigration of any other religious and cultural minorities. The case of the Jewish 'refuseniks' is complicated by such matters as the policies of the new state of Israel, but it has led to many other violations of human rights of importance to scientists, and undoubtedly remains a major human rights issue cutting across 'the one world of science'.

Underlying factors

At this point, it would be tempting to essay some kind of aetiology of oppression: to put forward hypotheses—and perhaps even a coherent theory or two—about why some governments in some countries are more prone than others to violate some of the human rights of some of their inhabitants. But this is a temptation we must resist, for it falls outside the areas of our competence. Besides, even the political philosophers and political scientists who have made this their special field of study differ profoundly, and often violently, on this question.

But the empirical evidence which we have examined leads to two quite clear conclusions. The first may be trite, but it cannot be reasserted too often: no political or economic system can claim any monopoly of good, or justify an accusation of a monopoly of evil, in the field of human rights. Within our 'Helsinki' set of 35 states, it is plain that the worst offenders all fall within the 'communist' group, and the 'capitalist' ones collectively come off much better. But then the 'Helsinki' group does not include avowedly 'capitalist' countries like South Africa or Chile, whose different records are just as deplorable as those of the USSR, nor countries like Iran and Uganda, which do not claim allegiance to either camp but where some horrifying things have recently happened.

The other conclusion is that there is no simple or facile answer to the question. History, geography, culture, and psychology seem to be quite as important factors as ideology. There is nothing particularly 'communist', for example, about despatching dissidents into internal exile: the Czars of the Russian Empire were doing it long before communism was invented. Likewise, nepotism and corruption are nothing new in the Balkans: they were endemic there long ago, when Bulgaria and Romania still formed part of the Ottoman or the Habsburg Empires. Nor is there a simple correlation with national poverty or lack of economic development: by world standards, the USSR, Iran, and South Africa are all quite rich.

If any correlation *is* discernible, it is rather with institutional constraints on the exercise of power: by and large, the level of all kinds of human rights violations seems to be at its lowest where those who exercise public power are chosen in free, secret, and frequent elections by those over whom they exercise it; where the performance of all power-holders, public and private, is constantly scrutinized by countervailing institutions such as trade unions, and by a free, plural, watchful and critical press; and where the propriety of everyone's actions, even those of the most mighty, can be tested at any time before independent tribunals, presided over by an independent and impartial judiciary assisted by an independent legal profession, and operating under the rule of law. Such domestic tribunals can and do protect human rights at the national level, and so facilitate their nations' compliance with the obligations they have undertaken in international law.

It so happens that, among the 'Helsinki' countries, these constraints on the exercise of power operate reasonably well most of the time in most of the 'capitalist' group, but they operate very sparsely, if at all, in most of the 'communist' group.[7] Doubtless there are good reasons for this, but we prefer to leave it to others to decide what they are.

---

[7] For a recent discussion of the role of 'legality' in the USSR, see Wrobel, B., 'Legality and illegality in Soviet criminal procedure'; *Yearbook of Socialist Law* (The Hague, 1985).

12

ONE SCIENCE FOR MANY NATIONS

Transnational science and individual freedom

The obstacles to the realization of 'the one world of science' are well enough known. Scientific organizations and governments address themselves to overcoming them, by a variety of means. What is far less well understood is that the whole notion of fostering transnational science for the benefit of international co-operation and security is self-defeating if national governments regard scientific research as an activity that must be made entirely subservient to their own interests, in peace or in war. One of the main theses of this book is that the effective existence of transnational science depends fundamentally on scientists being reasonably free to play their part in it as individuals, and not simply as state functionaries or as employees of commercial corporations.

Our study of the actual situation in the most scientifically advanced region of the world supports this thesis in detail. The infrastructure of transnational science — communication links, publication media, administrative organs, etc. — obviously cannot be improved unless scientists are able to communicate and travel internationally without serious hindrances and delays. Yet, as we saw in Chapters 6 and 8, a number of governments do impose such hindrances on all their citizens, including scientists. When this happens, their scientists are excluded from conferences, international projects, exchange visits, etc. which are also being hampered by limitations on freedom of assembly and association, and of expression and opinion, noted in Chapters 7 and 9. The usual method by which scientific ideas travel round the world — that is, inside people — is gravely restricted by official constraints on freedom of movement, including emigration (Chapter 8), and by the difficulties of getting scientific employment in many countries (Chapter 5). Again, educational discrimination (Chapter 4) is often linked with language issues, in circumstances where there can be little prospect of broadening the education of scientists to fit them for transnational research.

These are not only problems for science; they also pose moral problems for scientists. Transnational science brings scientists together as individuals, and gives them the opportunity to learn something of the social and cultural conditions in which they each work. When a scientist with whose work one is familiar, with whom one may have discussed scientific questions, and perhaps even formed a personal friendship, is subjected to grave injustice, this becomes something of a personal insult. Scientists normally manage to dissociate their strictly scientific work from the political background within which they operate, and are usually willing, when there is good reason, to collaborate scientifically with persons working under governments and corporations whose ideologies they deplore. But they are less able to overlook the plight of a respected colleague whose personal rights have been grossly violated—by dismissal from employment, by deprivation of honour and intellectual achievement, or, more brutally, by unjust imprisonment, exile, torture, or death. As we have seen in the previous chapters, such violations of individual rights continue to occur in some of the Helsinki countries, and they are apt to poison the atmosphere of transnational science in that region of the world.

Members of the international scientific community are thus faced with a dilemma. The whole spirit of transnational science is one of co-operation: scientists of every nation wish to do as much as they can to work with their colleagues in other nations, in a common cause. But to act in support of the human rights of some of those colleagues, they have to make known their criticism in public or in private to those who have violated these rights—that is, the very governments and other authorities that organize and control transnational science in practice. They feel that they should give priority to the positive values of co-operation—solving common problems, breaking down intellectual and cultural barriers, setting up joint projects and institutions, advancing technical knowledge, and so on; yet they have to balance this against their moral duty to react openly against cruelty and injustice, especially where it affects the workings of science itself, and thus adopt an attitude of non-co-operation and protest.

This dilemma will be discussed more fully in the final chapter, where we consider what can be done, by scientists especially, to strengthen and enhance the machinery of international law to protect freedom in science. But before we turn to those proposals, we must outline at least some of the ways in which the free and co-operative pursuit of transnational science could contribute to the betterment of our divided world.

Détente through science

The fundamental political purpose of the Helsinki Conference on Security and Co-operation in Europe ('CSCE') was to ease the tensions driving the nations of Europe into warlike confrontation. A major premiss of the Final Act is that transnational science is an effective instrument for this policy of *détente*. Co-operation in the one world of science is seen as one of the ways to security for many nations.

The disappointing history of the 'CSCE process' since the Final Act was signed in August 1975 merely emphasizes the desirability of such a policy. Military and diplomatic relationships between the NATO and Warsaw Pact groupings are more polarized and bitter than ever. There is little sign of any reconciliation between the two superpowers, the United States and the Soviet Union, whose antagonism springs from fundamental differences in their political and economic cultures. This is the harsh international climate in which our present study was born: we cannot pretend that the situation is otherwise, or that it will be significantly changed by what we say here.

Nevertheless, our investigation has confirmed in detail that science is indeed an activity that transcends national frontiers. The diametrically opposed cultures of the two blocs are united in their respect for, and their use of, science. All the nations which signed the Final Act, for example, accept the validity of the laws of thermodynamics, undertake research to clarify and extend those laws, and put enormous efforts into applying them technologically.

By an ironic paradox, the nuclear warheads and rocket motors that face one another so fearsomely across the Iron Curtain are derived, even-handedly, from just those universal laws of nature. But that is a perversion of a vital principle. There never was a time in which there was a more urgent need for universal *human* laws to preserve the peace of the world. As we have seen, such laws already exist, although they are still far too feebly enforced. Science and law, running in parallel, can be linked in practice. We have emphasized the role of international law as a means of protecting science and scientists in a disharmonious world. But the linkage also works the other way. Every step to extend the one world of science on behalf of international harmony reinforces the rule of law as a means of achieving and preserving precisely that harmony.

The deep involvement of science in war-making is not to be denied. Technologies based on science are a *threat* to co-operation and security in Europe. A cynical interpretation of the Helsinki Accords is that the Articles on human rights in Basket III were diplomatic bargaining counters to be set against the Articles on technical co-operation in Basket II: 'We will give you more access to our technological information if you will not imprison dissidents. ' But there is just as much truth, and a nobler purpose, embodied, for example, in a resolution of the United Nations Commission on Human Rights,[1] when it:

'1. Expresses its firm conviction that all peoples and all individuals have an inherent right to life, and that the safeguarding of this foremost right is an essential condition for the enjoyment of the entire range of economic, social and cultural, as well as civil and political, rights;

2. Stresses the urgent need for all possible efforts by the international community to strengthen peace, remove the threat of war, particularly nuclear war, halt the arms race and achieve general and complete disarmament under effective international control, thus contributing to assuring the right to life;

3. Calls upon all States to take the necessary measures to ensure that the results of scientific and technical progress are used exclusively in the interests of international peace and for the benefit of mankind and for promoting and encouraging respect for human rights and fundamental freedoms without distinction as to race, sex, language or religion . . .'

Co-operation in scientific work

As Basket II of the Helsinki Final Act makes clear, there are urgent and primarily non-political problems common to the whole world. Scientists have at least some of the information needed to foresee these problems, and they are often expected to find the answers to them. It must be admitted that many of them are not educated to look much beyond the boundaries of their immediate jobs and their national frontiers, or to comprehend the importance of the

---

[1] *Bulletin of Human Rights*, 35, 7; January/March 1982.

collective knowledge and effort which constitute 'the one world of science'. Nevertheless there are international bodies, official and unofficial, which have begun to tackle some of these problems, and through them essential scientific co-operation takes place which transcends perceived national interests. This is one of the most important ways in which the role of science as a transnational institution and of scientists as a transnational community can be fostered. It is also a means of improving personal contacts between scientists of different countries, even in the present climate of government and media-inspired antipathy on both sides of the Iron Curtain.

International scientific co-operation is already a reality in many fields of research. It is achieved in various ways, sometimes through official bodies such as the World Health Organization, the Food and Agriculture Organization, UNESCO, and the International Council of Scientific Unions (on which are represented the international unions concerned with the various branches of natural science, and the national academies or their equivalents); sometimes through bilateral arrangements between governments, sometimes through the operation of multi-national companies, and sometimes quite informally by agreement between individual scientists. Even during periods of international tension government-sponsored projects of this kind may continue without break.

The range of these activities is seldom appreciated by the outsider. It is instructive to look at some of them, in order to appreciate their value to humanity. The following list is not exhaustive:

Long-term weather prediction. This involves feeding local weather information for many countries into powerful computers, with the aim of eventually being able to predict the weather in any part of the world sufficiently well to enable farmers to sow, protect, and reap their crops much better and more safely.

Earthquake and volcanic prediction. Since earthquakes and volcanic eruptions depend upon movements of the earth's crust which extend across national frontiers, the sharing of information and theory about this phenomenon becomes essential even for local forecasting.

Effects on the stratosphere of carbon dioxide, fluorocarbons, and oxides of nitrogen. The possibility of significant heating of the earth's atmosphere due to the 'greenhouse' effect from increased concentration of carbon dioxide is now being taken seriously.

Predictions depend upon knowledge not only of the rate of combustion of fossil fuels (mainly coal and oil), but also of the production of carbon dioxide by organisms in the soil, and its removal by green plants and by dissolving in the oceans. Fluorocarbons from aerosols, and oxides of nitrogen produced by nuclear explosions or even by aeroplanes flying through the stratosphere, could deplete the ozone layer which protects the planet from strong ultraviolet irradiation, damaging to both plants and animals. These effects can only be studied on a global scale.

Stability of the biosphere. The existing atmosphere, with stable concentrations of oxygen, nitrogen, and other gases, is maintained largely by the balanced action of plants which produce oxygen and of other creatures which consume it. Major deforestation, and the conversion to desert of fertile soil or even bush, could seriously diminish the renewal of oxygen. International surveillance of these trends is therefore recognized as essential.

Exploitation of the oceans. The ecology of the oceans depends upon many factors—deep currents which affect temperature, the movement of essential nutrients, wind, etc.—all of which affect the growth of the algae and the krill on which fish and other creatures feed. As factory fishing and whaling have increased, the rate at which commercially used fish are harvested has in many cases exceeded their rate of reproduction. The results are poor catches and, in the case of some species of whale, the risk of extinction. Only if scientists of different nations can agree among themselves about the data, and about the legitimacy of predictions from them, can proper advice be provided about the permissible limits to exploitation of the seas. Whether or not the advice is followed, and long-term interests are put before short-term ones, is of course a political and often bitterly controversial matter.

Arid lands. In many tropical and subtropical countries, lands with low rainfall are turning into desert. The cause is thought to be faulty use of vegetation by man and domestic cattle, but this is a complex issue which demands the pooled experience of natural and social scientists from different countries.

Preservation and exploitation of genomes and genetic material. Man has adapted plants and animals to his uses by breeding (initially from wild species) for thousands of years. We have only recently come to realize the importance of preserving wild species, each of which has become adapted to its habitat by natural selection over very many generations. These species—apart from their intrinsic interest or value—contain genes which could be used to confer new properties on other species. The ability to transfer genes from one species to another has now been developed and continues to improve, but all over the world existing and possibly valuable species of plant and animal are being eliminated, mainly by human activity. International efforts to classify and preserve genetic materials before it becomes too late are recognized as enormously important, and 'banks' to preserve them have been set up.

Epidemic diseases. Infectious diseases do not respect national frontiers so long as insects, animal vectors, and humans can cross them. Surveillance of infectious diseases and attempts to combat them have long been areas in which international co-operation has been practised: the final elimination of smallpox illustrates how successful such co-operation can be.

Long-term energy resources. During the past fifty years, it has frequently been predicted that the world would soon run short of usable fossil fuels. Although the more pessimistic forecasts have been falsified through the discovery of hitherto untapped deposits, the prediction is sound in basic principle. The use of nuclear fission reactors to provide electricity has produced one solution to the problem, but only at the expense of accumulating large quantities of radioactive wastes which it may not prove easy to dispose of safely. In principle, a much safer and virtually inexhaustible source of energy could be provided by the fusion of hydrogen atoms at very high temperatures, as occurs in the sun and stars. But the technical problems of achieving controlled fusion are enormous, and may yet prove to be insurmountable. The apparatus involved is so costly that no single country has been able to 'go it alone' in testing all the possible ways of tackling the problem, and it is essential that experience be shared world-wide. Co-operation on fusion research between physicists and engineers in the industrially advanced countries of East and West has in fact proceeded smoothly on a large scale, despite the ups and downs of political relations between them.

Fundamental particle physics, radio astronomy, and space research. Our notions about the fundamental nature of matter, and about the origin and evolution of the universe, have been revolutionized during the past two decades as a result of observations made by scientists using apparatus to study the collision of particles moving at very high velocities, and also detectors mounted on satellites orbiting in space, or spacecraft sent to explore the planets. In some instances, the facilities have been built by single very large countries (the USA and the USSR), and in others by shared contributions from small countries (e.g. the giant particle accelerator of CERN at Geneva), but the scientists of all nations have benefited from their use.

Telecommunications. One of the greatest changes which has affected society all over the world has been the ability to communicate rapidly between one place and another by radio, television, and data links. A volcanic eruption, a war, a football match, or a visit by the Pope, wherever it takes place, can be heard or seen all over the world as it happens. Vast amounts of technical or commercial information can be moved around the world, in digital form, in fractions of seconds. However, radio frequency signals must be transmitted through space on narrow wavebands, and the useful wavebands have become seriously overcrowded, especially because of the reservation of bands for military communications. Other activities which generate electromagnetic waves can also interfere with radio communications. Out of sheer necessity, scientists from all countries which use telecommunications have had, and will continue to have, to co-operate in the allocation of wavebands for civilian, military, and scientific purposes.

Fostering transnational science

As we have seen, it is impossible to separate these long-term, large-scale projects from political, military, and industrial interests. Government policies and commercial profits are involved in the agricultural 'development' of the forest areas of the Amazon basin, the creation of genetic material banks, research into acid rain produced by industrial coal-burning, the exploitation of marine life, the development of renewable energy resources, satellites and space research, the sharing of radio frequency wavebands, and even in geophysical information which is relevant to detecting underground nuclear explosions or the concealment or detection of submarines. Scientists involved in the many projects outlined above are inevitably subject to internal or external pressures of national self-interest, and are often forced to tailor their findings to fit these interests. Yet scientific knowledge is only valid—only useful—if it has been reached by an unprejudiced search for facts, by sincere criticism and tests of hypotheses, and by mutual trust in the objectivity of the data. This approach to practical problems—the so-called 'scientific attitude'—is not sustained by mere technique: it is developed in the course of scientific work, learnt by young scientists from their elders, and passed on as a living tradition within the scientific community. It would quickly degenerate if this community were not a reality on a world-wide basis, actively engaged in scientific activities where these norms are openly observed and seen to be effective. In short, the material and social benefits of science and technology are closely linked to the health of science as a transnational institution in its own right.

Science in this sense—as a process of discovery, as well as a means of solving practical problems—is thus a fundamental ingredient of the security of the world and of the protection of human rights. It is not only the source of quite unexpected concepts, with entirely novel capabilities: it is also a 'gene bank' for the personal attitudes, styles of thought and argument, and interpersonal relations which make science so effective as a practical instrument. This is why Basket III of the Helsinki Accords concentrates on the means by which transnational science can be preserved and fostered as a 'cultural' force. Without such protection of its fundamental and universal standards, the science and technology of Basket II would become completely subservient to political and commercial expediency, and would lose much of its value as a means of achieving beneficial ends.

As we have already indicated, many of these large-scale, international, scientific projects are essentially 'discovery-oriented', and thus directly strengthen the world scientific community. This is particularly obvious in some of the basic sciences such as high energy physics, where international research teams collaborate with remarkable efficiency and harmony to carry out elaborate experiments in international institutions; or in human genetics, where regular international workshops are held at which the findings and methods used by geneticists all over the world are compared and checked for their validity. But transnational science is very dependent on an infrastructure of transnational communication, education, and exchange. This infrastructure needs to be strengthened in a number of practical ways.

Improving communication, education, and exchange

The communication system of science has many deficiences as a transnational network. The enormous bulk of the scientific literature has already been noted in Chapter 6: many countries cannot spare the foreign exchange to obtain adequate collections of journals and books for all their scientific libraries, so that their scientists may be put to great trouble and expense simply to consult a published paper. The practice of republishing some of the major journals, in the original language or in translation, is a makeshift device that is only feasible for a large country such as the Soviet Union, and does nothing to help the straitened finances of scientists in smaller countries. There is a good case for establishing a general procedure, on the model of the system of UNESCO coupons, whereby foreign scientific publications can be purchased with local currency credited to a central fund. The world system of scientific communication would also benefit from reductions in the costs, and improvements in the services, of the international postal system. Postal communications with some countries are scandalously hindered by inefficient bureaucratic procedures such as customs clearance, which often hold up and greatly add to the cost of scientific specimens and instruments, and can so delay the transit of short-lived or perishable materials that they are useless by the time they arrive.

The fact is that, if transnational science is to prosper, its infrastructure must take account of its transnational character. It is customary nowadays for international scientific conferences and congresses to take place under the auspices of international scientific unions, such as the International Union of Pure and Applied Chemistry (IUPAC), which brings together all the national learned societies concerned with a particular subject. These unions, in turn, are brought together in the International Council of Scientific Unions (ICSU), where the national scientific academies, such as the Royal Society, are also represented. However weak these organizations may be administratively, they have a genuine claim to speak for world science, and there is no doubt that their activities and functions ought to be augmented and strengthened.

A characteristic institution of world science is the international scientific journal. A journal produced by a national learned society, publishing articles drawn from a single country, usually covers too wide a range of subjects to appeal to scientists in other countries with highly specialized interests. For this reason, many journals are now deliberately produced for the world readership in a narrow specialty. Such a journal, whether published by a national learned society or by a commercial publisher, will be managed by an international editorial committee, will select its referees from scientists in different countries, and will publish papers by any competent scientific author, regardless of nationality. Thus (as one example amongst many), the editorial boards of the various sections of the *Journal of Physics*, which is published by the Institute of Physics in London, include members from all the countries belonging to the European Physical Society—that is, most of the countries of Eastern and Western Europe.

An inescapable problem for transnational science is the choice of language. There can be no doubt that written scientific communication is most efficiently conducted in a world-wide *lingua franca*, and that English—or, more precisely, 'Broken English'— has for historical reasons become firmly established in this role. Nevertheless, there are very sound reasons why scientists should not be forced to use just this one language, even for their formal communications. People find it easier to learn, and to express themselves, in their mother tongue than they do in a second language which they may have learnt later in life, and only imperfectly. Every nation is attached to, and proud of, its own language (or languages), and has a perfect right to protect its national culture. This is a delicate political issue, which has far wider implications than science and technology. Yet if journals produced in other languages are to make a contribution to transnational science— that is, to scientific knowledge in general—they need to make the substance of their articles accessible in English, by complete translations or at least by including an English summary of each paper.

Even though most scientists nowadays can puzzle through a written communication in the technical jargon of scientific English, many scientists in many great nations have little opportunity to learn it well enough to speak it fluently and understand it when spoken. This can prove to be a grave handicap in the direct, face-to-face communication that is so fruitful in international scientific conferences, and so essential in the management of the institutions of transnational science. The same applies to scientists from English-speaking countries, when they try to take part in the national meetings of scientists in other countries. An important component in the infrastructure of transnational science must be the means by which scientists learn a second language (and a third and a fourth, if necessary) in order not to be cut off from direct verbal communication with colleagues elsewhere.

Competence in foreign languages is only one element in the education which scientists need in order to fit themselves properly for 'the one world of science'. The educational tradition in science is narrow and vocational. This narrowness is enhanced by fierce competition for employment, especially in times of economic stringency. The misconceptions and prejudices of scientific nationalism and technical élitism can only be overcome by more general education, including some account of the ways in which the practical applications of basic science have come about, and the manner in which fundamental discoveries and inventions have been made, applied, and used by nationals of different countries. It might be said that participation in the transnational activities of science is itself an informal education in world citizenship: nevertheless, those who are technically trained to take part in these activities often need some formal preparation for the cultural and political background of life outside their own countries.

A very effective means of strengthening science transnationally is through scientific 'exchanges'—that is, individual scientists visiting and working in foreign scientific institutions for periods ranging from a few weeks to a year or more. In many cases, such visits are arranged privately: a British professor, for example, might choose to spend a sabbatical year at a French university, and might be offered a temporary appointment to cover the additional expenses of the stay. But such private arrangements are often difficult to establish, and there are now many official 'exchange programmes' to facilitate such visits. These programmes are often organized through national academies, and normally work on the principle that the sending country pays for travel, whilst accommodation and living expenses are paid in local currency by the receiving country. Other programmes which are not limited to strict exchange, but are based on opportunity and need, are run by international organizations such as the World Health Organization and the European Molecular Biology Organization, or by private foundations. Although the numbers are limited, such exchanges have proved an invaluable means of enabling individual scientists to experience scientific life and work in other countries. This applies particularly to exchanges between 'capitalist' and 'communist' countries, whose scientists often have grave misconceptions about each other.

Scientific exchange programmes are not, of course, without their problems. Knowledge of the language of the country to be visited may be very imperfect, and it may not be possible to arrange for the visitor to be accompanied by his or her family. Generally speaking, scientists are at ease with one another in their shared scientific interests, but this may not apply outside the laboratory. A visitor who is a state employee may have been instructed to act and speak circumspectly about working conditions and scientific achievements at home—and may, on the other hand, be regarded with some suspicion in the host country.

Outsiders sometimes allege that the main purpose of such exchange visits is industrial or scientific espionage. These allegations have never been validated. It is extremely important that there should be no foundation for them, since the whole function of scientific exhanges would be undermined if the scientists involved were engaged in any other mission than the free exchange of unclassified information and experience. Because of their symbolic significance as indicators of co-operation between nations, the official programmes are often curtailed in times of international tension. This has happened, for example, between the USA and the USSR, in response to the Soviet invasion of Afghanistan. In such circumstances, individual scientists may decide against undertaking visits to a country whose political system or political actions they deplore. In the long run, however, these programmes have to be seen as the means by which personal contact is established between scientists—and other citizens—of countries which may be very isolated from one another, and where unflattering stereotypes may have been created of each other's people.

In ways such as these, transnational science can be fostered and extended. But its proper functioning for the benefit of mankind is critically dependent on the parallel fostering and extension of respect for human rights—for people in general, and for scientists in particular. In our final chapter, we shall therefore outline some ways in which scientists can contribute to that endeavour more effectively than they yet do.

13

SUSTAINING HUMAN RIGHTS

Supporting international law

If people whose rights have been violated are to benefit from the international law of human rights, then *other* people must help them. In this final chapter we consider the various ways in which scientists can help other scientists, in their own or other countries. This is not to say, of course, that scientists should be less concerned about the fate of humanity in general than about the fate of their scientific colleagues. Nor does it mean that the fate of scientists need not concern the rest of humanity. As we have made clear throughout this study, freedom in science and for scientists is inseparable from freedom in society and for people in general. In this chapter, as in the rest of the book, we are concentrating on just one small part of a topic that percolates into every corner of politics, ethics, and law.

In principle, every person whose rights have been infringed should be able to seek a legal remedy for the infringement, first at home, and in the last resort at the international level. In practice, such a remedy may be difficult to obtain even at home; and a wronged person is seldom in a position to set in motion, unaided, the machinery of enforcement of international law which is remote, complex, and often unresponsive. Little can be done without the positive desire and organized efforts of enough people to make themselves heard on behalf of such individual calls for justice, and to amplify them in private and in public until justice is done.

Systematic support for human rights involves three activities: monitoring, validating, and sustaining. The situation needs to be continually *monitored*, to detect cases that might need support, to provide a network for receiving and co-ordinating reports of violations of rights, and to become aware of policies and practices affecting whole groups. Each claim for support then needs to be *validated*, by collecting and verifying the relevant facts and relating them to the detailed provisions of the human rights code. Finally, valid cases need to be *sustained* by a variety of means, ranging from informed approaches to initiating formal legal proceedings and organizing public protests on behalf of the victims. In practice, these activities merge into one another, but they may all be needed. Unless rights are regularly monitored, they are easily transgressed by authorities which can intimidate individual victims. Unless there are well-founded facts to justify it, a case cannot be taken to court or strongly supported in other ways. Unless this support is bold and determined, it is easily defeated by official denial or obfuscation.

These are broad and obvious considerations. The actual work of sustaining human rights, in science as in other sectors of society, is essentially practical. It is seldom difficult to realize that an injustice has been done, and that something should be done about it: the problem is usually to win allies and to devise some means of influencing very powerful opponents who do not acknowledge the injustice. In this chapter, therefore, we look mainly at the various organizations in the scientific world through which actions can be taken, and the various means they can employ to make them effective.

There is one problem of principle, however, which often faces scientists when they take part in such activities. The information that is available about a particular case is seldom so complete that one can be sure of knowing all the relevant facts: it is therefore often argued that action should be deferred until the facts can be determined with absolute certainty. This appeal to criteria which might apply to a scientific undertaking is often used by those scientists who speak on behalf of the oppressing authorities in order to delay criticism. It is also used by well-meaning scientists to rationalize their unwillingness to get involved in such matters. But it is not a sound argument. Legal decisions are not like scientific theories, whose final acceptance can be put off until they have been made convincing beyond any possible shadow of doubt. They have to be arrived at on the basis of the best available evidence, according to reasonable principles of inference, within the framework of a formal code: for justice delayed is almost always justice denied.

It is of the essence of cases where important human rights are at stake that they have to be sustained against authorities who will not agree the facts or their interpretation, and will not help an investigation. As much as possible should therefore be done to validate a claim that is initially based upon fragmentary information—but not to the extent of allowing a patent injustice to continue without protest.

Ad hoc action

Apart from the Holy See, Monaco, San Marino, and the USA, all the countries that signed the Helsinki Accords have adhered to one or more of the binding treaties of international human rights law (see Appendix 3). This means that they are bound to protect these same rights by their national laws. Yet, as we have seen throughout this book, in many of the Helsinki countries the national laws do not protect all these rights, and there are numerous cases where the guaranteed rights of an individual have been ruthlessly infringed by the very government that is legally bound to protect them. What is to be done then?

Clearly, the first thing to be established is whether in fact the law still rules in such a place. It is strange how seldom this question is actually asked or tested in countries with tyrannical regimes, which none the less continue to protest that they observe the rule of law. Yet, on occasions when it is, the results can sometimes prove surprisingly effective: it suddenly dawns on officials, prosecutors, and judges alike that a flagrant breach of legality will undermine a government's legitimacy more certainly, and more profoundly, than any act of mere administrative arbitrariness— especially if the eyes of the world are seen to be focussed on the trial.[1] There is therefore a strong case for helping such victims to institute appropriate legal proceedings in the national courts, in order to test the legality of the action that the public authorities have taken; to work through all the national legal remedies; and only then to take the matter to the international institutions— which anyway require the exhaustion of domestic legal remedies before they are willing to declare a case admissible before them.

Much can often be achieved by using these procedures to their maximum extent. But if the law fails to rule, what can be done then? For the victim's fellow citizens, there is a clear duty to continue to press for justice on his or her behalf, by whatever extra-legal means still remain available—and usually there are

---

[1] Poland, for example, has recently seen an upsurge of courageous—and often successful—litigation against its own governmental authorities; and some Polish officials have been heard to admit in private that this may be no bad thing.

some. True, this may sometimes be foolhardy or ineffective. A government that is acting illegally towards one of its citizens is unlikely to tolerate any organized protests. Thus, for example, when a number of citizens of Moscow, including Andrei Sakharov, clamoured for a fair trial for Sinyavsky and Daniel, their public demonstration was forcibly suppressed and their protests were ignored by the authorities. This is the harsh reality in most of the countries where human rights are systematically violated by the state.

To what extent, then, should the citizens of *other* countries feel obliged to act in such cases? This is a highly contentious issue, which arises inevitably out of the conception of certain fundamental rights as universal in scope, and their inclusion in universal laws. In so far as we are all under the protection of the same international laws, it becomes our duty to go to the aid of our fellow citizens under those laws, even though they may be subject to other national jurisdictions in other matters. But this duty cuts across the traditional claim of every nation to have exclusive sovereign jurisdiction over its own citizens, and to be entitled to ignore the opinions of foreign nations or foreign people. Yet the whole point of international human rights law is that it is *transnational* in its scope, giving individuals of all nations the legitimate standing to take up the just cause of every individual everywhere.

Most scientists, acting simply out of human concern for their colleagues or to safeguard their profession, would prefer not to get caught up in such matters. They do not yet realize that they already have an answer to the representative of the oppressive government of a foreign country who insists that their expressions of concern are unwarranted, that it is 'none of their business', and that they have no right to 'interfere in the internal affairs of another sovereign state'. Today, this is a fallacious defence. The answer is, simply, that they have more right to protest against a violation of international law, than the offending government has a right to break that law—and anyway, that their public expression of opinion is itself guaranteed under the same law.

The real questions about *ad hoc* action in support of human rights in other countries are not legal, but practical: does it help the victims, and could it do harm in other ways? The first question arises when the apologist for an offending government argues, say, that the verdict in a forthcoming trial, or the treatment of a political prisoner, may actually be worsened by public protest abroad. The answer to this, of course, is that the government concerned must take full responsibility for its own actions, and cannot thus shrug off its duty to act justly to its own citizens. In fact, the apologist's argument is morally disreputable: it casts the victim in the role of a helpless hostage, to be made to pay for the actions of others over whom he or she has no control. It is a bluff that asks to be called. The consistent testimony of the victims themselves is that pressure from abroad has never harmed them, and by bringing their case into the open has often saved them from an even worse fate. It has to be remembered that the decisions in such matters are often taken by middle-ranking officials whose careers depend on not getting into trouble. Such an official may be very vulnerable to the fear that a case for which he is responsible to his superiors may be blown up into an international issue, thus reflecting on his personal competence and discretion. One of us has direct experience of such a case in one of the Eastern Helsinki countries. Systematic exposure of such cases can be a powerful influence on the way in which such officials behave.

It is much more difficult to decide whether active concern about human rights in other countries can do harm in other ways. The Belgrade and Madrid Follow-up Conferences, which were supposed to lead to further progress in the 'Helsinki process', were hamstrung over this issue. Some commentators consider, for example, that the action of the Western countries in pressing their criticism of the human rights situation in the Eastern bloc may have been counterproductive of 'security and co-operation' in the region, while others hold that they were bound to comment on the poor performance of many countries in this vital aspect of the Accords.

We are not qualified to judge such high matters of foreign affairs and international diplomacy. But as we saw in the previous chapter, scientists in the Helsinki countries are faced with a dilemma: should they take a public stand against human rights violations in other countries of the region, at the possible expense of contacts and co-operation with the scientists of those countries? Does the unity of the world scientific community take precedence over support of the rights of individual scientists against their governments? At a time when the dangers of nuclear war loom larger than ever, many thoughtful scientific leaders argue[2] that Soviet scientists 'must not lose the feeling of being part of the world community of intellectuals', and that this is more important than fruitless efforts to protect a few individual dissidents such as Andrei Sakharov from persecution. Since most Soviet scientists, whatever their private opinions, are not responsible for but are nevertheless bound to support the actions of their own government whenever these are directly challenged in public, this issue arises continually in the practical affairs of the international scientific community.

Only the cold warriors on both sides have simple formulae for resolving this dilemma. We ourselves believe that this is a matter for individual decision and action on each occasion, taking into account the likely consequences for both the one world of science and the rule of law. Since these are not fundamentally inconsistent, but are really complementary goals, each barren without the other, it is often possible to act in ways that emphasize the connections. This will be our major consideration in the rest of this chapter.

A typical dilemma of this kind is the choice between private persuasion and public protest. Until quite recently it was the policy of the official leaders of the scientific communities in Western countries not to comment at all in public on cases where the rights of scientists in Eastern countries had been violated, even when these rights involved important scientific traditions, such as the recognition of priority of discovery (see Chapter 10). On the other hand, they would take the opportunity of a private conversation with their Soviet opposite numbers to raise such cases, and may, on occasion, have helped a few of the victims. This policy has the virtue of exploiting the international solidarity of science on behalf of individual victims of injustice, and may well achieve more, in its quiet way, than some of the louder protests. But if it does not succeed, there is nothing more to do at that level. It needs to be associated with a few public statements, temperately worded but strongly supporting scientific freedom, thus clearly indicating that these subjects are indeed being taken up seriously in private conversations between the scientific élites of both countries. This is the real value of several public statements by two successive Presidents of the Royal Society—Lord Todd[3] and Sir Andrew

---

[2] e. g. Victor Weisskopf, *Bulletin of the Atomic Scientists*, 40, 2; 1984.
[3] At the Hamburg Scientific Forum in 1980.

Huxley[4] —which made this matter quite clear, as does the 'Affirmation of Freedom of Inquiry and Expression' by the US National Academy of Sciences.[5]

The need to foster transnational science also argues against cutting off contacts with the scientists of a nation that persistently violates the international code of human rights law. There is often a strong case for action going beyond verbal protests, but a general boycott is a blunt instrument that can be as harmful to potential friends as to those whom it is designed to influence. For example, at the time of the invasion of Czechoslovakia by Soviet troops in 1968, some scientists refused to accept previously arranged visits by Russian colleagues. This gesture was misplaced, since the Russian visitors were not responsible for, and indeed quite ignorant about, the invasion. As we shall see later in this chapter, there is a whole range of selective sanctions and graded responses which can be applied in such circumstances, to indicate the seriousness with which the offence is regarded. But it must always be kept in mind that all such sanctions are *symbolic* acts, whose purpose is not to do real harm to science but to draw attention to a wrong and to indicate the indignation with which this wrong is regarded. This purpose is lost if they are pressed too far.

Many people believe that there is more to be gained from a 'missionary policy' of deliberately arranging personal contacts between the scientists of the two countries, and encouraging them to discuss outstanding issues together. It must be admitted, though, that human rights issues are regarded as too sensitive and divisive to figure in official agendas or published records of such meetings, even though they are often discussed between the participants in private.

There is one informal organization in which scientists, mostly rather senior, from many countries, including those signatory to the Helsinki Accords, meet regularly to discuss problems arising from the arms race and political confrontation between East and West. This is the Pugwash Continuing Conference on Science and World Affairs, which first met in 1957 in the village of Pugwash, Nova Scotia, in reponse to an appeal issued by Albert Einstein and Bertrand Russell, and has held several conferences each year ever since. Scientists come to these conferences in a personal ca-

---

[4] At an Aniversary Meeting of the Society; see *Royal Society News*, November 1982.
[5] *Science*, 21 May 1976.

pacity rather than as representatives of their governments (although they may in fact be government advisers), and free exchange of opinion and information—within limits—is the rule. The subjects discussed include the causes of tension, as well as technical aspects of arms control. Nevertheless, although human rights infringements are significant causes of political tension and may be brought up behind the scenes, they do not figure in the published summaries of conclusions and recommendations from these conferences.

A rather more limited and more recently founded organization is International Physicians for the Prevention of Nuclear War (IPPNW), founded in 1980 by two leading physicians, one American and one Russian. This is now composed of some 40 national physicians' organizations whose main purpose is to heighten public awareness of the medical consequences of any use of nuclear weapons, and is based on a shared medical ethic which includes a duty to prevent foreseeable threats to health and well-being.

IPPNW holds annual congresses which provide a forum in which quite influential physicians and others discuss informally not only medical aspects of the threat of nuclear weapons, but also causes of political tension. As is the case with the Pugwash conferences, the subject of human rights infringements can only be brought up, if at all, delicately and in private conversation, and they are officially regarded as minor side issues.

Scientific societies

Freedom is a *collective* good for scientists and for science. Its protection is therefore a responsibility for every organized group of scientists—universities, research institutes, and, above all, scientific societies. Until recently, this responsibility was treated as a theme for rhetorical addresses on celebratory occasions, rather than a cause for real activity. As we have indicated at various points in previous chapters, this attitude has changed, and many scientific societies in the West are now actively involved in human rights issues, at home and abroad.

This involvement has not gone unchallenged, even by scientists whose personal sympathies with the victims of oppression cannot be doubted. The traditional policy of almost all scientific societies has been to concentrate entirely on the advancement of their sub-

jects, through meetings, publications, prizes, research grants, and
so on, and to eschew involvement in other matters. Since the
beginnings of modern science in the seventeenth century, this
policy has been advocated as the only means of protecting the
internal affairs of the scientific community from political, ideological, or religious strife. As we saw in Chapter 9, there can be
no alternative to this policy, anyway, in countries where scientific
societies are simply not permitted to involve themselves in non-
technical issues.

In the last twenty or thirty years, however, scientists everywhere
have come to realize that research projects and achievements cannot
be isolated from their social origins and consequences, and that
scientists themselves cannot wholly escape responsibility for the
exploitation of their endeavours and products. Many scientific
societies now hold serious discussions on the social implications of
their professional work and the applications of their discoveries,
and are forced to take political, economic and cultural considerations into account. The rights and responsibilities of scientists themselves cannot be arbitrarily excluded from those
conditions. The members of such societies naturally use these
meetings and publications to keep themselves informed about the
welfare of their colleagues, not only in their own countries but
also in the rest of the world. If scandals and injustices are thus
disclosed, they can no longer be ignored: protest and other action
are bound to follow.

The national scientific society that has taken the main lead in
these matters is the American Association for the Advancement of
Science (AAAS). Through its standing Committee on Human
Rights and Responsibilities of Scientists, it has been effective in
monitoring, validating, and sustaining the human rights code, both
within the United States and abroad, especially in Latin America.
In particular, by its concern over current US Government constraints on scientific communication (see Chapter 6), the AAAS
has shown the way that scientists themselves should act collectively
to safeguard the pursuit of science within their own countries,
even in an open society.

The fact is, however, that most regular scientific societies in
Western countries have neither the resources nor the will to follow
this example. They do not give a high priority to human rights
issues, even where scientific freedom itself is at stake, and are still

very fearful of getting caught up in 'politics'. In adopting this attitude, scientific societies are, of course, usually reflecting the opinions of the majority of their members, who would rather leave such matters to the specialized groups of 'activists' who take up this or that cause outside the regular scientific proceedings of the society.

This point of view is perfectly understandable. Organizations such as the Committee of Concerned Scientists in New York draw heavily upon the conscientiousness and zeal of their supporters to collect information and orchestrate campaigns of protest about human rights abuses in various countries. They are able to keep in touch with other organizations with similar purposes, such as Amnesty International, and can monitor the activities of governmental and international bodies such as the Human Rights Commission of the United Nations. Some notable victims of injustice, in various parts of the world, owe their present health and liberty— perhaps their very lives—to protests and publicity stimulated by quite small ad hoc groups of scientists who have personally taken up their cause. Other organizations, such as Scientists for the Release of Soviet Refuseniks (formerly the Medical and Scientific Committee for Soviet Jewry) have worked for years on behalf of particular groups, and may well have helped several to obtain permission to emigrate. The relatively light 'punishment' of Victor Brailovsky (see Chapter 7) is thought to have been due to the pressure exerted on the Soviet authorities by this small but influential group, and other similar groups, in Western countries. Such ad hoc groups, however, cannot provide systematic coverage of human rights in the world of science. Their achievements are very real, but their enthusiasms are unco-ordinated and their interests often highly partisan.

Scientific trade unions

One might have thought that human rights cases, which involve the welfare of scientists as working people, would have been taken up systematically by the trade unions to which many scientists belong. Unfortunately, these organizations have not so far proved eager to take on this responsibility.

Before the second world war it was uncommon for scientists in 'capitalist' countries to belong to a trade union. In Britain, for example, scientists by and large regarded themselves as fortunate to be working in their chosen fields, and they enjoyed their work enough to accept uncertainty of continued employment and relatively low levels of remuneration compared with other professions. This changed with the recruitment of large numbers of scientists and engineers by the government and private firms during the war, mainly to help with the applications of science to the military effort. By the end of the war, although only a substantial minority had joined trade unions, these were already well-established. They concerned themselves with the role and future of science in society, as well as with bread-and-butter issues. However, human rights were taken for granted, and did not enter into these discussions. As the realities of job security and salary structures—strictly trade union business—came to preoccupy the trade unions, and were compounded by the preference of large employers such as the universities, government departments, and industry to negotiate terms and conditions of service of scientists and technicians with bodies which could claim to represent them, the trade unions have in practice become increasingly parochial, and their officials are less inclined to become involved in policy issues other than those which are of immediate interest to their members. As the GCHQ case shows, trade unions can and do effectively use the legal machinery on behalf of the rights of their members, but they have shown little inclination to use legal procedures—or even extra-legal pressures—on behalf of non-members in other countries.

In the USSR and other 'communist' countries, scientists belong to factory or institute or ministry based trade unions, whose function is mainly to improve the smooth running of the enterprise while at the same time concerning themselves with terms and conditions of work and labour relations generally. Such trade unions may take up the cases of dismissed individuals, but they are in no position to show any sympathy for individuals whose activities are regarded as 'anti-state'. There is no evidence that Jewish refuseniks or members of Helsinki Watch Committees have ever received support from their unions: rather, the unions have often actively approved their dismissal.

Scientific academies

In most of the countries with which we are concerned, the scientific community is headed by a national scientific academy (see Chapter

9). These play a key role in the international activities of the world of science.

Almost by definition, the members of a national academy constitute the scientific élite of the nation. Their members are scientists who at some period of their lives have been personally pre-eminent in their research. Many of the present-day academies—including the Soviet Academy of Sciences—are the heirs to a long historical tradition, and still follow the practices of an era when science and technology were not so highly organized and supported by the state as they are nowadays. But the membership of an academy tends to be drawn from able (and ambitious) scientists who are already well on in their careers, and are already directors of large laboratories and institutes. Since the competition for election is fierce, and election is for life, the average age of the members is always high. By their very nature, these are proud, independent, and conservative institutions, slow to move and to be moved.

In Britain, the United States, and other Western countries, the national scientific academies are indeed independent institutions, over whom the government has no official authority. But they do rely very heavily on government grants for much of their business, and are still regarded officially as the highest source of advice on scientific matters, although this traditional function is now shared by other bodies such as research councils. They play a particularly important part in the international activities of science, where they are regarded as the representatives of their national scientific communities.

The national scientific academies in countries where science is organized on the Soviet model have much greater responsibilities, since they run practically all the basic research. They directly control numerous specialized institutes, and directly employ many thousands of scientists. These responsibilities do not cover all the science in the country, since most of the applied research is done quite separately in institutes attached to various government ministries or to productive enterprises. But their official authority over the scientific life of the country is paramount, both in national and international affairs. This is why they are so important to our present subject, for they constitute the one channel, apart from the government itself, through which influence can flow from abroad.

In many respects, however, as we saw in Chapter 9, the formal independence of the Soviet-type academies is illusory. The fact that the Party Central Committee usually contains some senior Academicians merely indicates that these institutions are closely linked to the state apparatus. In reality, the power that they exercise within their own spheres is subject to approval by representatives of the Communist Party, and of the state security apparatus, in their higher administrative echelons. For many practical purposes, the scientific academies of the countries of the Eastern bloc have to be considered simply as specialized organs of the state.

Nevertheless, the views of the scientific leaders of an academy in a 'communist' country are not always subservient to political directives. The tensions thus generated are not, of course, made public, but information about them leaks out. A recent case was that of Dr David Goldfarb, a molecular biologist of international reputation who had been one of the first Soviet scientists sent abroad for training in the techniques of genetic engineering. When he sought to join his relatives in Israel, the KGB opposed his application, on the ground that research in genetic engineering involves access to state secrets. The Soviet Academy objected that Goldfarb had not, in fact, done any classified research, and eventually persuaded the Party authorities to grant him a visa. Among other considerations, it seems that the academicians feared that if all research on genetic engineering were classified they would not be able to publish their own work on the subject, and would thus fail to achieve international recognition. In this conflict, alas, the KGB eventually won: Goldfarb was arrested before he could leave the country, and at the time of writing awaits charges of planning to export state secrets.[6]

As this episode shows, the power of these academies to intervene on behalf of the human rights of scientists is not negligible, though it is severely limited. Their will to do so is also limited. As in other countries, most of the members have risen within the existing political system, and broadly support its structure and goals, even if they are critical of the way things are done in detail. In such circumstances, only an exceptionally strong-minded and personally secure individual—the late Peter Kapitza comes to mind—would dare to confront the state machinery directly. But there are certainly members who are willing to use such influence as they can muster to help in a quiet way with particular cases of injustice.

[6] *Nature*, 308, 766; 1984; 309, 104; 1984; 313, 10; 1985.

It is always worth remembering, moreover, that scientific academies and their members have a strong desire to be in good standing with the international scientific world, and are eager to participate in the kinds of co-operative project outlined in Chapter 12. This genuine desire to belong to 'the one world of science' should be taken seriously in dealing with them. It must also be remembered that their members rarely express their personal political opinions in public (except on topics such as environmental pollution), and are bound to conform outwardly to the current policies of their governments. In the present climate of diplomatic hostility and military rivalry between the NATO and Warsaw Pact countries, there is little hope of relaxation in the attitudes of the leading scientists on either side.

Nevertheless, the strength of intellect and character, and the experience of scientific work, that are required to become an academician are positive assets for the world of science. The scientific academies of the Soviet bloc do contain a number of independent-minded members who fully appreciate the value of freedom in science and for scientists. Representations to such academies on human rights issues may be publicly rejected or disregarded, but they do not always fall on entirely deaf ears. And on such practical matters as openness of publication and freedom of movement it may be assumed that their real interests and opinions coincide with those of their opposite numbers in the Royal Society or the US National Academy, and that they are as irked as their Western colleagues by bureaucratic nonsense.

Modes of response

Scientific societies (including national academies) are often uncertain how they should express their concern about the violation of the rights of scientists in other countries. There is an unfortunate tendency to jump from one extreme to another—from doing nothing to cutting off all scientific contact with the offending country. In reality there are many other possible responses between these extremes, each appropriate to particular circumstances. As it is put in an account of the work of the Committee on Human Rights of the US National Academy of Sciences: 'we have tried to develop a capability of patient sustained and persistent inquiry and support'.[7] The following list[8] is not exhaustive, but it will give some idea of the variety of ways in which the international code of human rights law can be sustained:

1. Sending a statement by the president of the society to a government authority in the country concerned, with copies to the relevant embassies and national academies;

2. Publishing such a statement or other formal protest in the society's bulletin or professional journal, together with any reply;

3. Providing facilities for protest meetings and press conferences, especially where these can attract attention at a nearby international scientific conference;

4. Writing an official letter to the head of a state, ruling party, or scientific academy, requesting information about a particular person or activity and expressing concern about the situation;

5. Collecting information about individual cases and disseminating it to members, so encouraging the sustained pressure that is often necessary, and giving them a 'human interest' in the work;

6. Organizing petitions by members on specific cases;

7. Granting recognition, publicity, or both, to 'alternative' meetings and seminars (see Chapter 9) organized by banned scientists in their own country;

8. Organizing or supporting meetings related to the scientific work of a distinguished foreign scientist suffering repression;

9. Sending free journals and other research aids to banned scientists;

10. Supporting exiled scientists financially; this can be done, for example, by scientific societies undertaking to help and place a refugee scientist in their own discipline, so that the scientist may find his or her feet in the country of refuge;

11. Sending a delegation to the offending country to investigate particular cases, assess the human rights problems of scientists, or discuss scientific exchanges and other co-operative programmes with governmental and scientific authorities in a human rights context;

12. Advising members whether they should attend meetings in an offending country, invite scientists from that country to conferences, or welcome them as visitors in scientific establishments or laboratories;

[7] Kates, R. W., 'Human issues in human rights', *Science*, 201, 502; 1978.
[8] Cohen, L., *Nature*, 287, 100; 1980.

13. Severing formal relationships with academies or societies in offending countries;

14. Campaigning to expel the academy or relevant society of an offending country from an international scientific organization.

This list of responses is very schematic, and obviously calls for detailed analysis in the light of experience. It is presented in approximate order of increasing severity, to indicate the wide range of actions that is actually open to a society at any given moment.

It seems to be the received opinion of many of those who have considered taking part in such work that the more extreme sanctions (i.e. options 12, 13, and 14) are likely to prove counterproductive, and should therefore not be considered except under correspondingly extreme provocation. But whether this is really so is decidedly debateable, especially in the light of the recent experience of the World Psychiatric Association. When evidence of the abuse of psychiatry in the Soviet Union first came to light (see Chapter 7), this highly respected organization set up a review committee to examine complaints received from member societies. However, for six years this committee failed to elicit any response from Soviet psychiatrists about individual cases. None the less, during the whole of that time the Association consistently refused to make any public statement about the growing and increasingly well-attested evidence of this abuse; indeed, its officers took much trouble to ensure that the issue was never formally debated at the Association's meetings. The rationale for this public silence was that pressure was being brought privately and informally, that open discussion might lead to an official Soviet resignation from the Association, and that such a rift could only damage the Association while doing nothing for the victims.

Meanwhile, the abuses increased, and so did the number and suffering of their victims. By then, all this was being widely reported in the world's press, and the Association came under increasing attack for its public silence. Finally, in 1982, three members of the Norwegian Psychiatric Association succeeded in having extensive discussions with leading Soviet psychiatrists; they concluded that, even allowing for the differences in psychiatric concepts and social values between them, psychiatric abuse for political purposes had occurred in the Soviet Union, and was continuing. Following their report, the UK Royal College of Psychiatrists put down a motion, for debate in July 1983, to withdraw membership of the World Psychiatric Association from the USSR All-Union Society of Neurologists and Psychiatrists. Predictably, the All-Union Society pre-empted the debate by resigning from the Association; equally predictably, the abuse continues.[9] But during the years of public silence, the World Psychiatric Association suffered a serious decline in the public respect which it had previously enjoyed, and a consequent decline in its weight and influence. By 1983, it cost the Soviet Union little to withdraw from it. Had the Association publicly asserted its condemnation of the abuses when they were first established as a systematic state-supported practice, matters might well have turned out differently—for the Association and the victims alike.

Undoubtedly, however, one of the most useful activities that scientific societies can undertake in this field is option 5—the collection and dissemination of reliable, up-to-date information about particular cases. There is a real need for an organization to monitor, validate, and sustain the human rights of scientists all over the world, and if this cannot be undertaken properly by an international body (see below), then it is in the first instance the responsibility of national scientific societies in free countries to see that it gets done. The need is plain; the opportunities are there; but they have not yet been taken.

International organizations

Human rights law is transnational in its scope: all truly transnational organizations have a stake in sustaining it. Unfortunately, most inter-govermental organizations are weak, or deeply divided over just such political issues as respect for human rights. As we have already remarked, this was one of the main reasons for the lack of progress at the Belgrade and Madrid Follow-up Conferences, where the 'Helsinki process' was supposed to have been reviewed and renewed. The same can be said of the human rights activities of the United Nations, which are sometimes useful as a source of information about abuses, but which achieve very little towards preventing them.

In a more general account, one would naturally describe in some detail the work of the non-governmental organizations, such as the

[9] See Bloch, S. and Reddaway, P., *Soviet Psychiatric Abuse* (Gollancz; London, 1984); Wynn, A., 'The Soviet Union and the World Psychiatric Association', *Lancet*, 1983, i, 406-8; Reich, W., 'The World of Soviet Psychiatry', *New York Times Magazine*, 30 January 1983.

International Commission of Jurists and Amnesty International, which play such a very important part in trying to increase respect for the international law of human rights, and giving aid to those whom it has failed to protect. But that is a large and important subject which deserves far more space than we can give it here. The main point is that these organizations have a great fund of specialized knowledge and practical experience which they are glad to make available to anyone starting work in this field. As we have continually emphasized, the rights claimed by scientists are the rights of all free men and women, and the tragic things that sometimes happen to them are not unique to their profession.

The one inter-governmental organization which is directly charged with ensuring the general welfare of science is UNESCO. It was UNESCO, for example, which formulated and agreed the important Recommendation on the Status of Scientific Researchers, the text of which is set out in Appendix 4. UNESCO has a human rights section which attempts to monitor and publish the extent to which the human rights of special concern to UNESCO are honoured in different countries. Since 1978, there has also been a Committee on Conventions and Recommendations which has a special (and confidential) procedure for considering 'communications' about specific violations of such human rights.

UNESCO procedures are thorough, but work through its bureaucracy very slowly, so that a pronouncement—even if in favour of a complainant—is liable to be made too late to affect the original issue, and may be disregarded by the offending state. In principle, the UNESCO machinery could provide a useful safeguard for the human rights of scientists; in practice, action is inhibited by the difficulty of persuading the representatives of the many countries which make up its General Assembly to agree to criticize one of their number. Only rarely, when a great deal of external pressure is also applied (as in the case of Professor L. Massera in Uruguay who was released from prison in 1984, having been sentenced 8 years before to 20 years' imprisonment), are governments likely to take any notice of such criticism.

Another international organization whose charter ought to make it particularly responsive to any abrogation of the individual rights of scientists is the World Federation of Scientific Workers (WFSW), which was founded in 1946 and provides a meeting place for representatives of scientific trade unions from both 'com-

munist' and 'capitalist' countries. This body has eminent scientists
from East and West on its Council, and its President has usually
been a prominent Western scientist. It has 47 affiliated organizations, including some professional bodies as well as trade unions
of scientific workers from 'capitalist', 'socialist', and 'developing'
countries. Its main concern has been with socio-economic problems
such as the dangers of the arms race, poverty and development in
the Third World, and science policy. It also formulated and adopted in 1969 a Declaration on the Rights of Scientific Workers
(set out in Appendix 5) which forthrightly enumerates the basic
rights with which their work is concerned. The fact that the
WSFW has been accepted and is well regarded in 'communist'
countries, and that its comments on world affairs have tended to
emphasize the achievements of 'socialist' societies and the defects
rather than the benefits of 'capitalistic' exploitation of resources,
have led to the organization being regarded in the West as
'communist-dominated' and of little importance. Nevertheless, its
pronouncements are regarded more seriously in 'socialist' and
'non-aligned' countries, and it could make private or public representations, if it chose to do so, about human rights infringements.
In fact, on this subject it has done very little. Although it made a
public protest about the imprisonment or disappearance of scientists in Latin America, it has made no statement about persecution
in the 'communist' countries. On 3 November 1981 a letter was
sent to the President of the Educational and Scientific Workers
Union of the USSR—its affiliated organization in that country—
concerning the denial of exit visas to certain scientists, but there
seems to be no report of a response nor of any further action by
the WFSW.[10] Further representations may have been made behind
the scenes, but no alleged infringements within the Helsinki countries have surfaced publicly through the WFSW.

The International Council of Scientific Unions
As we saw in Chapter 12, ICSU is the nearest approach to a
corporate representation of the world of science. Membership of
ICSU is open to all nations. It is composed of representatives of
national scientific academies, and of those specialized international
scientific unions whose scientific status is regarded as sufficiently
high. The international scientific unions in turn are voluntary

[10] *Nature* 295, 452; 1982: 298, 414; 1982.

associations of national scientific societies whose *bona fides* and status are acceptable. ICSU is governed by a General Assembly currently composed of 19 international unions and 70 national academies or their equivalents, which meets every three years. It elects officers and an Executive Board responsible for day-to-day decisions and for making policy recommendations, which reports annually to a General Committee composed of representatives of the international unions and a smaller number of elected representatives of the national academies. This structure is designed to ensure that the practical issues with which ICSU concerns itself are scientific, and not dominated by the national interests of the more numerous national academies.

During the second world war ICSU ceased to function, but it resumed in 1945, at the time when UNESCO was being formed. In 1946 an agreement was reached in which UNESCO recognized ICSU as providing a natural and appropriate forum for the international organization of science, and agreed that in these respects ICSU rather than UNESCO should be the co-ordinating and representative body. A close relationship is maintained between the two organizations, and UNESCO provides additional funds for projects of which its own General Assembly approves. The total budget available to ICSU is nevertheless meagre (about US$ 4 million in 1981), and does not reflect the immense amount of time freely given by scientists throughout the world who take part in its projects.

The USSR adhered to ICSU in 1954, but it was not until 1983 that a formula was agreed with the People's Republic of China which has enabled it to adhere to ICSU without demanding the expulsion of Taiwan, which had been a member for several years and had claimed still to represent all China. ICSU can now be considered to embrace all the world of natural science.

ICSU is not a very demonstrative organization: many scientists know little about it. It sponsors a large number of international congresses and smaller meetings, and of special and co-ordinating committees covering many of the international problems mentioned in Chapter 12, and others. It has, for example, organized worldwide simultaneous studies of geophysical problems during an International Geophysical Year; of astronomical problems during the Year of the Quiet Sun; of human, plant and animal ecology during an International Biological Year; and together with UNESCO it has set up a Bio-Sciences Network in Africa and South America. Although complaints are often heard that anything done through ICSU moves very slowly, this is almost inevitable because of the needs, firstly, to obtain the approval and collaboration of a significant number of scientists in order to ensure that any recommended activity is scientifically justified and worth while—and that those involved will actually carry out the recommendations—and, secondly, to obtain funding for any development for which there is not already a budget provision.

ICSU publicly recognizes the need for individual scientists to communicate with one another and to express freely their opinions on scientific and other matters, and to some extent ICSU acts to suggest this principle. During the years following the second world war, because of political hostility, governments of several countries banned the entry of nationals from some other countries even to attend scientific meetings. Consequently, the organizers of international meetings were faced with a situation in which some invited speakers or intending participants were refused entry visas, and even some nationals of the host country who were under a political cloud might not be allowed to attend. In 1963 ICSU formed a Standing Committee on the Free Circulation of Scientists, which undertook to advise the organizers of scientific meetings held under ICSU auspices whether intended host countries would guarantee the free entry, and safety from arrest, of all participants who were *bona fide* scientists entitled to attend the meeting. The enquiries are made discreetly, behind the scenes, and if the guarantee is not forthcoming the organizers are advised to seek another host country. Since holding an important meeting such as an international congress brings some prestige to the host country, the threat to transfer it elsewhere has usually sufficed to ensure that the guarantees are forthcoming.

Through ICSU, the world scientific community has thus managed to establish an informal and limited 'right of entry' for scientists attending scientific congresses. This is a significant example of the effectiveness of collective action, even against the sovereign power of national governments. Nevertheless, this pressure can only be sustained if it is fully backed up by all the scientists and scientific organizations that are free to do so. However, this need for solidarity in 'the one world of science' can lead to serious dilemmas for those involved. For example, should the organizers of an international conference cancel it at the last minute, if it becomes clear that 'administrative procedures' are in fact being used to block the participation of just a few individuals, despite prior guarantees? Such a drastic step not only imposes a heavy financial burden on all the other would-be participants: it also cuts across just those informal contacts with the scientists of the host country that make such meetings so valuable. Is it perhaps enough, in such cases, for the organizers to make a public fuss about it, and for the ICSU Committee to make embarrassing representations, after the event, to the national representative body of the offending country?

This was the dilemma facing the European Physical Society in the summer of 1984, on the eve of its Sixth General Conference in Prague, when one of its leading members, Professor Frantisek Janouch of Stockholm University, had been categorically refused an entry visa by the Czechoslovak authorities. In view of the way that Janouch had been treated when he was still a citizen of the CSSR (see Chapter 8), this was not altogether unexpected—but he had never been formally charged with any crime at that time, and having been unilaterally deprived of his Czechoslovak citizenship he had become a Swedish citizen. His exclusion from the meeting was particularly damaging to the EPS, since he was not only a theoretical physicist of international standing but also an elected representative of the EPS's individual members on its Council, which was to meet in Prague at the same time. Indeed, in September 1968 he had actually been instrumental in the decision to set up the EPS as originally planned, including all the East European countries, despite the Soviet invasion of Czechoslovakia.

Thus, the refusal of the Czechoslovak government even to allow Janouch to come to Prague for just a few days to take part in these proceedings was not only an act of arbitrary discrimination against him: it was a direct blow to the integrity and independence of the EPS as an international scientific organization. When, somewhat belatedly, the senior officers of the EPS realized what was happening, they made strong representations, in private, to the Czech government and scientific authorities, but they did not use the only real weapon in their hands—the threat to cancel the meeting altogether. The protests were of course ineffective, and in the event both the Conference and the Council meetings went ahead as planned—but without Frantisek Janouch. Many delegates at the Council meeting expressed their grave concern at this turn of events, but nothing further was done. Even the 'statement' that came out of the EPS General Assembly accepted the 'official' Czechoslovak account of Janouch's career, without any reference to a very different version which he would have given had he been allowed to present his case.[11]

Nor do such things only happen in the Eastern countries. In August 1982, two senior Soviet scientists wishing to attend a biochemistry congress in Perth were refused Australian visas, which drew a protest from the President of the Royal Society, Sir Andrew Huxley; [12] in September 1984, two Soviet delegates were refused Canadian visas to attend the meeting of the Twentieth General Assembly of ICSU in Ottawa;[13] and in February 1984 several Israeli scientists were prevented from attending the Seventh International Biotechnology Symposium in New Delhi. These episodes illustrate the difficulties faced by the international scientific bodies coming under the ICSU umbrella when they try to carry out their mission on behalf of 'the one world of science'. In general, these bodies are so anxious to maintain scientific contacts that they find it almost impossible to take harsh measures against any particular country, even under extreme provocation. Nevertheless, in the long run, the pressures exerted by such bodies as the ICSU Standing Committee on the Free Circulation of Scientists can have considerable effect, not least because all those countries which take their science seriously recognize that its work serves their own interests.

A second Standing Committee, this time on the Safeguard of the Pursuit of Science, was set up in 1972, largely to make recommendations about how to prevent the 'brain drain'—i.e. the emigration of able scientists from countries which offer limited opportunities to follow a scientific career, to countries where such opportunities are plentiful. In 1976 the Committee's remit was changed, by a large majority vote of the ICSU General Assembly, to embrace the task of identifying and making recommendations about unnecessary impediments to scientific progress (e.g. customs restrictions and delays on the import of perishable or short-lived research materials and scientific equipment, or the increasing tend-

[11] *Nature* 310, 617; 1984; F. Janouch, private communication.
[12] *Royal Society News*, Issue 18, November 1982.
[13] ICSU official minutes.

ency already mentioned to keep scientific findings secret), together with an entirely new remit. This was to collect, document and analyse individual cases where *bona fide* scientists have been seriously restricted in the pursuit of scientific research, or prevented from communicating with their fellow scientists. Its concern is limited to scientists in their professional capacity, especially those who have been dismissed or have been refused suitable scientific employment on unjust or arbitrary grounds—that is, for reasons other than proved scientific incompetence, breaking their contracts of employment, incapacitating illness, conviction for serious crime, or other reasons which demonstrate their unsuitability to continue as active scientists.

The Committee on the Safeguard of the Pursuit of Science reports to the Executive Board and the General Assembly of ICSU, but because it undertakes to preserve the confidentiality of its information about individuals (which is in fact seldom necessary since their cases are usually well known), its reports are couched in general terms only. Any action which might be taken outside ICSU requires the approval of the Executive Board and the General Assembly, and none—such as giving publicity to the Committee's findings—has ever yet been taken. The only published documents produced by this Committee (which have been circulated within the ICSU family) have been a summary of international human rights law, an account of agreements obtained by UNESCO about the importation of scientific equipment (often not acted upon by the countries which made them), and a draft Statement of Principles Required for the Safeguard of the Pursuit of Science. These seem to have had only a minimal impact so far.

Although, taken at its face value, this Committee might appear well placed to be the main custodian of the important human rights of scientists, little notice has been taken and little use made of it. The main reason is that, unlike the Committee on the Free Circulation of Scientists, it is less obviously in the immediate self-interest of all unions and national academies to make use of it; another is that the Soviet Academy of Sciences was initially opposed to its formation, and has only recently sent an observer to its meetings; a third is that very few individuals land in trouble for reasons exclusively related to their scientific activities, and even the number who are harassed for illegal but not specifically scientific activities (such as membership of a Helsinki Watch Committee) is still very small in relation to their colleagues who avoid getting into trouble, and who prefer not to become involved in controversial matters. It is possible, though not obvious, that the very existence of this Committee has had a prophylactic—even if not yet a therapeutic—effect.

In 1984, the Committee reported to the Executive Board that during its six years' existence its activities had excited little interest or support among the scientific unions, and that representations made to their respective national academies on behalf of individual scientists had usually gone unheeded. It requested that either it be given more support, or that it be disbanded. However, when the General Assembly was asked to approve the Committees's abolition this was not accepted, and the Executive Board was told to think again. Instead, the General Assembly adopted a resolution reaffirming its concern for the objectives of the Standing Committee for the Safeguard of the Pursuit of Science, and inviting the Executive Board to set up an *ad hoc* Committee to consider how the objectives of the Standing Committee could be most effectively carried out in the future.

At the time of writing, this is where the matter stands. It seems that ICSU, having once assumed—even if half-heartedly—some responsibility for the safeguard of the pursuit of science, is not now willing to relinquish it. However, what is clear is that only if the scientific community decides to make serious use of opportunities of this sort will anything effective come out of them.

Achieving one world of science, under the rule of law

From the foregoing account of the institutional means available for possible action by the scientific community about violations of its members' human rights, it becomes clear that such action would have to be grafted on to the activities of bodies whose primary interests are in co-operation for other more specific and more obvious purposes. Only ICSU, UNESCO, and a very few scientific societies in the West have clearly recognized that the human rights of scientists are their proper concern, and even then reported cases of infringement tend to be taken up delicately. This is partly because they are too few to appear to justify 'rocking the boat', and partly because it is hoped that rectification is more likely if the offending party is not required to lose public face in doing it. A further reason may be that the actions which led to the violations in the first place—e. g. a desire to emigrate, criticism of government policy, etc.—are ones with which little genuine sympathy is felt, or it is thought that other unknown reasons must be involved.

At the root of this apparent indifference lies the failure of the scientific community to recognize that their own work depends vitally on human rights, and that these cannot be taken for granted but need to be defended whenever they are threatened. Perhaps it does not yet appreciate the extent to which they are now based on agreed and objective international legal standards. Furthermore, scientists have been apt to display a certain timidity about criticizing authority in their own country, or in another with whose scientific community they aim to have good relations. When political tensions already exist, even fair criticism is liable to be regarded as made with hostile intent, and may be taken up by others for this purpose. This could change. Hope for the future lies partly in diminishing political tensions, which is out of the hands of the scientific community as such, and partly in educating this community to be more aware of its legitimate interests in human rights, and to make more effective use of the existing means whereby they can be safeguarded.

What needs to be clearly understood is that the only satisfactory environment for the pursuit of science is a society under the rule of law. As science itself is a transnational pursuit, so this law must be transnational: only the international code of human rights law satisfies that criterion.

This is not to say that everyone must be entirely satisfied with this code as now drafted, or to suppose that it must necessarily be fixed thus for all eternity. But it is not our business here to enter into all the niceties that judges, advocates, legal draftsmen, or academic commentators can discover in the interpretation and application of human rights instruments, whether national or international. As for the means available for enforcing such instruments, we can only regret the continued weaknesses of the system of international law in this respect (see Chapter 2), and we are therefore bound to consider various other ways of bringing pressure to bear on the most flagrant transgressors. Law, like science, is not something to be valued solely for its own sake, above and beyond the realities of life.

We share with most thoughtful people—and not least with working scientists—some scepticism about the power of any legal system to render justice and equity to all who are subject to it, without fear or favour. Nevertheless, we hold firmly to the principle that is deeply embedded in the constitution—written or unwritten—of every free society, that the right to exist as an individual is essentially defined and protected by the rule of law in that society, and must be considered primarily from this point of view. In so many of the cases reported in our earlier chapters, the true realization of the loss of a right occurred when the victim was unable to call on the law for support against arbitrary action— failure to provide an exit visa, racial discrimination against educational advancement, suppression of published work, imprisonment without charge, or worse. This is why scientists everywhere must be alive to these needs, and be ready to go to the aid of their fellows by every legal means.

But the well-being of science is not the concern of scientists alone. This book is addressed to all who care for the health of our civilization, where science is a powerful formative influence, and where respect for the rights of the individual is a sensitive indicator of a society's moral worth. An attack upon, say, a scientist's right to freedom of expression in a scientific controversy not only threatens the liberties of all other citizens; it may poison the wells of scientific truth in that nation, and pollute the channels of scientific communication throughout the world. It is not that scientists can claim special rights that are not equally due to other men and women; it is that their professional duties and responsibilities make them peculiarly vulnerable to restrictions on rights that other people seldom have to exercise. They deserve no greater protection from unlawful detention or torture than any bank clerk or district nurse, but like poets and historians their work is reduced to a nullity if it cannot be done freely and made public. This is the point where the subject of this book touches us all.

APPENDIX 1

In the texts reprinted here, the Universal Declaration is reproduced in full, but only the *substantive* material is reproduced from the four treaties—that is, the Preambles and the Articles which spell out the rights, obligations, restrictions, and limitations. The Articles omitted relate largely to the *procedures* for ratification, supervision, enforcement, etc.

Universal Declaration of Human Rights

Preamble

Whereas recognition of the inherent dignity and of the equal and inalienable rights of all members of the human family is the foundation of freedom, justice and peace in the world,

Whereas disregard and contempt for human rights have resulted in barbarous acts which have outraged the conscience of mankind, and the advent of a world in which human beings shall enjoy freedom of speech and belief and freedom from fear and want has been proclaimed as the highest aspiration of the common people,

Whereas it is essential, if man is not to be compelled to have recourse, as a last resort, to rebellion against tyranny and oppression, that human rights should be protected by the rule of law,

Whereas it is essential to promote the development of friendly relations between nations,

Whereas the peoples of the United Nations have in the Charter reaffirmed their faith in fundamental human rights, in the dignity and worth of the human person and in the equal rights of men and women and have determined to promote social progress and better standards of life in larger freedom,

Whereas Member States have pledged themselves to achieve, in cooperation with the United Nations, the promotion of universal respect for and observance of human rights and fundamental freedoms,

Whereas a common understanding of these rights and freedoms is of the greatest importance for the full realization of this pledge,

Now, therefore,

The General Assembly

Proclaims this Universal Declaration of Human Rights as a common standard of achievement for all peoples and all nations, to the end that every individual and every organ of society, keeping this Declaration constantly in mind, shall strive by teaching and education to promote respect for these rights and freedoms and by progressive measures, national and international, to secure their universal and effective recognition and observance, both among the peoples of Member States themselves and among the peoples of territories under their jurisdiction.

Article 1

All human beings are born free and equal in dignity and rights. They are endowed with reason and conscience and should act towards one another in a spirit of brotherhood.

Article 2

Everyone is entitled to all the rights and freedoms set forth in this Declaration, without distinction of any kind, such as race, colour, sex, language, religion, political or other opinion, national or social origin, property, birth or other status.

Furthermore, no distinction shall be made on the basis of the political, jurisdictional or international status of the country or territory to which a person belongs, whether it be independent, trust, non-self-governing or under any other limitation of sovereignty.

Article 3

Everyone has the right to life, liberty and security of person.

Article 4

No one shall be held in slavery or servitude; slavery and the slave trade shall be prohibited in all their forms.

Article 5

No one shall be subjected to torture or to cruel, inhuman or degrading treatment or punishment.

Article 6

Everyone has the right to recognition everywhere as a person before the law.

Article 7

All are equal before the law and are entitled without any discrimination to equal protection of the law. All are entitled to equal protection against any discrimination in violation of this Declaration and against any incitement to such discrimination.

Article 8

Everyone has the right to an effective remedy by the competent national tribunals for acts violating the fundamental rights granted him by the constitution or by law.

Article 9

No one shall be subjected to arbitrary arrest, detention or exile.

Article 10

Everyone is entitled in full equality to a fair and public hearing by an independent and impartial tribunal, in the determination of his rights and obligations and of any criminal charge against him.

Article 11

1. Everyone charged with a penal offence has the right to be presumed innocent until proved guilty according to law in a public trial at which he has had all the guarantees necessary for his defence.

2. No one shall be held guilty of any penal offence on account of any act or omission which did not constitute a penal offence, under national or international law, at the time when it was committed. Nor shall a heavier penalty be imposed than the one that was applicable at the time the penal offence was committed.

Article 12

No one shall be subjected to arbitrary interference with his privacy, family, home or correspondence, nor to attacks upon his honour and reputation. Everyone has the right to the protection of the law against such interference or attacks.

Article 13

1. Everyone has the right to freedom of movement and residence within the borders of each State.

2. Everyone has the right to leave any country, including his own, and to return to his country.

Article 14

1. Everyone has the right to seek and to enjoy in other countries asylum from persecution.

2. This right may not be invoked in the case of prosecutions genuinely arising from non-political crimes or from acts contrary to the purposes and principles of the United Nations.

Article 15

1. Everyone has the right to a nationality.

2. No one shall be arbitrarily deprived of his nationality nor denied the right to change his nationality.

Article 16

1. Men and women of full age, without any limitation due to race, nationality or religion, have the right to marry and to found a family. They are entitled to equal rights as to marriage, during marriage and at its dissolution.

2. Marriage shall be entered into only with the free and full consent of the intending spouses.

3. The family is the natural and fundamental group unit of society and is entitled to protection by society and the State.

Article 17

1. Everyone has the right to own property alone as well as in association with others.

2. No one shall be arbitrarily deprived of his property.

Article 18

Everyone has the right to freedom of thought, conscience and religion; this right includes freedom to change his religion or belief, and freedom, either alone or in community with others and in public or private, to manifest his religion or belief in teaching, practice, worship and observance.

Article 19

Everyone has the right to freedom of opinion and expression; this right includes freedom to hold opinions without interference and to seek, receive and impart information and ideas through any media and regardless of frontiers.

Article 20

1. Everyone has the right to freedom of peaceful assembly and association.

2. No one may be compelled to belong to an association.

Article 21

1. Everyone has the right to take part in the government of his country, directly or through freely chosen representatives.

2. Everyone has the right of equal access to public service in his country.

3. The will of the people shall be the basis of the authority of government; this will shall be expressed in periodic and genuine elections which shall be by universal and equal suffrage and shall be held by secret vote or by equivalent free voting procedures.

Article 22

Everyone, as a member of society, has the right to social security and is entitled to realization, through national effort and international co-operation and in accordance with the organization and resources of each State, of the economic, social and cultural rights indispensable for his dignity and the free development of his personality.

Article 23

1. Everyone has the right to work, to free choice of employment, to just and favourable conditions of work and to protection against unemployment.

2. Everyone, without any discrimination, has the right to equal pay for equal work.

3. Everyone who works has the right to just and favourable remuneration ensuring for himself and his family an existence worthy of human dignity, and supplemented, if necessary, by other means of social protection.

4. Everyone has the right to form and to join trade unions for the protection of his interests.

Article 24

Everyone has the right to rest and leisure, including reasonable limitation of working hours and periodic holidays with pay.

Article 25

1. Everyone has the right to a standard of living adequate for the health and well-being of himself and of his family, including food, clothing, housing and medical care and necessary social services, and the right to security in the event of unemployment, sickness, disability, widowhood, old age or other lack of livelihood in circumstances beyond his control.

2. Motherhood and childhood are entitled to special care and assistance. All children, whether born in or out of wedlock, shall enjoy the same social protection.

Article 26

1. Everyone has the right to education. Education shall be free, at least in the elementary and fundamental stages. Elementary education shall be compulsory. Technical and professional education shall be made generally available and higher education shall be equally accessible to all on the basis of merit.

2. Education shall be directed to the full development of the human personality and to the strengthening of respect for human rights and fundamental freedoms. It shall promote understanding, tolerance and friendship among all nations, racial or religious groups, and shall further the activities of the United Nations for the maintenance of peace.

3. Parents have a prior right to choose the kind of education that shall be given to their children.

Article 27

1. Everyone has the right freely to participate in the cultural life of the

community, to enjoy the arts and to share in scientific advancement and its benefits.

2. Everyone has the right to the protection of the moral and material interests resulting from any scientific, literary or artistic production of which he is the author.

Article 28

Everyone is entitled to a social and international order in which the rights and freedoms set forth in this Declaration can be fully realized.

Article 29

1. Everyone has duties to the community in which alone the free and full development of his personality is possible.

2. In the exercise of his rights and freedoms, everyone shall be subject only to such limitations as are determined by law solely for the purpose of securing due recognition and respect for the rights and freedoms of others and of meeting the just requirements of morality, public order and the general welfare in a democratic society.

3. These rights and freedoms may in no case be exercised contrary to the purposes and principles of the United Nations.

Article 30

Nothing in this Declaration may be interpreted as implying for any State, group or person any right to engage in any activity or to perform any act aimed at the destruction of any of the rights and freedoms set forth herein.

International Covenant on Civil and Political Rights

PREAMBLE

The States Parties to the present Covenant,

Considering that, in accordance with the principles proclaimed in the Charter of the United Nations, recognition of the inherent dignity and of the equal and inalienable rights of all members of the human family is the foundation of freedom, justice and peace in the world,

Recognizing that these rights derive from the inherent dignity of the human person,

Recognizing that, in accordance with the Universal Declaration of Human Rights, the ideal of free human beings enjoying civil and political freedom and freedom from fear and want can only be achieved if conditions are created whereby everyone may enjoy his civil and political rights, as well as his economic, social and cultural rights,

Considering the obligation of States under the Charter of the United Nations to promote universal respect for, and observance of, human rights and freedoms,

Realizing that the individual, having duties to other individuals and to the community to which he belongs, is under a responsibility to strive for the promotion and observance of the rights recognized in the present Covenant,

Agree upon the following articles:

PART I

Article 1

1. All peoples have the right of self-determination. By virtue of that right they freely determine their political status and freely pursue their economic, social and cultural development.

2. All peoples may, for their own ends, freely dispose of their natural wealth and resources without prejudice to any obligations arising out of international economic co-operation, based upon the principle of mutual benefit, and international law. In no case may a people be deprived of its own means of subsistence.

3. The States Parties to the present Covenant, including those having responsibility for the administration of Non-Self-Governing and Trust Territories, shall promote the realization of the right of self-determination, and shall respect that right, in conformity with the provisions of the Charter of the United Nations.

Part II

Article 2

1. Each State Party to the present Covenant undertakes to respect and to ensure to all individuals within its territory and subject to its jurisdiction the rights recognized in the present Covenant, without distinction of any kind, such as race, colour, sex, language, religion, political or other opinion, national or social origin, property, birth or other status.

2. Where not already provided for by existing legislative or other measures, each State Party to the present Covenant undertakes to take the necessary steps, in accordance with its constitutional processes and with the provisions of the present Covenant, to adopt such legislative or other measures as may be necessary to give effect to the rights recognized in the present Covenant.

3. Each State Party to the present Covenant undertakes:

(*a*) To ensure that any person whose rights or freedoms as herein recognized are violated shall have an effective remedy, notwithstanding that the violation has been committed by persons acting in an official capacity;

(*b*) To ensure that any person claiming such a remedy shall have his right thereto determined by competent judicial, administrative or legislative authorities, or by any other competent authority provided for by the legal system of the State, and to develop the possibilities of judicial remedy;

(*c*) To ensure that the competent authorities shall enforce such remedies when granted.

Article 3

The State Parties to the present Covenant undertake to ensure the equal right of men and women to the enjoyment of all civil and political rights set forth in the present Covenant.

Article 4

1. In time of public emergency which threatens the life of the nation and the existence of which is officially proclaimed, the States Parties to the present Covenant may take measures derogating from their obligations under the present Covenant to the extent strictly required by the exigencies of the situation, provided that such measures are not inconsistent with their other obligations under international law and do not involve discrimination solely on the ground of race, colour, sex, language, religion or social origin.

2. No derogation from articles 6, 7, 8 (paragraphs 1 and 2), 11, 15, 16 and 18 may be made under this provision.

3. Any State Party to the present Covenant availing itself of the right of

derogation shall immediately inform the other States Parties to the present Covenant, through the intermediary of the Secretary-General of the United Nations, of the provisions from which it has derogated and of the reasons by which it was actuated. A further communication shall be made, through the same intermediary, on the date on which it terminates such derogation.

Article 5

1. Nothing in the present Covenant may be interpreted as implying for any State, group or person any right to engage in any activity or perform any act aimed at the destruction of any of the rights and freedoms recognized herein or at their limitation to a greater extent than is provided for in the present Covenant.

2. There shall be no restriction upon or derogation from any of the fundamental human rights recognized or existing in any State Party to the present Covenant pursuant to law, conventions, regulations or custom on the pretext that the present Covenant does not recognize such rights or that it recognizes them to a lesser extent.

PART III

Article 6

1. Every human being has the inherent right to life. This right shall be protected by law. No one shall be arbitrarily deprived of his life.

2. In countries which have not abolished the death penalty, sentence of death may be imposed only for the most serious crimes in accordance with the law in force at the time of the commission of the crime and not contrary to the provisions of the present Covenant and to the Convention on the Prevention and Punishment of the Crime of Genocide. This penalty can only be carried out pursuant to a final judgement rendered by a competent court.

3. When deprivation of life constitutes the crime of genocide, it is understood that nothing in this article shall authorize any State Party to the present Covenant to derogate in any way from any obligation assumed under the provisions of the Convention on the Prevention and Punishment of the Crime of Genocide.

4. Anyone sentenced to death shall have the right to seek pardon or commutation of the sentence. Amnesty, pardon or commutation of the sentence of death may be granted in all cases.

5. Sentence of death shall not be imposed for crimes committed by persons below eighteen years of age and shall not be carried out on pregnant women.

6. Nothing in this article shall be invoked to delay or to prevent the abolition of capital punishment by any State Party to the present Covenant.

Article 7

No one shall be subjected to torture or to cruel, inhuman or degrading treatment or punishment. In particular, no one shall be subjected without his free consent to medical or scientific experimentation.

Article 8

1. No one shall be held in slavery; slavery and the slave-trade in all their forms shall be prohibited.

2. No one shall be held in servitude.

3. (*a*) No one shall be required to perform forced or compulsory labour;

(*b*) Paragraph 3(*a*) shall not be held to preclude, in countries where imprisonment with hard labour may be imposed as a punishment for a crime, the performance of hard labour in pursuance of a sentence to such punishment by a competent court;

(*c*) For the purpose of this paragraph the term "forced or compulsory labour" shall not include:

(i) Any work or service, not referred to in subparagraph (*b*), normally required of a person who is under detention in consequence of a lawful order of a court, or of a person during conditional release from such detention;

(ii) Any service of a military character and, in countries where conscientious objection is recognized, any national service required by law of conscientious objectors;

(iii) Any service exacted in cases of emergency or calamity threatening the life or well-being of the community;

(iv) Any work or service which forms part of normal civil obligations.

Article 9

1. Everyone has the right to liberty and security of person. No one shall be subjected to arbitrary arrest or detention. No one shall be deprived of his liberty except on such grounds and in accordance with such procedure as are established by law.

2. Anyone who is arrested shall be informed, at the time of arrest, of the reasons for his arrest and shall be promptly informed of any charges against him.

3. Anyone arrested or detained on a criminal charge shall be brought promptly before a judge or other officer authorized by law to exercise judicial power and shall be entitled to trial within a reasonable time or to release. It shall not be the general rule that persons awaiting trial shall be detained in custody, but release may be subject to guarantees to appear for

trial, at any other stage of the judicial proceedings, and, should occasion arise, for execution of the judgement.

4. Anyone who is deprived of his liberty by arrest or detention shall be entitled to take proceedings before a court, in order that that court may decide without delay on the lawfulness of his detention and order his release if the detention is not lawful.

5. Anyone who has been the victim of unlawful arrest or detention shall have an enforceable right to compensation.

Article 10

1. All persons deprived of their liberty shall be treated with humanity and with respect for the inherent dignity of the human person.

2. (a) Accused persons shall, save in exceptional circumstances, be segregated from convicted persons and shall be subject to separate treatment appropriate to their status as unconvicted persons;

(b) Accused juvenile persons shall be separated from adults and brought as speedily as possible for adjudication.

3. The penitentiary system shall comprise treatment of prisoners the essential aim of which shall be their reformation and social rehabilitation. Juvenile offenders shall be segregated from adults and be accorded treatment appropriate to their age and legal status.

Article 11

No one shall be imprisoned merely on the ground of inability to fulfil a contractual obligation.

Article 12

1. Everyone lawfully within the territory of a State shall, within that territory, have the right to liberty of movement and freedom to choose his residence.

2. Everyone shall be free to leave any country, including his own.

3. The above-mentioned rights shall not be subject to any restrictions except those which are provided by law, are necessary to protect national security, public order (*ordre public*), public health or morals or the rights and freedoms of others, and are consistent with the other rights recognized in the present Covenant.

4. No one shall be arbitrarily deprived of the right to enter his own country.

Article 13

An alien lawfully in the territory of a State Party to the present Covenant may be expelled therefrom only in pursuance of a decision reached in accordance with law and shall, except where compelling reasons of national security otherwise require, be allowed to submit the reasons against his expulsion and to have his case reviewed by, and be represented for the purpose before, the competent authority or a person or persons especially designated by the competent authority.

Article 14

1. All persons shall be equal before the courts and tribunals. In the determination of any criminal charge against him, or of his rights and obligations in a suit at law, everyone shall be entitled to a fair and public hearing by a competent, independent and impartial tribunal established by law. The Press and the public may be excluded from all or part of a trial for reasons of morals, public order (*ordre public*) or national security in a democratic society, or when the interest of the private lives of the parties so requires, or to the extent strictly necessary in the opinion of the court in special circumstances where publicity would prejudice the interests of justice; but any judgement rendered in a criminal case or in a suit at law shall be made public except where the interest of juvenile persons otherwise requires or the proceedings concern matrimonial disputes or the guardianship of children.

2. Everyone charged with a criminal offence shall have the right to be presumed innocent until proved guilty according to law.

3. In the determination of any criminal charge against him, everyone shall be entitled to the following minimum guarantees, in full equality:

(*a*) To be informed promptly and in detail in a language which he understands of the nature and cause of the charge against him;

(*b*) To have adequate time and facilities for the preparation of his defence and to communicate with counsel of his own choosing;

(*c*) To be tried without undue delay;

(*d*) To be tried in his presence, and to defend himself in person or through legal assistance of his own choosing; to be informed, if he does not have legal assistance, of this right; and to have legal assistance assigned to him, in any case where the interests of justice so require, and without payment by him in any such case if he does not have sufficient means to pay for it;

(*e*) To examine, or have examined, the witnesses against him and to obtain the attendance and examination of witnesses on his behalf under the same conditions as witnesses against him;

(*f*) To have the free assistance of an interpreter if he cannot understand or speak the language used in court;

(*g*) Not to be compelled to testify against himself or to confess guilt.

4. In the case of juvenile persons, the procedure shall be such as will take account of their age and the desirability of promoting their rehabilitation.

5. Everyone convicted of a crime shall have the right to his conviction and sentence being reviewed by a higher tribunal according to law.

6. When a person has by a final decision been convicted of a criminal offence and when subsequently his conviction has been reversed or he has been pardoned on the ground that a new or newly discovered fact shows conclusively that there has been a miscarriage of justice, the person who has suffered punishment as a result of such conviction shall be compensated according to law, unless it is proved that the non-disclosure of the unknown fact in time is wholly or partly attributable to him.

7. No one shall be liable to be tried or punished again for an offence for which he has already been finally convicted or acquitted in accordance with the law and penal procedure of each country.

Article 15

1. No one shall be held guilty of any criminal offence on account of any act or omission which did not constitute a criminal offence, under national or international law, at the time when it was committed. Nor shall a heavier penalty be imposed than the one that was applicable at the time when the criminal offence was committed. If, subsequent to the commission of the offence, provision is made by law for the imposition of the lighter penalty, the offender shall benefit thereby.

2. Nothing in this article shall prejudice the trial and punishment of any person for any act or omission which, at the time when it was committed, was criminal according to the general principles of law recognized by the community of nations.

Article 16

Everyone shall have the right to recognition everywhere as a person before the law.

Article 17

1. No one shall be subjected to arbitrary or unlawful interference with his privacy, family, home or correspondence, nor to unlawful attacks on his honour and reputation.

2. Everyone has the right to the protection of the law against such interference or attacks.

Article 18

1. Everyone shall have the right to freedom of thought, conscience and religion. This right shall include freedom to have or to adopt a religion or belief of his choice, and freedom, either individually or in community with others and in public or private, to manifest his religion or belief in worship, observance, practice and teaching.

2. No one shall be subject to coercion which would impair his freedom to have or to adopt a religion or belief of his choice.

3. Freedom to manifest one's religion or beliefs may be subject only to such limitations as are prescribed by law and are necessary to protect public safety, order, health, or morals or the fundamental rights and freedoms of others.

4. The States Parties to the present Covenant undertake to have respect for the liberty of parents and, when applicable, legal guardians to ensure the religious and moral education of their children in conformity with their own convictions.

Article 19

1. Everyone shall have the right to hold opinions without interference.

2. Everyone shall have the right to freedom of expression; this right shall include freedom to seek, receive and impart information and ideas of all kinds, regardless of frontiers, either orally, in writing or in print, in the form of art, or through any other media of his choice.

3. The exercise of the rights provided for in paragraph 2 of this article carries with it special duties and responsibilities. It may therefore be subject to certain restrictions, but these shall only be such as are provided by law and are necessary:

(*a*) For respect of the rights or reputations of others;

(*b*) For the protection of national security or of public order (*ordre public*), or of public health or morals.

Article 20

1. Any propaganda for war shall be prohibited by law.

2. Any advocacy of national, racial or religious hatred that constitutes incitement to discrimination, hostility or violence shall be prohibited by law.

Article 21

The right of peaceful assembly shall be recognized. No restrictions may be placed on the exercise of this right other than those imposed in conformity with the law and which are necessary in a democratic society in the interests of national security or public safety, public order (*ordre public*), the protection of public health or morals or the protection of the rights and freedoms of others.

Article 22

1. Everyone shall have the right to freedom of association with others, including the right to form and join trade unions for the protection of his interests.

2. No restrictions may be placed on the exercise of this right other than

those which are prescribed by law and which are necessary in a democratic society in the interests of national security or public safety, public order (*ordre public*), the protection of public health or morals or the protection of the rights and freedoms of others. This article shall not prevent the imposition of lawful restrictions on members of the armed forces and of the police in their exercise of this right.

3. Nothing in this article shall authorize States Parties to the International Labour Organisation Convention of 1948 concerning Freedom of Association and Protection of the Right to Organize to take legislative measures which would prejudice, or to apply the law in such a manner as to prejudice, the guarantees provided for in that Convention.

Article 23

1. The family is the natural and fundamental group unit of society and is entitled to protection by society and the State.

2. The right of men and women of marriageable age to marry and to found a family shall be recognized.

3. No marriage shall be entered into without the free and full consent of the intending spouses.

4. States Parties to the present Covenant shall take appropriate steps to ensure equality of rights and responsibilities of spouses as to marriage, during marriage and at its dissolution. In the case of dissolution, provision shall be made for the necessary protection of any children.

Article 24

1. Every child shall have, without any discrimination as to race, colour, sex, language, religion, national or social origin, property or birth, the right to such measures of protection as are required by his status as a minor, on the part of his family, society and the State.

2. Every child shall be registered immediately after birth and shall have a name.

3. Every child has the right to acquire a nationality.

Article 25

Every citizen shall have the right and the opportunity, without any of the distinctions mentioned in article 2 and without unreasonable restrictions:

(*a*) To take part in the conduct of public affairs, directly or through freely chosen representatives;

(*b*) To vote and to be elected at genuine periodic elections which shall be by universal and equal suffrage and shall be held by secret ballot, guaranteeing the free expression of the will of the electors;

(*c*) To have access, on general terms of equality, to public service in his country.

Article 26

All persons are equal before the law and are entitled without any discrimination to the equal protection of the law. In this respect, the law shall prohibit any discrimination and guarantee to all persons equal and effective protection against discrimination on any ground such as race, colour, sex, language, religion, political or other opinion, national or social origin, property, birth or other status.

Article 27

In those States in which ethnic, religious or linguistic minorities exist, persons belonging to such minorities shall not be denied the right, in community with the other members of their group, to enjoy their own culture, to profess and practise their own religion, or to use their own language.

. . . .

Article 47

Nothing in the present Covenant shall be interpreted as impairing the inherent right of all peoples to enjoy and utilize fully and freely their natural wealth and resources.

. . . .

International Covenant on Economic, Social and Cultural Rights

PREAMBLE

The States Parties to the present Covenant,

Considering that, in accordance with the principles proclaimed in the Charter of the United Nations, recognition of the inherent dignity and of the equal and inalienable rights of all members of the human family is the foundation of freedom, justice and peace in the world,

Recognizing that these rights derive from the inherent dignity of the human person,

Recognizing that, in accordance with the Universal Declaration of Human Rights, the ideal of free human beings enjoying freedom from fear and want can only be achieved if conditions are created whereby everyone may enjoy his economic, social and cultural rights, as well as his civil and political rights,

Considering the obligation of States under the Charter of the United Nations to promote universal respect for, and observance of, human rights and freedoms,

Realizing that the individual, having duties to other individuals and to the community to which he belongs, is under a responsibility to strive for the promotion and observance of the rights recognized in the present Covenant,

Agree upon the following articles:

PART I

Article 1

1. All peoples have the right of self-determination. By virtue of that right they freely determine the political status and freely pursue their economic, social and cultural development.

2. All peoples may, for their own ends, freely dispose of their natural wealth and resources without prejudice to any obligations arising out of international economic co-operation, based upon the principle of mutual benefit, and international law. In no case may a people be deprived of its own means of subsistence.

3. The States Parties to the present Covenant, including those having responsibility for the administration of Non-Self-Governing and Trust Territories, shall promote the realization of the right of self-determi-

nation, and shall respect that right, in conformity with the provisions of the Charter of the United Nations.

PART II

Article 2

1. Each State Party to the present Covenant undertakes to take steps, individually and through international assistance and cooperation, especially economic and technical, to the maximum of its available resources, with a view to achieving progressively the full realization of the rights recognized in the present Covenant by all appropriate means, including particularly the adoption of legislative measures.

2. The States Parties to the present Covenant undertake to guarantee that the rights enunciated in the present Covenant will be exercised without discrimination of any kind as to race, colour, sex, language, religion, political or other opinion, national or social origin, property, birth or other status.

3. Developing countries, with due regard to human rights and their national economy, may determine to what extent they would guarantee the economic rights recognized in the present Covenant to non-nationals.

Article 3

The States Parties to the present Covenant undertake to ensure the equal right of men and women to the enjoyment of all economic, social and cultural rights set forth in the present Covenant.

Article 4

The States Parties to the present Covenant recognize that, in the enjoyment of those rights provided by the State in conformity with the present Covenant, the State may subject such rights only to such limitations as are determined by law only in so far as this may be compatible with the nature of these rights and solely for the purpose of promoting the general welfare in a democratic society.

Article 5

1. Nothing in the present Covenant may be interpreted as implying for any State, group or person any right to engage in any activity or to perform any act aimed at the destruction of any of the rights or freedoms recognized herein, or at their limitation to a greater extent than is provided for in the present Covenant.

2. No restriction upon or derogation from any of the fundamental human rights recognized or existing in any country in virtue of law, conventions, regulations or custom shall be admitted on the pretext that the

present Covenant does not recognize such rights or that it recognizes them to a lesser extent.

PART III

Article 6

1. The States Parties to the present Covenant recognize the right to work, which includes the right of everyone to the opportunity to gain his living by work which he freely chooses or accepts, and will take appropriate steps to safeguard this right.

2. The steps to be taken by a State Party to the present Covenant to achieve the full realization of this right shall include technical and vocational guidance and training programmes, policies and techniques to achieve steady economic, social and cultural development and full and productive employment under conditions safeguarding fundamental political and economic freedoms to the individual.

Article 7

The States Parties to the present Covenant recognize the right of everyone to the enjoyment of just and favourable conditions of work which ensure, in particular:

(*a*) Remuneration which provides all workers, as a minimum, with:
   (i) Fair wages and equal remuneration for work of equal value without distinction of any kind, in particular women being guaranteed conditions of work not inferior to those enjoyed by men, with equal pay for equal work;
   (ii) A decent living for themselves and their families in accordance with the provisions of the present Covenant;

(*b*) Safe and healthy working conditions;

(*c*) Equal opportunity for everyone to be promoted in his employment to an appropriate higher level, subject to no considerations other than those of seniority and competence;

(*d*) Rest, leisure and reasonable limitation of working hours and periodic holidays with pay, as well as remuneration for public holidays.

Article 8

1. The States Parties to the present Covenant undertake to ensure:

(*a*) The right of everyone to form trade unions and join the trade union of his choice, subject only to the rules of the organization concerned, for the promotion and protection of his economic and social interests. No restrictions may be placed on the exercise of this right other than those prescribed by law and which are necessary in a democratic society in the interests of national security or public order or for the protection of the rights and freedoms of others;

(*b*) The right of trade unions to establish national federations or confederations and the right of the latter to form or join international trade-union organizations;

(*c*) The right of trade unions to function freely subject to no limitations other than those prescribed by law and which are necessary in a democratic society in the interests of national security or public order or for the protection of the rights and freedoms of others;

(*d*) The right to strike, provided that it is exercised in conformity with the laws of the particular country.

2. This article shall not prevent the imposition of lawful restrictions on the exercise of these rights by members of the armed forces or of the police or of the administration of the State.

3. Nothing in this article shall authorize States Parties to the International Labour Organisation Convention of 1948 concerning Freedom of Association and Protection of the Right to Organize to take legislative measures which would prejudice, or apply the law in such a manner as would prejudice, the guarantees provided for in that Convention.

Article 9

The States Parties to the present Covenant recognize the right of everyone to social security, including social insurance.

Article 10

The States Parties to the present Covenant recognize that:

1. The widest possible protection and assistance should be accorded to the family, which is the natural and fundamental group unit of society, particularly for its establishment and while it is responsible for the care and education of dependent children. Marriage must be entered into with the free consent of the intending spouses.

2. Special protection should be accorded to mothers during a reasonable period before and after childbirth. During such period working mothers should be accorded paid leave or leave with adequate social security benefits.

3. Special measures of protection and assistance should be taken on behalf of all children and young persons without any discrimination for reasons of parentage or other conditions. Children and young persons should be protected from economic and social exploitation. Their employment in work harmful to their morals or health or dangerous to life or likely to hamper their normal development should be punishable by law. States should also set age limits below which the paid employment of child labour should be prohibited and punishable by law.

Article 11

1. The States Parties to the present Covenant recognize the right of everyone to an adequate standard of living for himself and his family, including adequate food, clothing and housing, and to the continuous improvement of living conditions. The States Parties will take appropriate steps to ensure the realization of this right, recognizing to this effect the essential importance of international co-operation based on free consent.

2. The States Parties to the present Covenant, recognizing the fundamental right of everyone to be free from hunger, shall take, individually and through international co-operation, the measures, including specific programmes, which are needed:

(*a*) To improve methods of production, conservation and distribution of food by making full use of technical and scientific knowledge, by disseminating knowledge of the principles of nutrition and by developing or reforming agrarian systems in such a way as to achieve the most efficient development and utilization of natural resources;

(*b*) Taking into account the problems of both food-importing and food-exporting countries, to ensure an equitable distribution of world food supplies in relation to need.

Article 12

1. The States Parties to the present Covenant recognize the right of everyone to the enjoyment of the highest attainable standard of physical and mental health.

2. The steps to be taken by the States Parties to the present Covenant to achieve the full realization of this right shall include those necessary for:

(*a*) The provision for the reduction of the stillbirth-rate and of infant mortality and for the healthy development of the child;

(*b*) The improvement of all aspects of environmental and industrial hygiene;

(*c*) The prevention, treatment and control of epidemic, endemic, occupational and other diseases;

(*d*) The creation of conditions which would assure to all medical service and medical attention in the event of sickness.

Article 13

1. The States Parties to the present Covenant recognize the right of everyone to education. They agree that education shall be directed to the full development of the human personality and the sense of its dignity, and shall strengthen the respect for human rights and fundamental freedoms. They further agree that education shall enable all persons to participate effectively in a free society, promote understanding, tolerance and friend-

ship among all nations and all racial, ethnic or religious groups, and further the activities of the United Nations for the maintenance of peace.

2. The States Parties to the present Covenant recognize that, with a view to achieving the full realization of this right:

(*a*) Primary education shall be compulsory and available free to all;

(*b*) Secondary education in its different forms, including technical and vocational secondary education, shall be made generally available and accessible to all by every appropriate means, and in particular by the progressive introduction of free education;

(*c*) Higher education shall be made equally accessible to all, on the basis of capacity, by every appropriate means, and in particular by the progressive introduction of free education;

(*d*) Fundamental education shall be encouraged or intensified as far as possible for those persons who have not received or completed the whole period of their primary education;

(*e*) The development of a system of schools at all levels shall be actively pursued, an adequate fellowship system shall be established, and the material conditions of teaching staff shall be continuously improved.

3. The States Parties to the present Covenant undertake to have respect for the liberty of parents and, when applicable, legal guardians to choose for their children schools, other than those established by the public authorities, which conform to such minimum educational standards as may be laid down or approved by the State and to ensure the religious and moral education of their children in conformity with their own convictions.

4. No part of this article shall be construed so as to interfere with the liberty of individuals and bodies to establish and direct educational institutions, subject always to the observance of the principles set forth in paragraph 1 of this article and to the requirement that the education given in such institutions shall conform to such minimum standards as may be laid down by the State.

Article 14

Each State Party to the present Covenant which, at the time of becoming a Party, has not been able to secure in its metropolitan territory or other territories under its jurisdiction compulsory primary education, free of charge, undertakes, within two years, to work out and adopt a detailed plan of action for the progressive implementation, within a reasonable number of years, to be fixed in the plan, of the principle of compulsory education free of charge for all.

Article 15

1. The States Parties to the present Covenant recognize the right of everyone:

(*a*) To take part in cultural life;

(*b*) To enjoy the benefits of scientific progress and its applications;

(*c*) To benefit from the protection of the moral and material interests resulting from any scientific, literary or artistic production of which he is the author.

2. The steps to be taken by the States Parties to the present Covenant to achieve the full realization of this right shall include those necessary for the conservation, the development and the diffusion of science and culture.

3. The States Parties to the present Covenant undertake to respect the freedom indispensable for scientific research and creative activity.

4. The States Parties to the present Covenant recognize the benefits to be derived from the encouragement and development of international contacts and co-operation in the scientific and cultural fields.

.   .   .   .

Article 25

Nothing in the present Covenant shall be interpreted as impairing the inherent rights of all peoples to enjoy and utilize fully and freely their natural wealth and resources.

.   .   .   .

European Convention for the Protection of Human Rights and Fundamental Freedoms

The Governments signatory hereto, being Members of the Council of Europe,

Considering the Universal Declaration of Human Rights proclaimed by the General Assembly of the United Nations on 10 December 1948;

Considering that this Declaration aims at securing the universal and effective recognition and observance of the Rights therein declared;

Considering that the aim of the Council of Europe is the achievement of greater unity between its Members and that one of the methods by which that aim is to be pursued is the maintenance and further realization of Human Rights and Fundamental Freedoms;

Reaffirming their profound belief in those Fundamental Freedoms which are the foundation of justice and peace in the world and are best maintained on the one hand by an effective political democracy and on the other by a common understanding and observance of the Human Rights upon which they depend;

Being resolved, as the Governments of European countries which are likeminded and have a common heritage of political traditions, ideals, freedom and the rule of law to take the first steps for the collective enforcement of the Rights stated in the Universal Declaration;

Have agreed as follows:

Article 1

The High Contracting Parties shall secure to everyone within their jurisdiction the rights and freedoms defined in Section I of this Convention.

Section I

Article 2

1. Everyone's right to life shall be protected by law. No one shall be deprived of his life intentionally save in the execution of a sentence of a court following his conviction of a crime for which this penalty is provided by law.

2. Deprivation of life shall not be regarded as inflicted in contravention of this Article when it results from the use of force which is no more than absolutely necessary:

    (*a*) in defence of any person from unlawful violence;

    (*b*) in order to effect a lawful arrest or to prevent the escape of a person lawfully detained;

(*c*) in action lawfully taken for the purpose of quelling a riot or insurrection.

Article 3

No one shall be subjected to torture or to inhuman or degrading treatment or punishment.

Article 4

1. No one shall be held in slavery or servitude.
2. No one shall be required to perform forced or compulsory labour.
3. For the purpose of this Article the term 'forced or compulsory labour' shall not include:
    (*a*) any work required to be done in the ordinary course of detention imposed according to the provisions of Article 5 of this Convention or during conditional release from such detention;
    (*b*) any service of a military character or, in case of conscientious objectors in countries where they are recognized, service exacted instead of compulsory military service;
    (*c*) any service exacted in case of an emergency or calamity threatening the life or well-being of the community;
    (*d*) any work or service which forms part of normal civic obligations.

Article 5

1. Everyone has the right to liberty and security of person.
   No one shall be deprived of his liberty save in the following cases and in accordance with a procedure prescribed by law;
    (*a*) the lawful detention of a person after conviction by a competent court;
    (*b*) the lawful arrest or detention of a person for non-compliance with the lawful order of a court or in order to secure the fulfilment of any obligation prescribed by law;
    (*c*) the lawful arrest or detention of a person effected for the purpose of bringing him before the competent legal authority on reasonable suspicion of having committed an offence or when it is reasonably considered necessary to prevent his committing an offence or fleeing after having done so;
    (*d*) the detention of a minor by lawful order for the purpose of educational supervision or his lawful detention for the purpose of bringing him before the competent legal authority;
    (*e*) the lawful detention of persons for the prevention of the spreading of infectious diseases, of persons of unsound mind, alcoholics or drug addicts, or vagrants;
    (*f*) the lawful arrest or detention of a person to prevent his effecting

an unauthorized entry into the country or of a person against whom action is being taken with a view to deportation or extradition.

2. Everyone who is arrested shall be informed promptly, in a language which he understands, of the reasons for his arrest and of any charge against him.

3. Everyone arrested or detained in accordance with the provisions of paragraph 1 (*c*) of this Article shall be brought promptly before a judge or other officer authorized by law to exercise judicial power and shall be entitled to trial within a reasonable time or to release pending trial. Release may be conditioned by guarantees to appear for trial.

4. Everyone who is deprived of his liberty by arrest or detention shall be entitled to take proceedings by which the lawfulness of his detention shall be decided speedily by a court and his release ordered if the detention is not lawful.

5. Everyone who has been the victim of arrest or detention in contravention of the provisions of this Article shall have an enforceable right to compensation.

Article 6

1. In the determination of his civil rights and obligations or of any criminal charge against him, everyone is entitled to a fair and public hearing within a reasonable time by an independent and impartial tribunal established by law. Judgement shall be pronounced publicly but the press and public may be excluded from all or part of the trial in the interest of morals, public order or national security in a democratic society, where the interest of juveniles or the protection of the private life of the parties so require, or to the extent strictly necessary in the opinion of the court in special circumstances where publicity would prejudice the interests of justice.

2. Everyone charged with a criminal offence shall be presumed innocent until proved guilty according to law.

3. Everyone charged with a criminal offence has the following minimum rights:

(*a*) to be informed promptly, in a language which he understands and in detail, of the nature and cause of the accusation against him;

(*b*) to have adequate time and facilities for the preparation of his defence;

(*c*) to defend himself in person or through legal assistance of his own choosing or, if he has not sufficient means to pay for legal assistance, to be given it free when the interests of justice so require;

(*d*) to examine or have examined witnesses against him and to obtain the attendance and examination of witnesses on his behalf under the same conditions as witnesses against him;

(*e*) to have the free assistance of an interpreter if he cannot understand or speak the language used in court.

Article 7

1. No one shall be held guilty of any criminal offence on account of any
act or omission which did not constitute a criminal offence under national
or international law at the time when it was committed. Nor shall a heavier
penalty be imposed than the one that was applicable at the time the criminal offence was committed.
2. This Article shall not prejudice the trial and punishment of any person
for any act or omission which, at the time when it was committed, was
criminal according to the general principles of law recognized by civilized
nations.

Article 8

1. Everyone has the right to respect for his private and family life, his
home and his correspondence.
2. There shall be no interference by a public authority with the exercise of
this right except such as is in accordance with the law and is necessary in a
democratic society in the interests of national security, public safety or the
economic well-being of the country, for the prevention of disorder or
crime, for the protection of health or morals, or for the protection of the
rights and freedoms of others.

Article 9

1. Everyone has the right to freedom of thought, conscience and religion;
this right includes freedom to change his religion or belief, and freedom,
either alone or in community with others and in public or private, to manifest his religion or belief, in worship, teaching, practice and observance.
2. Freedom to manifest one's religion or beliefs shall be subject only to
such limitations as are prescribed by law and are necessary in a democratic
society in the interests of public safety, for the protection of public order,
health or morals, or for the protection of the rights and freedoms of others.

Article 10

1. Everyone has the right to freedom of expression. This right shall
include freedom to hold opinions and to receive and impart information
and ideas without interference by public authority and regardless of frontiers. This Article shall not prevent States from requiring the licensing of
broadcasting, television or cinema enterprises.
2. The exercise of these freedoms, since it carries with it duties and
responsibilities, may be subject to such formalities, conditions, restrictions
or penalties as are prescribed by law and are necessary in a democratic
society in the interests of national security, territorial integrity or public

safety, for the prevention of disorder or crime, for the protection of health or morals, for the protection of the reputation or rights of others, for preventing the disclosure of information received in confidence, or for maintaining the authority and impartiality of the judiciary.

Article 11

1. Everyone has the right to freedom of peaceful assembly and to freedom of association with others, including the right to form and to join trade unions for the protection of his interests.

2. No restrictions shall be placed on the exercise of these rights other than such as are prescribed by law and are necessary in a democratic society in the interests of national security or public safety, for the prevention of disorder or crime, for the protection of health or morals to for the protection of the rights and freedoms of others. This Article shall not prevent the imposition of lawful restrictions on the exercise of these rights by members of the armed forces, of the police or of the administration of the State.

Article 12

Men and women of marriageable age have the right to marry and to found a family, according to the national laws governing the exercise of this right.

Article 13

Everyone whose rights and freedoms as set forth in this Convention are violated shall have an effective remedy before a national authority notwithstanding that the violation has been committed by persons acting in an official capacity.

Article 14

The enjoyment of the rights and freedoms set forth in this Convention shall be secured without discrimination on any ground such as sex, race, colour, language, religion, political or other opinion, national or social origin, association with a national minority, property, birth or other status.

Article 15

1. In time of war or other public emergency threatening the life of the nation any High Contracting Party may take measures derogating from its obligations under this Convention to the extent strictly required by the exigencies of the situation, provided that such measures are not inconsistent with its obligations under international law.

2. No derogation from Article 2, except in respect of deaths resulting from lawful acts of war, or from Articles 3, 4 (paragraph 1) and 7 shall be made under this provision.

3. Any High Contracting Party availing itself of this right of derogation shall keep the Secretary-General of the Council of Europe fully informed

of the measures which it has taken and the reasons therefor. It shall also inform the Secretary-General of the Council of Europe when such measures have ceased to operate and the provisions of the Convention are again fully executed.

Article 16

Nothing in Articles 10, 11, and 14 shall be regarded as preventing the High Contracting Parties from imposing restrictions on the political activity of aliens.

Article 17

Nothing in this Convention may be interpreted as implying for any State, group or person any right to engage in any activity or perform any act aimed at the destruction of any of the rights and freedoms set forth herein or at their limitation to a greater extent than is provided for in the Convention.

Article 18

The restrictions permitted under this Convention to the said rights and freedoms shall not be applied for any purpose other than those for which they have been prescribed.

. . . .

PROTOCOL 1—ENFORCEMENT OF CERTAIN RIGHTS AND FREEDOMS NOT INCLUDED IN SECTION I OF THE CONVENTION

The Governments signatory hereto, being Members of the Council of Europe,

Being resolved to take steps to ensure the collective enforcement of certain rights and freedoms other than those already included in Section 1 of the Convention for the Protection of Human Rights and Fundamental Freedoms signed at Rome on 4th November, 1950 (hereinafter referred to as 'the Convention'),

Have agreed as follows:

Article 1

Every natural or legal person is entitled to the peaceful enjoyment of his possessions. No one shall be deprived of his possessions except in the public interest and subject to the conditions provided for by law and by the general principles of international law.

The preceding provisions shall not, however, in any way impair the right of a State to enforce such laws as it deems necessary to control the use of property in accordance with the general interest or to secure the payment of taxes or other contributions or penalties.

Article 2

No person shall be denied the right to education. In the exercise of any functions which it assumes in relation to education and to teaching, the State shall respect the right of parents to ensure such education and teaching in conformity with their own religious and philosophical convictions.

Article 3

The High Contracting Parties undertake to hold free elections at reasonable intervals by secret ballot, under conditions which will ensure the free expression of the opinion of the people in the choice of the legislature.

. . . .

PROTOCOL 4—PROTECTING CERTAIN ADDITIONAL RIGHTS

The Governments signatory hereto, being Members of the Council of Europe,

Being resolved to take steps to ensure the collective enforcement of certain rights and freedoms other than those already included in Section 1 of the Convention for the Protection of Human Rights and Fundamental Freedoms signed at Rome on 4 November 1950 (hereinafter referred to as 'the Convention') and in Articles 1 to 3 of the First Protocol to the Convention, signed at Paris on 20 March 1952,

Have agreed as follows:

Article 1

No one shall be deprived of his liberty merely on the ground of inability to fulfil a contractual obligation.

Article 2

1. Everyone lawfully within the territory of a State shall, within that territory, have the right to liberty of movement and freedom to choose his residence.
2. Everyone shall be free to leave any country, including his own.
3. No restrictions shall be placed on the exercise of these rights other than such as are in accordance with law and are necessary in a democratic society in the interests of national security or public safety, for the maintenance of 'ordre public', for the prevention of crime or for the protection of the rights and freedoms of others.
4. The rights set forth in paragraph 1 may also be subject, in particular

areas, to restrictions imposed in accordance with law and justified by the public interest in a democratic society.

Article 3

1. No one shall be expelled, by means either of an individual or of a collective measure, from the territory of the State of which he is a national.
2. No one shall be deprived of the right to enter the territory of the State of which he is a national.

Article 4

Collective expulsion of aliens is prohibited.

.   .   .   .

European Social Charter

The Governments signatory hereto, being Members of the Council of Europe,

Considering that the aim of the Council of Europe is the achievement of greater unity between its Members for the purpose of safeguarding and realizing the ideals and principles which are their common heritage and of facilitating their economic and social progress, in particular by the maintenance and further realization of human rights and fundamental freedoms;

Considering that in the European Convention for the Protection of Human Rights and Fundamental Freedoms signed at Rome on 4th November 1950, and the Protocol thereto signed at Paris on 20th March 1952, the member States of the Council of Europe agreed to secure to their populations the civil and political rights and freedoms therein specified;

Considering that the enjoyment of social rights should be secured without discrimination on grounds of race, colour, sex, religion, political opinion, national extraction or social origin;

Being resolved to make every effort in common to improve the standard of living and to promote the social well-being of both their urban and rural populations by means of appropriate institutions and action;

Have agreed as follows:

Part I

The Contracting Parties accept as the aim of their policy, to be pursued by all appropriate means, both national and international in character, the attainment of conditions in which the following rights and principles may be effectively realized:

(1) Everyone shall have the opportunity to earn his living in an occupation freely entered upon.

(2) All workers have the right to just conditions of work.

(3) All workers have the right to safe and healthy working conditions.

(4) All workers have the right to a fair remuneration sufficient for a decent standard of living for themselves and their families.

(5) All workers and employers have the right to freedom of association in national or international organizations for the protection of their economic and social interests.

(6) All workers and employers have the right to bargain collectively.

(7) Children and young persons have the right to a special protection against the physical and moral hazards to which they are exposed.

(8) Employed women, in case of maternity, and other employed women as appropriate, have the right to a special protection in their work.

(9) Everyone has the right to appropriate facilities for vocational guidance with a view to helping him choose an occupation suited to his personal aptitude and interests.

(10) Everyone has the right to appropriate facilities for vocational training.

(11) Everyone has the right to benefit from any measures enabling him to enjoy the highest possible standard of health attainable.

(12) All workers and their dependants have the right to social security.

(13) Anyone without adequate resources has the right to social and medical assistance.

(14) Everyone has the right to benefit from social welfare services.

(15) Disabled persons have the right to vocational training, rehabilitation and resettlement, whatever the origin and nature of the disability.

(16) The family as a fundamental unit of society has the right to appropriate social, legal and economic protection to ensure its full development.

(17) Mothers and children, irrespective of marital status and family relations, have the right to appropriate social and economic protection.

(18) The nationals of any one of the Contracting Parties have the right to engage in any gainful occupation in the territory of any one of the others on a footing of equality with the nationals of the latter, subject to restrictions based on cogent economic or social reasons.

(19) Migrant workers who are nationals of a Contracting Party and their families have the right to protection and assistance in the territory of any other Contracting Party.

Part II

The Contracting Parties undertake, as provided for in Part III, to consider themselves bound by the obligations laid down in the following Articles and paragraphs.

Article 1—The Right to Work

With a view to ensuring the effective exercise of the right to work, the Contracting Parties undertake:

    (1) to accept as one of their primary aims and responsibilities the

achievement and maintenance of as high and stable a level of employment as possible, with a view to the attainment of full employment;

(2) to protect effectively the right of the worker to earn his living in an occupation freely entered upon;

(3) to establish or maintain free employment services for all workers;

(4) to provide or promote appropriate vocational guidance, training and rehabilitation.

Article 2—The Right to Just Conditions of Work

With a view to ensuring the effective exercise of the right to just conditions of work, the Contracting Parties undertake:

(1) to provide for reasonable daily and weekly working hours, the working week to be progressively reduced to the extent that the increase of productivity and other relevant factors permit;

(2) to provide for public holidays with pay;

(3) to provide for a minimum of two weeks' annual holiday with pay;

(4) to provide for additional paid holidays or reduced working hours for workers engaged in dangerous or unhealthy occupations as prescribed;

(5) to ensure a weekly rest period which shall, as far as possible, coincide with the day recognized by tradition or custom in the country or region concerned as a day of rest.

Article 3—The Right to Safe and Healthy Working Conditions

With a view to ensuring the effective exercise of the right to safe and healthy working conditions, the Contracting Parties undertake:

(1) to issue safety and health regulations;

(2) to provide for the enforcement of such regulations by measures of supervision;

(3) to consult, as appropriate, employers' and workers' organizations on measures intended to improve industrial safety and health.

Article 4—The Right to a Fair Remuneration

With a view to ensuring the effective exercise of the right to a fair remuneration, the Contracting Parties undertake:

(1) to recognize the right of workers to a remuneration such as will give them and their families a decent standard of living;

(2) to recognize the right of workers to an increased rate of remuneration for overtime work, subject to exceptions in particular cases;

(3) to recognize the right of men and women workers to equal pay for work of equal value;

(4) to recognize the right of all workers to a reasonable period of notice for termination of employment;

(5) to permit deductions from wages only under conditions and to the extent prescribed by national laws or regulations or fixed by collective agreements or arbitration awards.

The exercise of these rights shall be achieved by freely concluded collective agreements, by statutory wage-fixing machinery, or by other means appropriate to national conditions.

Article 5—The Right to Organize

With a view to ensuring or promoting the freedom of workers and employers to form local, national or international organizations for the protection of their economic and social interests and to join those organizations, the Contracting Parties undertake that national law shall not be such as to impair, nor shall it be so applied as to impair, this freedom. The extent to which the guarantees provided for in this Article shall apply to the police shall be determined by national laws or regulations. The principle governing the application to the members of the armed forces of these guarantees and the extent to which they shall apply to persons in this category shall equally be determined by national laws or regulations.

Article 6—The Right to Bargain Collectively

With a view to ensuring the effective exercise of the right to bargain collectively, the Contracting Parties undertake:
  (1) to promote joint consultation between workers and employers;
  (2) to promote, where necessary and appropriate, machinery for voluntary negotiations between employers or employers' organizations and workers' organizations, with a view to the regulation of terms and conditions of employment by means of collective agreements;
  (3) to promote the establishment and use of appropriate machinery for concilation and voluntary arbitration for the settlement of labour disputes;
and recognize:
  (4) the right of workers and employers to collective action in cases of conflicts of interest, including the right to strike, subject to obligations that might arise out of collective agreements previously entered into.

Article 7—The Right of Children and Young Persons to Protection

With a view to ensuring the effective exercise of the right of children and young persons to protection, the Contracting Parties undertake:
  (1) to provide that the minimum age of admission to employment shall be 15 years, subject to exceptions for children employed in

prescribed light work without harm to their health, morals or education;

(2) to provide that a higher minimum age of admission to employment shall be fixed with respect to prescribed occupations regarded as dangerous or unhealthy;

(3) to provide that persons who are still subject to compulsory education shall not be employed in such work as would deprive them of the full benefit of their education;

(4) to provide that the working hours of persons under 16 years of age shall be limited in accordance with the needs of their development, and particularly with their need for vocational training;

(5) to recognize the right of young workers and apprentices to a fair wage or other appropriate allowances;

(6) to provide that the time spent by young persons in vocational training during the normal working hours with the consent of the employer shall be treated as forming part of the working day;

(7) to provide that employed persons of under 18 years of age shall be entitled to not less than three weeks' annual holiday with pay;

(8) to provide that persons under 18 years of age shall not be employed in night work with the exception of certain occupations provided for by national lawas or regulations;

(9) to provide that persons under 18 years of age employed in occupations prescribed by national laws or regulations shall be subject to regular medical control;

(10) to ensure special protection against physical and moral dangers to which children and young persons are exposed, and particularly against those resulting directly or indirectly from their work.

Article 8—The Right of Employed Women to Protection

With a view to ensuring the effective exercise of the right of employed women to protection, the Contracting Parties undertake:

(1) to provide either by paid leave, by adequate social security benefits or by benefits from public funds, for women to take leave before and after childbirth up to a total of at least 12 weeks;

(2) to consider it as unlawful for an employer to give a woman notice of dismissal during her absence on maternity leave or to give her notice of dismissal at such a time that the notice would expire during such absence;

(3) to provide that mothers who are nursing their infants shall be entitled to sufficient time off for this purpose;

(4) (a) to regulate the employment of women workers on night work in industrial employment;

(b) to prohibit the employment of women workers in underground mining, and, as appropriate, on all other work which is unsuitable for them by reason of its dangerous, unhealthy, or arduous nature.

Article 9—The Right to Vocational Guidance

With a view to ensuring the effective exercise of the right to vocational guidance, the Contracting Parties undertake to provide or promote, as necessary, a service which will assist all persons, including the handicapped, to solve problems related to occupational choice and progress, with due regard to the individual's characteristics and their relation to occupational opportunity: this assistance should be available free of charge, both to young persons, including school children, and to adults.

Article 10—The Right to Vocational Training

With a view to ensuring the effective exercise of the right to vocational training, the Contracting Parties undertake:

(1) to provide or promote, as necessary, the technical and vocational training of all persons, including the handicapped, in consultation with employers' and workers' organizations, and to grant facilities for access to higher technical and university education, based solely on individual aptitude;

(2) to provide or promote a system of apprenticeship and other systematic arrangements for training young boys and girls in their various employments;

(3) to provide or promote, as necessary:

    (a) adequate and readily available training facilities for adult workers;

    (b) special facilities for the re-training of adult workers needed as a result of technological developments or new trends in employment;

(4) to encourage the full utilization of the facilities provided by appropriate measures such as:

    (a) reducing or abolishing any fees or charges;

    (b) granting financial assistance in appropriate cases;

    (c) including in the normal working hours time spent on supplementary training taken by the worker, at the request of his employer, during employment;

    (d) ensuring, through adequate supervision, in consultation with the employers' and workers' organizations, the efficiency or apprenticeship and other training arrangements for young workers, and the adequate protection of young workers generally.

Article 11—The Right to Protection of Health

With a view to ensuring the effective exercise of the right to protection of health, the Contracting Parties undertake, either directly or in co-operation with public or private organizations, to take appropriate measures designed *inter alia*:

(1) to remove as far as possible the causes of ill-health;
(2) to provide advisory and educational facilities for the promotion of health and the encouragement of individual responsibility in matters of health;
(3) to prevent as far as possible epidemic, endemic and other diseases.

Article 12—The Right to Social Security

With a view to ensuring the effective exercise of the right to social security, the Contracting Parties undertake:

(1) to establish or maintain a system of social security;
(2) to maintain the social security system at a satisfactory level at least equal to that required for ratification of International Labour Convention (No. 102) Concerning Minimum Standards of Social Security;
(3) to endeavour to raise progressively the system of social security to a higher level;
(4) to take steps, by the conclusion of appropriate bilateral and multilateral agreements, or by other means, and subject to the conditions laid down in such agreements, in order to ensure:
   (*a*) equal treatment with their own nationals of the nationals of other Contracting Parties in respect of social security rights, including the retention of benefits arising out of social security legislation, whatever movements the persons protected may undertake between the territories of the Contracting Parties;
   (*b*) the granting, maintenance and resumption of social security rights by such means as the accumulation of insurance or employment periods completed under the legislation of each of the Contracting Parties.

Article 13—The Right to Social and Medical Assistance

With a view to ensuring the effective exercise of the right to social and medical assistance, the Contracting Parties undertake:

(1) to ensure that any person who is without adequate resources and who is unable to secure such resources either by his own efforts or from other sources, in particular by benefits under a social security scheme, be granted adequate assistance, and, in case of sickness, the care necessitated by his condition;

(2) to ensure that persons receiving such assistance shall not, for that reason, suffer from a diminution of their policital or social rights;

(3) to provide that everyone may receive by appropriate public or private services such advice and personal help as may be required to prevent, to remove, or to alleviate personal or family want;

(4) to apply the provisions referred to in paragraphs 1, 2 and 3 of this Article on an equal footing with their nationals to nationals of other Contracting Parties lawfully within their territories, in accordance with their obligations under the European Convention on Social and Medical Assistance, signed at Paris on 11th December 1953.

Article 14—The Right to Benefit from Social Welfare Services

With a view to ensuring the effective exercise of the right to benefit from social welfare services, the Contracting Parties undertake:

(1) to promote or provide services which, by using methods of social work, would contribute to the welfare and development of both individuals and groups in the community, and to their adjustment to the social environment;

(2) to encourage the participation of individuals and voluntary or other organizations in the establishment and maintenance of such services.

Article 15—The Right of Physically or Mentally Disabled Persons to Vocational Training, Rehabilitation and Social Resettlement

With a view to ensuring the effective exercise of the right of the physically or mentally disabled to vocational training, rehabilitation and resettlement, the Contracting Parties undertake:

(1) to take adequate measures for the provision of training facilities, including, where necessary, specialized institutions, public or private;

(2) to take adequate measures for the placing of disabled persons in employment, such as specialized placing services, facilities for sheltered employment and measures to encourage employers to admit disabled persons to employment.

Article 16—The Right of the Family to Social, Legal and Economic Protection

With a view to ensuring the necessary conditions for the full development of the family, which is a fundamental unit of society, the Contracting Parties undertake to promote the economic, legal and social protection of family life by such means as social and family benefits, fiscal arrangements, provision of family housing, benefits for the newly married, and other appropriate means.

Article 17—The Right of Mothers and Children to Social and Economic Protection

With a view to ensuring the effective exercise of the right of mothers and children to social and economic protection, the Contracting Parties will take all appropriate and necessary measures to that end, including the establishment or maintenance of appropriate institutions of services.

Article 18—The Right to Engage in a Gainful Occupation in the Territory of Other Contracting Parties

With a view to ensuring the effective exercise of the right to engage in a gainful occupation in the territory of any other Contracting Party, the Contracting Parties undertake:

(1) to apply existing regulations in a spirit of liberality;

(2) to simplify existing formalities and to reduce or abolish chancery dues and other charges payable by foreign workers or their employers;

(3) to liberalize, individually or collectively, regulations governing the employment of foreign workers;

and recognize:

(4) the right of their nationals to leave the country to engage in a gainful occupation in the territories of the other Contracting Parties.

Article 19—The Right of Migrant Workers and their Families to Protection and Assistance

With a view to ensuring the effective exercise of the right of migrant workers and their families to protection and assistance in the territory of any other Contracting Party, the Contracting Parties undertake:

(1) to maintain or to satisfy themselves that there are maintained adequate and free services to assist such workers, particularly in obtaining accurate information, and to take all appropriate steps, so far as national laws and regulations permit, against misleading propaganda relating to emigration and immigration;

(2) to adopt appropriate measures within their own jurisdiction to facilitate the departure, journey and reception of such workers and their families, and to provide, within their own jurisdiction, appropriate services for health, medical attention and good hygienic conditions during the journey;

(3) to promote co-operation, as appropriate, between social services, public and private, in emigration and immigration countries;

(4) to secure for such workers lawfully within their territories, insofar as such matters are regulated by law or regulations or are subject to the control of administrative authorities, treatment not less

favourable than that of their own nationals in respect of the following matters:
    (a) remuneration and other employment and working conditions;
    (b) membership of trade unions and enjoyment of the benefits of
        collective bargaining;
    (c) accommodation;
(5) to secure for such workers lawfully within their territories treat-
    ment not less favourable than that of their own nationals with
    regard to employment taxes, dues or contributions payable in
    respect of employed persons;
(6) to facilitate as far as possible the reunion of the family of a foreign
    worker permitted to establish himself in the territory;
(7) to secure for such workers lawfully within their territories treat-
    ment not less favourable than that of their own nationals in respect
    of legal proceedings relating to matters referred to in this Article;
(8) to secure that such workers lawfully residing within their terri-
    tories are not expelled unless they endanger national security or
    offend against public interest or morality;
(9) to permit, within legal limits, the transfer of such parts of the ear-
    nings and savings of such workers as they may desire;
(10) to extend the protection and assistance provided for in this Article
    to self-employed migrants insofar as such measures apply.

PART III

Article 20—Undertakings

1. Each of the Contracting Parties undertakes:
    (a) to consider Part I of this Chapter as a declaration of the aims
        which it will pursue by all appropriate means, as stated in the
        introductory paragraph of that Part;
    (b) to consider itself bound by at least five of the following Articles of
        Part II of this Charter: Articles 1, 5, 6, 12, 13, 16 and 19;
    (c) in addition to the Articles selected by it in accordance with the
        preceding sub-paragraph, to consider itself bound by such a
        number of Articles or numbered paragraphs of Part II of the
        Charter as it may select, provided that the total number of Articles
        or numbered paragraphs by which it is bound is not less than 10
        Articles or 45 numbered paragraphs.
2. The Articles or paragraphs selected in accordance with sub-paragraphs
(b) and (c) or paragraph 1 of this Article shall be notified to the Secretary-
General of the Council of Europe at the time when the instrument of ratification or approval of the Contracting Party concern is deposited.
3. Any Contracting Party may, at a later date, declare by notification to the

Secretary-General that it considers itself bound by any Articles or any numbered paragraphs of Part II of the Charter which is has not already accepted under the terms of paragraph 1 of this Article. Such undertakings subsequently given shall be deemed to be an integral part of the ratification or approval, and shall have the same effect as from the thirtieth day after the date of the notification.

4. The Secretary-General shall communicate to all the signatory Governments and to the Director-General of the International Labour Office any notification which he shall have received pursuant to this Part of the Charter.

5. Each Contracting Party shall maintain a system of labour inspection appropriate to national conditions.

. . . .

PART V

Article 30—Derogations in time of War or Public Emergency

1. In time of war or other public emergency threatening the life of the nation any Contracting Party may take measures derogating from its obligation under this Charter to the extent strictly required by the exigencies of the situation, provided that such measures are not inconsistent with its other obligations under international law.

2. Any Contracting Party which has availed itself of this right of derogation shall, within a reasonable lapse of time, keep the Secretary-General of the Council of Europe fully informed of the measures taken and of the reasons therefor. It shall likewise inform the Secretary-General when such measures have ceased to operate and the provisions of the Charter which it has accepted are again being fully executed.

3. The Secretary-General shall in turn inform other Contracting Parties and the Director-General of the International Labour Office of all communications received in accordance with paragraph 2 of this article.

Article 31—Restrictions

1. The rights and principles set forth in Part I when effectively realized, and their effective exercise as provided for in Part II, shall not be subject to any restrictions or limitations not specified in those Parts, except such as are prescribed by law and are necessary in a democratic society for the protection of the rights and freedoms of others or for the protection of public interest, national security, public health, or morals.

2. The restrictions permitted under this Charter to the rights and obli-

gations set forth herein shall not be applied for any purpose other than that for which they have been prescribed.

. . . .

APPENDIX 2

Rights and Articles

Right	UDHR	ICCPR	ICESCR	ECHR*	ESC
Right to life	3	6		2	
Right to liberty and security of person	3, 9	9, 11		5, P4: 1	
Freedom from torture, or cruel, inhuman, or degrading treatment or punishment	5	7, 10		3	
Freedom of movement	9, 13	12, 13		P4: 2, 3, 4	18, 19
Right to asylum	14				
Right to an adequate standard of living	25		11		3, 4
Right to health	25		12		11
Family rights	16	23	10		16
Rights of children	25	24	10		7, 8, 17
Right to work	23		6		1
Right to just and favourable conditions of work	23		7		2, 3, 4
Right to rest and leisure	24		7		2
Freedom from slavery, servitude, and forced labour	4	8		4	
Right to social security, assistance, and welfare	22, 25		9		12, 13, 14, 15
Right to education	26	18	13, 14	P1: 2	9, 10
Right to property	17			P1: 1	
Right to nationality	15	24			
Right to recognition as a person before the law	6	16			
Right to equality before the law, and equal protection of the law	7	14, 26			

*P1 = First Protocol; P4 = Fourth Protocol.

Right	UDHR	ICCPR	ICESCR	ECHR*	ESC
Right to a fair trial	10	14		6	
Right not to be punished under a retroactive law	11	15		7	
Rights of accused persons	11, 14	14		6	
Right to privacy, honour, and reputation	12	17		8	
Freedom of thought, con-science, and religion	18	18		9, P1: 2	
Freedom of opinion and expression	19	19		10	
Right to culture, and to intellectual property		27		15	
Freedom of peaceful assembly	20	21		11	
Freedom of association	20	22		11	
Right to form and join trade unions	23	22	8	11	5, 6
Right to participate in government and public affairs	21 (1)	25			
Right to genuine and periodic elections	21 (3)	25		P1: 3	
Right of access to the public service	21 (2)	25			
Right of self-determination		1	1		
Right to international peace and security	28	20			
Right to use of natural wealth and resources		1	1, 25		
Rights of minorities to enjoy own culture, profess and practise own religion, and use own language		27			

APPENDIX 3

Dates of Adherence of 'Helsinki' States to Human Rights Treaties

	ICCPR	ICESCR	ECHR	ESC
Austria	10. 9.78	10. 9.78	3. 9.58	29.10.69
Belgium	21. 4.83	21. 4.83	14. 6.55	
Bulgaria	21. 9.70	21. 9.70		
Canada	19. 5.76*	19. 5.76		
Cyprus	2. 4.69	2. 4.69	6.10.62	7. 3.68
Czechoslovakia	23.12.75	23.12.75		
Denmark	6. 1.72*	6. 1.72	13. 4.53	3. 3.65
Finland	19. 8.75*	19. 8.75		
France	4.11.80	4.11.80	3. 5.74	9. 3.73
Germany, Dem. Rep.	8.11.73	8.11.73		
Germany, Fed. Rep.	17.12.73	17.12.73	5.12.52	27. 1.65
Greece			28.11.74	6. 6.84
Holy See				
Hungary	17. 1.74	17. 1.74		
Iceland	22. 8.79	22. 8.79	29. 6.53	15. 1.76
Ireland			25. 2.53	7.10.64
Italy	15. 9.78*	15. 9.78	26.10.55	22.10.65
Liechtenstein			8. 9.82	
Luxembourg	18. 8.83*	18. 8.83	3. 9.53	
Malta			23. 1.67	
Monaco				
Netherlands	11.12.78*	11.12.78	31. 8.54	22. 4.80
Norway	13. 9.72*	13. 9.72	15. 1.52	26.10.62
Poland	18. 3.77	18. 3.77		
Portugal	15. 6.78*	31. 7.78	9.11.78	28. 5.82
Romania	9.12.74	9.12.74		
San Marino				
Spain	27. 4.77	27. 4.77	4.10.79	6. 5.80
Sweden	6.12.71*	6.12.71	4. 2.52	17.12.62
Switzerland			28.11.74	
Turkey			18. 5.54	
UK	20. 5.76	20. 5.76	8. 3.51	11. 7.62
USA				
USSR	16.10.73	16.10.73		
Yugoslavia	2. 6.71	2. 6.71		

* Also a party to the Optional Protocol to the ICCPR, allowing individual 'communications' to be adjudicated by the Human Rights Committee.

APPENDIX 4

UNESCO Recommendation on the Status of Scientific Researchers

The General Conference of the United Nations Educational, Scientific and Cultural Organization, meeting in Paris from 17 October to 23 November 1974, at its eighteenth session,

Recalling that, by the terms of the final paragraph of the Preamble to its Constitution, Unesco seeks—by means of promoting (*inter alia*) the scientific relations of the peoples of the world—to advance the objectives of international peace and of the common welfare of mankind for which the United Nations was established and which its Charter proclaims,

Considering the terms of the Universal Declaration of Human Rights adopted by the United Nations General Assembly on 10 December 1948, and in particular Article 27.1 thereof which provides that everyone has the right freely to participate in the cultural life of the community, and to share in scientific advancement and its benefits,

Recognizing that:

    (*a*) scientific discoveries and related technological developments and applications open up vast prospects for progress made possible in particular by the optimum utilization of science and scientific methods for the benefit of mankind and for the preservation of peace and the reduction of international tensions but may, at the same time, entail certain dangers which constitute a threat, especially in cases where the results of scientific research are used against mankind's vital interests in order to prepare wars involving destruction on a massive scale or for purposes of the exploitation of one nation by another, and in any event give rise to complex ethical and legal problems;

    (*b*) to face this challenge, Member States should develop or devise machinery for the formulation and execution of adequate science and technology policies, that is to say, policies designed to avoid the possible dangers and fully realize and exploit the positive prospects inherent in such discoveries, technological developments and applications,

Recognizing also:

(*a*) that a cadre of talented and trained personnel is the cornerstone of an indigenous research and experimental development capability and indispensable for the utilization and exploitation of research carried out elsewhere;

(*b*) that open communication of the results, hypotheses and opinions—as suggested by the phrase 'academic freedom'—lies at the very heart of the scientific process, and provides the strongest guarantee of accuracy and objectivity of scientific results;

(*c*) the necessity of adequate support and essential equipment for performance of research and experimental development,

Observing that, in all parts of the world, this aspect of policy-making is coming to assume increasing importance for the Member States; having in mind the intergovernmental initiatives set out in the annex to this recommendation, demonstrating recognition by Member States of the growing value of science and technology for tackling various world problems on a broad international basis, thereby strengthening co-operation among nations as well as promoting the development of individual nations; and confident that these trends predispose Member States to the taking of concrete action for the introduction and pursuit of adequate science and technology policies,

Persuaded that such governmental action can considerably assist in the creation of those conditions which encourage and assist indigenous capability to perform research and experimental development in an enhanced spirit of responsibility towards man and his environment,

Believing that one of the foremost of these conditions must be to ensure a fair status for those who actually perform research and experimental development in science and technology, taking due account of the responsibilities inherent in and the rights necessary to the performance of that work,

Considering that scientific research activity is carried out in exceptional working conditions and demands a highly responsible attitude on the part of the scientific researchers towards that work, towards their country and towards the international ideals and objectives of the United Nations, and that workers in this profession accordingly need an appropriate status,

Convinced that the current climate of governmental, scientific and public opinion makes the moment opportune for the General Conference to formulate principles for the assistance of member governments desirous of ensuring fair status for the workers concerned,

Recalling that much valuable work in this respect has already been accomplished both in respect of workers generally and in respect of scientific researchers in particular, notably by the international instruments and other texts recalled in this Preamble, and in the annex to this recommendation,

Conscious that the phenomenon frequently known as the 'brain drain' of scientific researchers has in the past caused widespread anxiety, and that to certain Member States it continues to be a matter of considerable preoccupation; having present in mind, in this respect, the paramount needs of the developing countries; and desiring accordingly to give scientific researchers stronger reasons for serving in countries and areas which stand most in need of their services,

Convinced that similar questions arise in all countries with regard to the status of scientific researchers and that these questions call for the adoption of the common approaches and so far as practicable the application of the common standards and measures which it is the purpose of this recommendation to set out,

However, taking fully into account, in the adoption and application of this recommendation, the great diversity of the laws, regulations and customs which, in different countries, determine the pattern and organization of research work and experimental development in science and technology,

Desiring for these reasons to complement the standards and recommendations set out in the laws and decrees of every country and sanctioned by its customs and those contained in the international instruments and other documents referred to in this Preamble and in the annex to this recommendation, by provisions relating to questions of central concern to scientific researchers,

Having before it, as item 26 of the agenda of the session, proposals concerning the status of scientific researchers,

Having decided, at its seventeenth session, that these proposals should take the form of a recommendation to Member States,

Adopts this recommendation this twentieth day of November 1974.

The General Conference recommends that Member States should apply the following provisions by taking whatever legislative or other steps may be required to apply within their respective territories the principles and norms set forth in this recommendation.

The General Conference recommends that Member States should bring this recommendation to the attention of the authorities, institutions and enterprises responsible for the conduct of research and experimental development and the application of its results, and of the various organizations representing or promoting the interests of scientific researchers in association, and other interested parties.

The General Conference recommends that Member States should report to it, on dates and in a manner to be determined by it, on the action they have taken to give effect to this recommendation.

I. Scope of application

1. For the purposes of this recommendation:
   - (*a*) (i) The word 'science' signifies the enterprise whereby mankind, acting individually or in small or large groups, makes an organized attempt, by means of the objective study of observed phenomena, to discover and master the chain of causalities; brings together in a co-ordinated form the resultant subsystems of knowledge by means of systematic reflection and conceptualization, often largely expressed in the symbols of mathematics; and thereby furnishes itself with the opportunity of using, to its own advantage, understanding of the processes and phenomena occurring in nature and society;
     - (ii) The expression 'the sciences' signifies a complex of fact and hypothesis, in which the theoretical element is normally capable of being validated, and to that extent includes the sciences concerned with social facts and phenomena;
   - (*b*) The word 'technology' signifies such knowledge as relates directly to the production or improvement of goods or services;
   - (*c*) (i) The expression 'scientific research' signifies those processes of study, experiment, conceptualization and theory-testing involved in the generation of scientific knowledge, as described in paragraphs 1(*a*)(i) and 1(*a*)(ii) above;
     - (ii) The expression 'experimental development' signifies the processes of adaptation, testing and refinement which lead to the point of practical applicability;
   - (*d*) (i) The expression 'scientific researchers' signifies those persons responsible for investigating a specific domain in science or technology;
     - (ii) On the basis of the provisions of this recommendation, each Member State may determine the criteria for inclusion in the category of persons recognized as scientific researchers (such as possession of diplomas, degrees, academic titles or functions), as well as the exceptions to be allowed for;
   - (*e*) The word 'status' as used in relation to scientific researchers signifies the standing or regard accorded them, as evidenced, first, by the level of appreciation both of the duties and responsibilities inherent in their function and of their competence in performing

them, and, secondly, by the rights, working conditions, material assistance and moral support which they enjoy for the accomplishment of their task.

2. This recommendation applies to all scientific researchers, irrespective of:
   (a) the legal status of their employer, or the type of organization or establishment in which they work;
   (b) their scientific or technological fields of specialization;
   (c) the motivation underlying the scientific research and experimental development in which they engage;
   (d) the kind of application to which that scientific research and experimental development relates most immediately.
3. In the case of scientific researchers performing scientific research and experimental development on a part-time basis, this recommendation applies to them only at such times and in such contexts as they are engaged upon the activity of scientific research and experimental development.

II. Scientific researchers in the context of national policy-making

4. Each Member State should strive to use scientific and technological knowledge for the enhancement of the cultural and material well-being of its citizens, and to further the United Nations ideals and objectives. To attain this objective, each Member State should equip itself with the personnel, institutions and mechanisms necessary for developing and putting into practice national science and technology policies aimed at directing scientific research and experimental development efforts to the achievement of national goals while according a sufficient place to science *per se*. By the policies they adopt in respect of science and technology, by the way in which they use science and technology in policy-making generally, and by their treatment of scientific researchers in particular, Member States should demonstrate that science and technology are not actvities to be carried on in isolation but part of the nations' integrated effort to set up a society that will be more humane and really just.
5. At all appropriate stages of their national planning generally, and of their planning in science and technology specifically, Member States should:
   (a) treat public funding of scientific research and experimental development as a form of public investment the returns on which are, for the most part, necessarily long term;
   (b) take all appropriate measures to ensure that the justification for,

and indeed the indispensability of, such expenditure is held constantly before public opinion.

6. Member States should make every effort to translate into terms of international policies and practices, their awareness of the need to apply science and technology in a great variety of specific fields of wider than national concern: namely, such vast and complex problems as the preservation of international peace and the elimination of want and other problems which can only be effectively tackled on an international basis, such as pollution monitoring and control, weather forecasting and earthquake prediction.

7. Member States should cultivate opportunities for scientific researchers to participate in the outlining of national scientific research and experimental development policy. In particular, each Member State should ensure that these processes are supported by appropriate institutional mechanisms enjoying adequate advice and assistance from scientific researchers and their professional organizations.

8. Each Member State should institute procedures adapted to its needs for ensuring that, in the performance of publicly supported scientific research and experimental development, scientific researchers respect public accountability while at the same time enjoying the degree of autonomy appropriate to their task and to the advancement of science and technology. It should be fully taken into account that creative activities of scientific researchers should be promoted in the national science policy on the basis of utmost respect for the autonomy and freedom of research necessary to scientific progress.

9. With the above ends in view, and with respect for the principle of freedom of movement of scientific researchers, Member States should be concerned to create that general climate, and to provide those specific measures for the moral and material support and encouragement of scientific researchers, as will:

(a) ensure that young people of high calibre find sufficient attraction in the vocation, and sufficient confidence in scientific research and experimental development as a career offering reasonable prospects and a fair degree of security, to maintain a constantly adequate regeneration of the nation's scientific and technological personnel;

(b) facilitate the emergence and stimulate the appropriate growth, among its own citizens, of a body of scientific researchers regarding themselves and regarded by their colleagues throughout the world as worthy members of the international scientific and technological community;

(c) encourage a situation in which the majority of scientific researchers or young people who aspire to become scientific researchers are provided with the necessary incentives to work in the service of their country and to return there if they seek some of their education, training or experience abroad.

III. The initial education and training of scientific researchers

10. Member States should have regard for the fact that effective scientific research calls for scientific researchers of integrity and maturity, combining high moral and intellectual qualities.

11. Among the measures which Member States should take to assist the emergence of scientific researchers of this high calibre are:

   (a) ensuring that, without discrimination on the basis of race, colour, sex, language, religion, political or other opinion, national or social origin, economic condition or birth, all citizens enjoy equal opportunities for the initial education and training needed to qualify for scientific research work, as well as ensuring that all citizens who succeed in so qualifying enjoy equal access to available employment in scientific research;

   (b) encouragement of the spirit of community service as an important element in such education and training for scientific workers.

12. So far as is compatible with the necessary and proper independence of educators, Member States should lend their support to all educational initiatives designed to foster that spirit, such as:

   (a) the incorporation or development, in the curricula and courses concerning the natural sciences and technology, of elements of social and environmental sciences;

   (b) the development and use of educational techniques for awakening and stimulating such personal qualities and habits of mind as:

   (i) disinterestedness and intellectual integrity;

   (ii) the ability to review a problem or situation in perspective and in proportion, with all its human implications;

   (iii) skill in isolating the civic and ethical implications in issues involving the search for new knowledge and which may at first sight seem to be of a technical nature only;

   (iv) vigilance as to the probable and possible social and ecological consequences of scientific research and experimental development activities;

   (v) willingness to communicate with others not only in scientific and technological circles but also outside those circles, which implies willingness to work in a team and in a multi-occupational context.

IV. The vocation of the scientific researcher

13. Member States should bear in mind that the scientific researcher's sense of vocation can be powerfully reinforced if he is encouraged to think of his work in terms of service both to his fellow countrymen and to his fellow human beings in general. Member States should seek, in their treatment of and attitude towards scientific researchers, to express encouragement for scientific research and experimental development performed in this broad spirit of community service.

The civic and ethical aspect of scientific research

14. Member States should seek to encourage conditions in which scientific researchers, with the support of the public authorities, have the responsibility and the right:
    (a) to work in a spirit of intellectual freedom to pursue, expound and defend the scientific truth as they see it;
    (b) to contribute to the definition of the aims and objectives of the programmes in which they are engaged and to the determination of the methods to be adopted which should be humanely, socially and ecologically responsible;
    (c) to express themselves freely on the human, social or ecological value of certain projects and in the last resort withdraw from those projects if their conscience so dictates;
    (d) to contribute positively and constructively to the fabric of science, culture and education in their own country, as well as to the achievement of national goals, the enhancement of their fellow citizens' well-being, and the furtherance of the international ideals and objectives of the United Nations;
    it being understood that Member States, when acting as employers of scientific researchers, should specify as explicitly and narrowly as possible the cases in which they deem it necessary to depart from the principles set out in paragraphs (a) to (d) above.
15. Member States should take all appropriate steps to urge all other employers of scientific researchers to follow the recommendations contained in paragraph 14.

The international aspect of scientific research

16. Member States should recognize that scientific researchers encounter, with increasing frequency, situations in which the scientific research and experimental development on which they are engaged has an international dimension; and should endeavour to assist scientific researchers to exploit such situations in the furtherance of international peace, co-operation and understanding, and the common welfare of mankind.

17. Member States should in particular provide all possible support to the initiatives of scientific researchers undertaken in search of improved understanding of factors involved in the survival and well-being of mankind as a whole.

18. Each Member State should enlist the knowledge, industry and idealism of those of its citizens who are scientific researchers, especially of the younger generation, in the task of furnishing as generous a contribution as its resources can permit to the world's scientific and technological research effort. Member States should welcome all the advice and assistance scientific researchers can provide, in socio-economic development efforts that will contribute to the consolidation of an authentic culture and of national sovereignty.

19. In order that the full potentialities of scientific and technological knowledge be promptly geared to the benefit of all peoples, Member States should urge scientific researchers to keep in mind the principles set out in paragraphs 16, 17 and 18.

V. Conditions for success on the part of scientific researchers

20. Member States should:
    (a) bear in mind that the public interest, as well as that of scientific researchers, requires moral support and material assistance conducive to successful performance in scientific research and experimental development by scientific researchers;
    (b) recognize that in this respect they have, as employers of scientific researchers, a leading responsibility and should attempt to set an example to other employers of such researchers;
    (c) urge all other employers of scientific researchers to pay close attention to the provision of satisfactory working conditions for scientific researchers, notably in repsect of all the provisions of the present section;
    (d) ensure that scientific researchers enjoy conditions of work and pay commensurate with their status and performance without discrimination on the basis of sex, language, age, religion or national origin.

Adequate career development prospects and facilities

21. Member States should draw up, preferably within the framework of a comprehensive national manpower policy, policies in respect of employment which adequately cover the needs of scientific researchers, in particular by:
    (a) providing scientific researchers in their direct employment with adequate career development prospects and facilities though not

necessarily exclusively in the fields of scientific research and experimental development: and encouraging non-governmental employers to do likewise;

(*b*) making every effort to plan scientific research and experimental development in such a way that the scientific researchers concerned are not subjected, merely by the nature of their work, to avoidable hardship;

(*c*) considering the provision of the necessary funds for facilities for readaptation and redeployment in respect of the scientific researchers in their permanent employ, as an integral part of scientific research and experimental development planning, especially, but not exclusively, in the case of programmes or projects as limited duration activities; and where these facilities are not possible, providing appropriate compensatory arrangements;

(*d*) offering challenging opportunities for young scientific researchers to do significant scientific research and experimental development, in accordance with their abilities.

Permanent self re-education

22. Member States should seek to encourage that:

(*a*) like other categories of workers facing similar problems, scientific researchers enjoy opportunities for keeping themselves up to date in their own and in related subjects, by attendance at conferences, by free access to libraries and other sources of information, and by participation in educational or vocational courses; and where necessary, scientific researchers should have the opportunity to undergo further scientific training with a view to transferring to another branch of scientific activity;

(*b*) appropriate facilities are provided for this purpose.

Mobility in general and the civil service in particular

23. Member States would take measures to encourage and facilitate, as part of a comprehensive national policy for highly qualified manpower, the interchange or mobility of scientific researchers as between scientific research and experimental development service in the government and in the higher education and productive enterprise contexts.

24. Member States should also bear in mind that the machinery of government at all levels can benefit from the special skills and insights provided by scientific researchers. All Member States could therefore profitably benefit from a careful comparative examination of the experience gained in those Member States which have introduced salary scales and other conditions of

employment specially designed for scientific researchers, with a view to determining to what extent such schemes would help meet their own national needs. Matters which appear to require particular attention in this respect are:

(a) optimum utilization of scientific researchers within the framework of a comprehensive national policy of highly qualified manpower;

(b) the desirability of providing procedures with all the necessary guarantees allowing for the periodic review of the material conditions of scientific researchers to ensure that they remain equitably comparable with those of other workers having equivalent experience and qualifications and in keeping with the country's standard of living;

(c) the possibility of providing adequate career development prospects in public research bodies; as well as the need to give scientifically or technologically qualified researchers the option of transferring from scientific research and experimental development positions to administrative positions.

25. Member States should furthermore turn to advantage the fact that science and technology can be stimulated by close contact with other spheres of national activity, and vice versa. Member States should accordingly take care not to discourage scientific researchers whose predilections and talents, initially cultivated in the scientific research and experimental development context proper, lead them to progress into cognate activities. Member States should on the contrary be vigilant to encourage those scientific researchers, whose original scientific research and experimental development training and subsequently acquired experience reveal potentialities lying in such fields as management of scientific research and experimental development or the broader field of science and technology policies as a whole, to develop to the full their talents in these directions.

Participation in international scientific and technological gatherings

26. Member States should actively promote the interplay of ideas and information among scientific researchers throughout the world, which is vital to the healthy development of science and technology; and to this end should take all measures necessary to ensure that scientific researchers are enabled, throughout their careers, to participate in international scientific and technological gatherings and to travel abroad.

27. Member States should furthermore see to it that all governmental or quasi-governmental organizations in which or under whose authority scientific research and experimental development are performed, regularly devote a portion of their budget to financing the

participation, at such international scientific and technological gatherings, of scientific researchers in their employ.

Access by scientific researchers to postitions of greater responsibility with corresponding rewards

28. Member States should encourage in practice that decisions as to access by scientific researchers in their employ to positions of greater responsibility, and correspondingly higher rewards, are formulated essentially on the basis of fair and realistic appraisal of the capacities of the persons concerned, as evidenced by their current or recent performances, as well as on the basis of formal or academic evidence of knowledge acquired or skills demonstrated by them.

Protection of health; social security

29. (*a*) Member States should accept that, as employers of scientific researchers, the onus is on them—in accordance with national regulations, and the international instruments concerned with the protection of workers in general from hostile or dangerous environments—to guarantee so far as is reasonably possible the health and safety of the scientific researchers in their employ, as of all other persons likely to be affected by the scientific research and experimental development in question. They should accordingly ensure that the managements of scientific establishments enforce appropriate safety standards; train all those in their employ in the necessary safety procedures; monitor and safeguard the health of all persons at risk; take due note of warnings of new (or possible new) hazards brought to their attention, in particular by the scientific researchers themselves, and act accordingly; ensure that the working day and rest periods are of reasonable length, the latter to include annual leave on full pay;

(*b*) Member States should take all appropriate steps to urge like practices on all other employers of scientific researchers.

30. Member States should ensure that provision is made for scientific researchers to enjoy (in common with all other workers) adequate and equitable social security arrangements appropriate to their age, sex, family situation, state of health and to the nature of the work they perform.

Promotion, appraisal, expression and recognition of creativity

Promotion

31. Member States should be actively concerned to stimulate creative performance in the field of science and technology by all scientific researchers.

Appraisal

32. Member States should, as regards scientific researchers in their employ:

    (*a*) take due account, in all procedures for appraisal of the creativity of scientific researchers, of the difficulty inherent in measuring a personal capacity which seldom manifests itself in a constant and unfluctuating form;

    (*b*) enable, and as appropriate encourage, scientific researchers in whom it appears this capacity might be profitably stimulated:

        (i) either to turn to a new field of science or technology;

        (ii) or else to progress from scientific research and experimental development to other occupations in which the experience they have acquired and the other personal qualities of which they have given proof can be put to better use in a new context.

33. Member States should urge like practices upon other employers of scientific researchers.

34. As elements pertinent to appraisal of creativity, Member States should seek to ensure that scientific researchers may:

    (*a*) receive without hindrance the questions, criticisms and suggestions addressed to them by their colleagues throughout the world, as well as the intellectual stimulus afforded by such communications and the exchanges to which they give rise;

    (*b*) enjoy in tranquillity international acclaim warranted by their scientific merit.

Expression by publication

35. Member States should encourage and facilitate publication of the results obtained by scientific researchers, with a view to assisting them to acquire the reputation which they merit as well as with a view to promoting the advancement of science and technology, education and culture generally.

36. To this end, Member States should ensure that the scientific and technological writings of scientific researchers enjoy appropriate legal protection, and in particular the protection afforded by copyright law.

37. Member States should, in consultation with scientific researchers' organizations and as a matter of standard practice, encourage the employers of scientfic researchers, and themselves as employers seek:

    (*a*) to regard it as the norm that scientific researchers be at liberty and encouraged to publish the results of their work;

    (*b*) to minimize the restrictions placed upon scientific researchers' right to publish their findings, consistent with public interest and the right of their employers and fellow workers;

(c) to express as clearly as possible in writing in the terms and conditions of their employment the circumstances in which such restrictions are likely to apply;

(d) similarly, to make clear the procedures by which scientific researchers can ascertain whether the restrictions mentioned in this paragraph apply in a particular case and by which he can appeal.

Recognition

38. Member States should demonstrate that they attach high importance to the scientific researcher's receiving appropriate moral support and material compensation for the creative effort which is shown in his work.

39. Accordingly, Member States should:
    (a) bear in mind that:
        (i) the degree to which scientific researchers receive credit for and acknowledgement of their proven creativity may affect their level of perceived job satisfaction;
        (ii) job satisfaction is likely to affect performance in scientific research generally, and may affect specifically the creative element in that performance;
    (b) adopt, and urge the adoption of, appropriate treatment of scientific researchers with respect to their proven creative effort.

40. Member States should adopt, and urge the adoption of, the following standard practices;
    (a) written provisions to be included in the terms and conditions of employment of scientific researchers, stating clearly what rights (if any) belong to them (and, where appropriate, other interested parties) in respect of any discovery, invention, or improvement in technical know-how which may arise in the course of the scientific research and experimental development which these researchers undertake;
    (b) the attention of scientific researchers to be always drawn by the employer to such written provisions before the scientific researchers enter employment.

Reasonable flexibility in the interpretation and application of texts setting out the terms and conditions of employment of scientific researchers

41. Member States should seek to ensure that the performance of scientific research and experimental development be not reduced to pure routine. They should therefore see to it that all texts setting out terms of employment for, or governing the conditions of work

of, scientific researchers be framed and interpreted with all the desirable flexibility to meet the requirements of science and technology. This flexibility should not however be invoked in order to impose on scientific researchers conditions that are inferior to those enjoyed by other workers of equivalent qualifications and responsibility.

The advancement of their various interests by scientific researchers in association

42. Member States should recognize it as wholly legitimate, and indeed desirable, that scientific researchers should associate to protect and promote their individual and collective interests, in bodies such as trade unions, professional associations and learned societies, in accordance with the rights of workers in general and inspired by the principles set out in the international instruments listed in the annex to this recommendation. In all cases where it is necessary to protect the rights of scientific researchers, these organizations should have the right to support the justified claims of such researchers.

VI. Utilization and exploitation of the present recommendation

43. Member States should strive to extend and complement their own action in respect of the status of scientific researchers, by co-operating with all national and international organizations whose activities fall within the scope and objectives of this recommendation, in particular National Commissions for Unesco; international organizations; organizations representing science and technology educators; employers generally; learned societies, professional associations and trade unions of scientific researchers; associations of science writers; youth organizations.

44. Member States should support the work of the bodies mentioned above by the most appropriate means.

45. Member States should enlist the vigilant and active co-operation of all organizations representing scientific researchers, in ensuring that the latter may, in a spirit of community service, effectively assume the responsibilities, enjoy the rights and obtain the recognition of the status described in this recommendation.

VII. Final provision

46. Where scientific researchers enjoy a status which is, in certain respects, more favourable than that provided for in this recommendation, its terms should not be invoked to diminish the status already acquired.

APPENDIX 5

World Federation of Scientific Workers
Declaration on the Rights of Scientific Workers

(adopted by the General Assembly in April 1969)

1. PREAMBLE

Science and scientific research can contribute increasingly to the improvement of the living conditions of mankind, can become a reliable source of welfare, and can create conditions of the realisation of social justice within society. Furthermore, science and science teaching are expanding at an increasing rate, so that the importance of ensuring the application of the enormous forces made available by scientific discovery to the needs of mankind increases correspondingly.

The profession of scientist and science teacher is therefore characterised by special features arising out of the great social responsibility of these workers. Their activities have a particular significance and importance due, on the one hand, to the broad possibilities of using science and its achievements for the benefit of society as a whole and for solving important social and economic problems and, on the other, to the danger that the results of scientific research will be used against the vital interests of mankind either in preparations for wars of mass destruction or for the exploitation of one country by another. Scientific workers have an important role in promoting the most effective use of science and scientific methods of human welfare and in contributing to the preservation of peace and reduction of international tensions.

2. GENERAL

2.1 *Definition*

A scientific worker is considered to be a suitably qualified person engaged in professional work in natural, technological or social science, in fundamental or applied science, and in the teaching of science.

2.2 *Nature of Qualifications*

A professional scientific worker is deemed to be qualified by the possession of a university degree or diploma of equivalent standing in one of the sciences.

Notwithstanding this basic requirement, and without lowering the

general standard, individuals who lack some of the formal academic cer-
tificates, may qualify by possession of valuable experience and by holding
responsible posts demanding high scientific attainments, or by publications or achievements of acknowledged standing.

Steps should be taken towards international agreement on professional
standards for scientific workers.

2.3 Places of Employment

Scientific workers are employed in universities, technical colleges, scientific research establishments, in industry and in governmental and private
organisations, or may be self-employed as consultants, writers, etc.

2.4 Field of Recruitment

All citizens should be given equal opportunities to become members of a
scientific profession regardless of race, nationality, sex, creed, or social
status.

2.5 Advancement of Science

Governments should support and promote the development of science,
should allocate the necessary means for training scientists, and should
encourage the employment of suitably qualified scientific workers in
research work.

With the future of mankind vitally involved in the correct application of
science and scientific methods to the problems of our time, scientific
workers should be given opportunities to influence the ways in which
science is used, and to make its potentialities known to the general public.

Scientific workers should have the support of governments in resisting
pressures to compromise their scientific integrity.

3. BASIC RIGHTS OF SCIENTIFIC WORKERS

3.1 Civil Rights

Scientific workers regardless of their sex, race, nationality, creed, and political conviction should have all civil rights defined in the General Declaration of Human Rights and in the Agreement on Human Rights accepted
by the United Nations Organisation.

3.2 Right to Employment

Scientific workers should have the right to work in accordance with their
scientific capacities and Governments should endeavour to ensure this
right.

3.3 Right to Exchange Experiences

If science is to contribute actively to the growth of the welfare of mankind,
it is necessary to give scientific workers the right of free exchange of views

and experiences on scientific work and its economic and social consequences, on both a national and international scale.

Governments should refrain from interference with the freedom to
express scientific views or to publish the results of scientific research and
should take steps to prevent other interference with this freedom.

3.4 Right to Representation on Managing Bodies

Authorities should recognise the importance of the participation of scientific workers in steps designed to improve the quality and direction of
scientific research and development. Authorities and organisations of
scientific workers should collaborate to this end. Scientists should be
represented on governing bodies directing science and research.

Authorities should ensure that the management of scientific and
research institutions should be entrusted to scientific workers with appropriate experience and ability.

3.5 Non-discrimination

Scientific workers should have equal rights in their professions regardless
of sex, race, nationality, creed, or political conviction.

3.6 Right of Defence

Scientific workers should be entitled to defend their rights.

4. Rights of Scientific Workers in their Employment

4.1 Contract of Employment

The rights, duties and responsibilities of the employing body and of each
scientific worker should be stated clearly either by legislative measures or
by contracts of work concluded between the employing body and the
scientific worker. This should include measures for special cases when the
scientific worker is transferred, temporarily or permanently, to other
scientific work within the same organisation.

4.2 Type of Employment

The employing body should ensure that each scientific worker is given
work commensurate with his qualifications and knowledge, and that
favourable conditions are created for him to be able properly to perform
duties as stipulated in the contract.

4.3 Redundancy at Place of Employment

If a situation arises where there appears to be a surplus or redundancy of
particular grades of scientific worker in an establishment, due to changed
circumstances, there should be consultations between the trade unions
and the employing bodies in order to seek means of minimising or avoiding the dismissal of staff. If, nonetheless, redundancy remains, each scien-

tific worker should be given adequate assistance and time on full pay to transfer to other suitable employment, or paid compensation on a predetermined scale.

4.4 *Dismissal from Employment*

The circumstances under which a scientific worker may be dismissed should be defined by law.

4.5 *Certification on Change of Employment*

At the termination of an employment, a scientific worker should have the right to obtain a certificate in which all important facts about his activities during the period of employment are stated; the organisation would be bound to discuss the contents of the certificate with the scientific worker before issuing it; this document should not contain anything detrimental to the scientific worker.

4.6 *Conditions for Effective Scientific Work*

Because of the value and importance of the work of scientists and science teachers, it should be so organised and assisted as to avoid wastage of their time and energy, and carried out under favourable conditions.

Total hours of work of scientific workers should not exceed those determined for other occupations. Some flexibility should be recognised in certain classes of creative work, and adherence to a rigid timetable should not be required where this would be detrimental to the progress of the work as a whole, taking into account the supporting activities of technicians and other staff.

To raise the professional standard scientific workers should be given leave and opportunities to participate in courses leading to post-graduate qualification.

Scientific workers should be provided with adequate opportunities and facilities for devoting a part of their working hours to scientific conferences or to other means of communication with their professional colleagues, and to deepening their knowledge and qualifications by keeping up to date with current developments through published literature.

4.7 *Determination of Salaries*

Salaries for scientific workers should be determined through the process of negotiation between the trade unions and the employing bodies. Salary rates for scientific workers should be determined having regard to qualifications, skill and experience in scientific work, but regardless of sex, race, creed, or nationality.

4.8 *Holidays*

All scientific workers should enjoy a right to adequate annual holidays with full pay, and this should be not less than one month, in addition to public holidays.

4.9 *Leave*

After some years of employment a scientific worker should be granted a substantial period of leave with full pay for purposes of study either in a related branch of science or in his individual field. This period of study-leave should be counted for seniority and pension purposes and be additional to the opportunities accorded for keeping up to date with current developments referred to in Section 4.6.

Leave of absence without loss of seniority or pension rights should be granted to scientific workers within the framework of bilateral or multi-lateral agreements on secondment between the organisations in the developing and the developed countries. In addition special arrangements should be made to cover their extraordinary expenses.

Scientific workers should be granted leave of absence with full pay to enable them to participate in the activities of their trade union and professional organisations.

Scientific workers should be granted leave of absence with full pay for adequate personal reasons under arrangements specified in advance of employment.

4.10 *Protection in Case of Dangerous Work*

Scientific workers who are carrying out dangerous work or are working under unusual conditions should be accorded appropriate protection by legislation of their governments. These scientific workers may have shorter working hours and longer holidays and be paid special hardship allowances. They should be guaranteed full compensation in case of disease or accidents caused by their occupation.

4.11 *Maternity Leave*

Women scientific workers should—apart from maternity care and relief granted by national law—be given special facilities such as: leave before and after confinement, the right to return to their original place of work or to a job on the same level as the one they had before their maternity leave.

4.12 *Sick Leave and Pension*

Scientific workers should be entitled to leave with full pay throughout any period of incapacity for work by reason of sickness or temporary disability. Old-age and permanent disability pensions should be so related to earnings from employment that the scientific worker may continue to maintain an adequate living standard.

Where the level of benefits under governmental general social security provisions is lower than that provided for in this Declaration, it should be brought up to the recommended standard by means of supplementary schemes agreed between the appropriate trade unions and the employers. It should be made possible for all pension and social security rights to be transferred when a scientific worker changes his employment, either in his own country or another.

5. TRADE UNION RIGHTS OF SCIENTIFIC WORKERS

5.1 *Right to Organise*

Scientific workers should have the right to organize trade unions for the protection of their status and economic conditions, to be members of such trade unions, and to recruit others into membership in accordance with ILO Convention number 98. Members should not suffer discrimination in the activities of such organisations.

5.2 *Independence of Trade Unions*

Trade unions of scientific workers should be independent of the State and employers, and they should be free from interference and control.

5.3 *Defence of Rights and Interests of Members*

Trade unions of scientific workers should have the right in law to defend themselves and the interests of scientific workers by means accepted in individual countries.

5.4 *Right of Free Association*

Trade unions of scientific workers should have the right to free association with other organisations, both nationally and internationally.

5.5 *Legal Status*

Trade unions of scientific workers should be recognised as negotiating bodies and legally empowered to act on behalf of scientific workers in membership and should have the right in law to represent scientific workers and defend their interests.

INDEX OF NAMES

INDEX OF NATIONS; NATIONAL
INSTITUTIONS AND ORGANIZATIONS

INDEX OF INTERNATIONAL INSTITUTIONS
AND ORGANIZATIONS

INDEX OF TREATIES AND OTHER INSTRUMENTS

INDEX OF HUMAN RIGHTS SUBJECTS

INDEX OF MISCELLANEOUS SUBJECTS

DATE DUE